High Calling

The Courageous Life and Faith of
Space Shuttle Columbia
Commander Rick Husband

Evelyn Husband

with

Donna VanLiere

THOMAS NELSON PUBLISHERS®
Nashville

A Division of Thomas Nelson, Inc.
www.ThomasNelson.com

Published in Nashville, Tennessee, by Thomas Nelson, Inc.

Published in association with Yates & Yates, LLP, Attorneys and Counselors, Orange, California.

Library of Congress Cataloging-in-Publication Data

Husband, Evelyn.
    High calling : the courageous life and faith of space shuttle Columbia commander Rick Husband / Evelyn Husband with Donna VanLiere.
    p. cm.
    ISBN 0-7852-6068-4 (IE)
    ISBN 0-7852-6195-8 (hardcover)
    1. Husband, Rick Douglas, 1957–2003 2. Astronauts—United States—Biography.
    3. Columbia (Spacecraft)—Accidents. I. VanLiere, Donna, 1966– II. Title.
    TL789.85.H87H87 2004
    629.45'0092—dc22   2003023676

For Laura and Matthew

Contents

1

Coming Home

ON SATURDAY MORNING, FEBRUARY 1, 2003, I WATCHED THE sun come up over the ocean in Florida. It was a beautiful, huge orange ball of fire. I stood on the balcony of our hotel room and said, "Rick is finally coming home today!" My husband, Rick, was the commander of the space shuttle *Columbia*. He and the six other STS-107 crew members left on January 16 for a sixteen-day mission to space.

I was filled with absolute joy on February 1 because the mission was finished and Rick was coming back. I watched the sunrise, which is unusual for me. I am not a morning person, and neither are my children—Laura, twelve, and Matthew, seven. I can count on one hand the number of sunrises I have watched in my lifetime. But that morning, I watched it and was amazed at its beauty; it was spectacular. I thanked God that everything had gone so well for Rick and his crew. When fog started to roll over the ocean, I became concerned. I knew that if it didn't lift, the landing would have to be rescheduled. I prayed that God would lift the fog so Rick and the crew could make a safe landing, the kind Rick had trained and prayed for from the beginning.

At six o'clock I woke Laura so she could experience part of the sunrise. She went out onto the balcony, and I watched her silhouette against the sky. She was so pretty and innocent. I walked next to her and put my arm around her. "Laura, you're going to remember this sunrise for the rest of your life," I said. While I made her something to eat, she began to watch her last devotional video from Rick. About a week prior to the crew's quarantine, Rick told me he wanted to record videotapes for Laura and Matthew.

"I want to make a videotape for Laura and one for Matthew that they can watch each day I'm in orbit," he said. "I want the children to know how much I love them and that I'll be thinking about them every day."

Rick wanted to give the kids something that would show his love for them, but a toy or game just wasn't good enough—a toy couldn't express the depth of Rick's love for his children. What he prized more than anything was time with his family, so he wanted to spend "time" with the kids while he was in space, and he wanted to make that time worthwhile for them. Rick couldn't think of anything better than telling them about the God he desperately loved. God wasn't the "man upstairs" to Rick; He was Lord of his life. Jesus wasn't a kind character with good morals out of a book; He was the Son of God who loved Rick so much that He left heaven to live on earth for thirty-three years before dying on the cross for him. Jesus wasn't a fictitious character; He was real to Rick. Rick wanted more than anything on earth for his children to have a relationship with Him that was real.

We figured that prior to the launch, once he was in quarantine, he could work on the tapes. "I can at least talk to them over the videotape and let them know that I'm praying for them and thinking of them," he said. It was a familiar habit with Laura and Matthew for Rick to pray with them every night before going to bed, so this was his way of still praying with them every day.

Laura watched her video devotional while I woke Matthew. "Hi, Sweetie Pie," Rick said on the tape. "It's landing day, and hopefully, if the weather's good, I'll be landing today in Florida. I'm certainly looking forward to seeing you and Matthew and Mama very much."

Rick read from Laura's devotional book, and when he finished, he prayed for her: "Lord, thank You for bringing us to this point in the journey that our family has taken toward this mission. I pray that You'll be with us in the shuttle and help us to have a great entry and landing today. We look forward to being back together as a family again." Rick looked into the camera and smiled. "Okay, Laura, it won't be long before I get to see you! I love you very, very much . . . I'm looking forward to seeing you and Mama and Matthew. I'll see you in just a little while! I love you. Bye-bye!"

I prepared Matthew's breakfast as he watched his last devotional. When he was finished, I turned off the TV and put both videotapes inside the entertainment cabinet so I'd know where to find them when we packed our things to head back to Houston. The days had dwindled down to this, and Laura, Matthew, and I could barely contain our excitement about watching the landing. Daddy was coming home! I looked out the window and noticed the ground fog hadn't lifted. I prayed again that God would lift the fog so the crew could have a safe landing.

At 7:00 A.M. eastern standard time (EST), Rick and the crew finished the last of the systems checks and confirmed that the *Columbia* was in the correct position for entry.

Steve Lindsey picked us up about 8:00 A.M. to take us to the landing site. Rick met Steve in his astronaut candidate class in 1995. Steve is a colonel in the U.S. Air Force, and he and Rick were two of the ten pilots accepted by NASA for astronaut training that year. Each crew selects astronaut escorts who help with all the logistics of both launch and landing days, and our escorts were Steve, Scott Parazynski, Clay Anderson, and Terry Virts. Usually, each crew selects two escorts (Rick was family escort for two of Steve's three flights and for two of Scott's four missions), but because security was especially tight for STS-107 with the first Israeli astronaut on board, the crew's families had a total of four escorts. Rick named Steve our lead escort and also designated him as CACO (Casualty Assistance Calls Officer) for our family, which meant Steve would take on a heavy burden of responsibility in case of tragedy. In such an instance, a CACO's duties would be long and complex and include acting as liaison between NASA and the suffering family, screening all media inquiries, assisting with mortuary affairs, and helping with legal and financial needs. Seventeen years after the shuttle *Challenger* exploded, some CACOs are still assisting crew family members because the job never ends.

We needed to be at Kennedy Space Center thirty minutes before landing. The shuttle was scheduled to land at 9:15 A.M. (EST). I looked down at my watch: we had only another hour and fifteen minutes before Rick was home. I shuffled Laura and Matthew into the car and opened my mouth to ask Steve how concerned I should be about the ground fog, but he was already on his cell phone to see if the weather was clear for landing.

At 8:15 A.M. EST, when Rick and the crew were over the Indian Ocean at an altitude of 150 miles, Mission Control gave Rick and Willie McCool, the *Columbia*'s pilot, approval for what is called the deorbit burn. At that time, the shuttle was flying upside down and backward, but because of weightlessness in space, all altitudes "feel" the same—there is no feeling of being up or down. Rick and Willie fired off the two six-thousand-pound thrust orbital maneuvering rocket engines to slow the shuttle for descent as it entered the earth's atmosphere, and then the shuttle's computers slowly moved the *Columbia* around into a nose-up position. It was ready for entry.

This part of entry is somewhat difficult because the shuttle needs to reach the landing site with sufficient energy, so altitude and airspeed are crucial for keeping the shuttle on trajectory. As the vehicle hits the atmosphere, a tremendous amount of friction is generated—more friction and heat are created as the shuttle descends at a steep angle. Energy is controlled by banking the shuttle, but that turns the vehicle away from the landing site, so then the bank angle must be reversed. From the ground, it looks as if the shuttle is making a series of S turns. Rick and Willie had to constantly monitor deceleration, temperature, hydraulics, and other systems to make sure the shuttle was flying on course and approaching the landing area at just the right angle.

The viewing area near the landing site is divided into sections at Kennedy Space Center: there are bleachers for the crew families and their invited guests in one section, NASA officials sit in one section, and general spectators are in yet another section. I was able to walk back and forth and visit with Rick's mom, Jane; his brother, Keith; Keith's fiancée, Kathy; and many of our invited guests. I was in such a joyful mood that morning that I was very social, talking and laughing with all our guests as we waited for the shuttle.

Laura and Matthew were playing in a grassy area that faced the runway with the other crew children, chasing each other and laughing. The fog had lifted and the sun was shining. Though it was a bit cold, it was an absolutely beautiful day, just perfect for landing. There was a party atmosphere within the stands. Everyone was celebrating a very successful mission.

NASA has never had a bad landing; the only disaster has been the explosion of the space shuttle *Challenger* in 1986, which occurred seventy-three seconds after liftoff. No one at Mission Control in

Houston or on board the *Columbia* was nervous or worried that day; no one had any reason to believe that this entry would be any different from the previous 112 shuttle flights (27 of them made by the *Columbia*). Everything was going as expected.

"It was picture perfect, all the way through," Steve Lindsey says. "Nobody really thinks about landing as a dangerous time, even though we know it is, but nobody thinks about it because everybody has *Challenger* in their heads, which was launch."

Inside the orbiter, the crew on the flight deck—Rick, Willie, Laurel Clark, and Kalpana Chawla (K. C.)—were videotaping their last minutes aboard the *Columbia*, just prior to the scheduled landing. Their conversation was easygoing and light. Around 8:43 A.M. EST the crew prepared to enter the earth's atmosphere. "Two minutes to entry interface," Rick said on the video.

At 8:45 A.M. the *Columbia* penetrated the outer fringes of the earth's atmosphere just north of Hawaii, at an altitude of 400,000 feet. Close to two minutes later, Laurel had the video camera and was pointing it at K. C.

LAUREL: K. C., can you look at the camera for a sec? Look at me.

K. C.: Can you see me?

LAUREL: Yep.

K. C. waved at the camera, and it was evident in all their voices that the members of the crew were excited about coming home.

In the background at Kennedy Space Center, I could hear Mission Control talking with the shuttle, but I wasn't paying attention to anything that was being said. As far as I was concerned, it was just background noise. I grabbed my cell phone and called my parents, Dan and Jean Neely, in Amarillo.

"Are you watching, Daddy?" I asked. "Rick's just a few minutes from landing now."

"We've got the TV on, Darlin'," he said, sharing my excitement.

I hung up the phone and walked over to Steve Lindsey and asked him exactly what to expect for the landing. It had been four years since Rick's previous flight with STS-96 on board the shuttle *Discovery* so I couldn't remember everything that was going to take place.

"About a minute out, you'll hear the sonic boom," Steve said, "then they'll be coming in from the west." He told me some of the calls Rick would be making to Mission Control when they were close to landing and said those calls would be coming in soon.

Meanwhile, inside the orbiter, Laurel was pointing the camera toward the overhead window, recording the plasma that was burning as the orbiter entered the earth's atmosphere, turning from orange to pink. The crew on the flight deck looked out the windows in amazement at what was happening.

> **LAUREL:** Tell me when there's good stuff out front. I'm filming the overhead now.
>
> **WILLIE:** Starting to glow a little bit more now, Laurel.
>
> **RICK:** Yep.
>
> **LAUREL:** Okay.
>
> **WILLIE:** Can you see over my shoulder, Laurel?
>
> **LAUREL:** I was filming it. It doesn't show up nearly as much as the back.
>
> **WILLIE:** It's glowing pretty good now. Ilan, it's really neat. It's a bright orange yellow out over the nose, all around the nose.

There was no trace of uncertainty in anyone's voice and absolutely no fear. They were minutes from home. Willie looked out over the nose of the orbiter.

> **RICK:** Wait till you start seeing the swirl patterns out your left or right windows.
>
> **WILLIE:** Wow.
>
> **RICK:** Looks like a blast furnace. Let's see here. Look at that.
>
> **WILLIE:** This is amazing. It's really getting fairly bright out there.
>
> **RICK:** You definitely don't want to be outside now.

At that point, the crew saw a pink glow from the windows as the atmospheric friction heated the 25,000-plus protective tiles on the shuttle to nearly 3,000 degrees Fahrenheit. As the shuttle descended, the glow went from pink to red to searing white, normal for every shuttle entry. So far, Mission Control was pleased; there was no reason to anticipate any problems. The biggest concern that day had been the fog, but it had lifted, paving the way for a smooth landing.

At 8:53 A.M., as the *Columbia* flew over San Francisco, data on various monitors at Mission Control in Houston began to indicate vehicle problems. Some hydraulic systems temperature sensors in the shuttle's left wing were indicating unusual temperature changes. Occasional data dropouts occur during entry so the crew wasn't notified, but these dropouts are very short in duration and only temporary. The changes in the *Columbia*'s wing began to cascade.

As Rick and the crew were over Nevada and Utah, the temperature in the left landing gear and brake lining peaked higher than normal. An amateur astronomer videotaped chunks falling from the *Columbia*. Two minutes later, as the *Columbia* flew over Arizona, another home video recorded pieces falling from the orbiter, but neither the crew nor Mission Control was aware that anything was breaking off the shuttle. Then, three temperature sensors in the left wing went dead, and the shuttle experienced an increased drag on its left side, something the automatic control systems on board were trying to correct. The *Columbia* was flying at the equivalent of eighteen times the speed of sound, or approximately 13,200 miles per hour. Rick was now 1,400 miles from landing and sixteen minutes from seeing us again.

As the *Columbia* flew over Texas at an altitude of 207,000 feet, Jeff Kling, the shuttle's mechanical systems officer, read something on his monitor at Mission Control.

JEFF: We just lost tire pressure on the left outboard and left inboard, both tires.

At 8:59 A.M. EST, Capsule Communicator (CAPCOM) Charlie Hobaugh radioed the crew from Mission Control in Houston.

CHARLIE: And *Columbia*, Houston. We see your tire pressure messages. And we did not copy your last.

RICK: Roger, buh—

It would be the last communication Mission Control had with Rick. Charlie tried to regain contact with the shuttle.

CHARLIE: Columbia, Houston. Comm check.

Mission Control heard static. The seconds were excruciating as Mission Control waited.

CHARLIE: *Columbia,* Houston. U.H.F. comm check.

Phil Engelauf, a mission operations directorate official, received word from a colleague who had seen the shuttle breaking up over Texas. Phil shared the news with Flight Director LeRoy Cain. The report was staggering. LeRoy immediately called Ground Control over the flight loop, a common audio channel used by the flight director to communicate with Mission Control front room flight controllers.

CAIN: GC, Flight. *[No response. Cain called again.]* GC, Flight.

GROUND CONTROL: Flight, GC.

CAIN: Lock the doors.

GROUND CONTROL: Copy.

CAIN: No data, no phone calls, no transmissions anywhere, into or out.

The reality of what was happening was setting in at Mission Control, but at Kennedy Space Center, as we anticipated the landing, I had no idea what was going on.

In Amarillo, my parents were quiet as they watched the images on their TV screen. Several bright streaks filled the sky, and when Daddy saw them, his heart sank. CNN was broadcasting that contact had been lost with the shuttle. He turned off the TV.

"Something was wrong with the camera," Mother said, desperately wanting to believe that what they were seeing was a technical error. "The camera was out of focus."

Daddy felt nauseous. "It's not the camera, Jean," he said. "Something's terribly wrong."

Within moments, the doorbell rang. Mother answered it.

"I'm so sorry, Jean," a friend said, grabbing Mother's hand. It was then that Mother knew the camera wasn't out of focus.

When the shuttle was eleven minutes from landing, Matthew, Laura, and I stood for a picture in front of the huge landing clock at

Kennedy Space Center, and our faces revealed how excited we were. As far as we knew, Rick was just minutes away. I wasn't aware at the time but found out later that some of the other crew spouses had started listening to communication between Mission Control and the shuttle and knew something was wrong. Steve Lindsey realized it when he heard the dialogue at Mission Control and the attempts to repeatedly contact Rick.

"About the third time I heard them call, the hair started standing up on the back of my neck," Steve says. "It's common to lose transmission for ten seconds or twenty seconds, but not a long time. It was a terrible, sickening feeling."

Although Steve had just told me minutes earlier which direction I should be looking for the shuttle, I had forgotten. When the shuttle was still about a minute out, I asked again: "I'm sorry, Steve. Which direction did you say I should be looking?"

He was listening to Mission Control and held up his finger as if to say, "Wait a minute." Then I saw the color drain out of his face. He couldn't answer.

I saw movement in the corner of my eye and slowly looked to my left. NASA executives and personnel were pouring out of their bleacher seats with cell phones to their ears. My stomach dropped. I could feel my heart beating, but my body was numb. Something was wrong. *Oh, God, what's happening?*

From that moment on, everything moved in slow motion, even my brain. I couldn't think straight. I looked for Laura and Matthew and saw they were still playing with the other crew children. I looked to my right and saw Keith standing beside Jane. His face was ashen. He had been listening to the communication between Mission Control and the shuttle and had already suspected that something terrible had happened. I moved toward him, but it was difficult to lift my legs; my body wasn't working.

"Keith, I think something's wrong," I whispered.

"I think there is too," he said.

I tried to process what was taking place. There was no way this was happening. This was Rick's dream. It couldn't be ending. Not today. Not like this.

2
Dreams of Space

From the time I was about four years old, I wanted to be an astronaut.

—Rick Husband

ON JANUARY 24, 1977, I WENT WITH MY COLLEGE ROOMMATE to a basketball game at the Texas Tech coliseum in Lubbock. I got up to buy a Coke and saw a good-looking guy (at six-two he stood out in the seats) in the row in front of me and immediately recognized him from high school. He had graduated a year ahead of me, and although we lived less than two miles apart, we didn't really know each other. But I remembered him! It was Rick Husband.

Even in high school, I was a faraway fan of Rick's and admired his singing and acting ability. I thought he was very handsome and remembered hearing him sing at a dinner theater one summer. I was on a date but was watching Rick, hoping that the boy I was with wouldn't notice. Rick had a tremendous voice, and his personality was magnetic. I couldn't take my eyes off him; it didn't hurt that he was pretty fun to look at, either.

In high school, I didn't know that Rick wanted to be an astronaut, but his friends knew. "From the time I met him in fourth grade, I knew," David Jones says. "And he never wavered from that dream. All through school I knew he was going to be an astronaut."

Rick's parents knew earlier than that. If a plane flew over their home in Amarillo, four-year-old Rick would run into the yard to watch it. He'd crane his neck and squint into the sun, wondering what it was like to soar above the clouds. "He'd get so excited," Jane says. "For whatever reason, he was drawn to airplanes and space from the time he was just a little boy."

If he knew there was going to be something on TV about the space program, Rick was glued to the set, making his mom and dad watch it with him.

"Where's the camera, Mama?" Rick asked, running into the kitchen.

"I'm not sure, Rick," she said. "What do you need the camera for?"

"I have to take a picture of the TV when the spaceship comes on," he said, flapping his arms in excitement. "I have to find the camera!"

Jane didn't laugh. She knew he was serious.

"Well, look in the hall closet, Honey. Maybe it's there."

Rick bounded through the hall and threw open the closet door. There it was, on the top shelf, where his parents assumed it was out of Rick's reach. He put a foot up on the shelf closest to the floor and climbed up, reaching for the camera. "Come on! I've got it," he said, plopping down in front of the TV set. "Come on, Mama! Come on, Daddy!"

Rick and his parents watched Gus Grissom rocket up 117 miles above the earth, and Rick was mesmerized. He snapped a picture of the TV when the rocket came on the screen. "There it is!" he shouted, snapping another picture. "There's the rocket!" He was captivated and hooked.

One evening in February of 1962, Rick, Jane, and Doug watched the news coverage of John Glenn orbiting the earth. "I want to be an astronaut when I grow up," Rick said, watching the screen. "That's what I want to do."

Jane and Doug looked at their little boy and smiled. From the time Rick and Keith were little, both Jane and Doug encouraged them to follow their dreams.

"Rick," his father said, "you can be anything you want to be."

From that time on, Rick set his sights on the stars. Doug and Jane bought him a telescope, and he'd run to the backyard and point the 'scope toward the heavens, straining to see the constellations or a close-up of the moon. Jane found a toy space helmet in a store one day and bought it for Rick. One morning, when he was still in his pajamas, he put the helmet on. "Look at me, Mama," he said. "I'm already an astronaut."

"Are you going to fly to the moon today?" Jane asked.

"Yep," Rick said, running around the living room.

"Well, let me take your picture before you go," Jane said. He posed in front of the fireplace, and Jane snapped the picture.

"I'll try to be back for dinner," Rick said, carrying on with his space business.

Jane laughed and put the camera away, thankful she had said yes to a blind date years earlier. As a young woman, Jane Barbagallo was content working in the House of Representatives office in Washington, D.C., and never had any intention of moving. When someone suggested she go out with a man named Doug Husband from Texas, she didn't see any harm in it; she assumed she'd gain a new friend. She had no idea she would soon fall in love with the Southerner with a smile as big as Texas and marry him in 1953. She moved sixteen hundred miles away to Amarillo, in the heart of the Texas panhandle, and soon discovered that it was where she wanted to raise her family. Rick Douglas Husband was born on July 12, 1957, and Keith followed less than three years later.

From the moment I met them, I knew the Husbands were a close, tight-knit family. There were always genuine love and respect for each other, which you could feel whenever you were around them. Doug ran the Amarillo Packing Company for years, and Jane stayed home, raising their sons. Rick was an easygoing, happy child who was ready at any time with a kiss for his mother. He'd walk by her and say, "I love you, Mama," or he'd stop and give her a hug before going out to play.

Although they had different personalities, Rick loved having Keith as a brother, and the feeling was mutual. Keith has said that Rick had the patience of a saint growing up. Rick's parents taught him that he should never hurt Keith, and Keith took full advantage of that knowledge, aggravating Rick to the point of meltdown. When both boys were little, Doug took Rick aside one day.

"The next time Keith hits you," Doug said, "you need to hit him back."

Rick patiently waited for that time to come. While playing in the back room one day, Keith punched Rick in the arm, and Rick hauled back and socked Keith in the shoulder. Keith's mouth dropped open. He was shocked.

"Mama! Rick hit me," he yelled. But he didn't get any sympathy.

"You finally got what you deserved," Doug said.

None of Rick and Keith's arguments lasted long, though. Neither held a grudge, and they were always soon playing together again.

Rick and his family could entertain me for hours with stories of their family vacations. When Rick and Keith were little, the family traveled across the country in their station wagon. Everything would go smoothly until Rick and Keith finally got on Doug's nerves. He'd fire off warning signals first: "Boys, knock it off," or "Boys, don't let me tell you again." If they continued to argue, the next step was what Rick called "The Long Arm of the Law." Doug's muscular right arm and large hand, complete with big college ring, would reach around the back of the front seat and start swiping the air. Rick and Keith would squish up against the doors, trying to avoid The Long Arm of the Law as Doug made big, sweeping swats from one side of the car to the other.

On a summer vacation to New Mexico, Rick and Keith climbed the steps into the camper attached to the back of the pickup truck. Doug took his place behind the wheel.

"I don't want to hear from either of you unless there are serious injuries," Jane said, closing the camper door. She took her seat next to Doug in the truck and held her breath, waiting for the inevitable. Rick and Keith saw their parents through a window and waved at them, but that was the extent of their communication. Several hours into the journey, Rick and Keith were playing checkers. Everything was going well until Keith started losing. Keith looked at Rick and grabbed hold of the checkerboard and flipped it. Checker pieces flew everywhere.

"Are you nuts?" Rick asked.

"You're cheating, and I don't want to play anymore," Keith said.

Unable to think of a good response, Rick threw himself on Keith and a tussle ensued. Keith started banging on the window. Jane turned around and saw him flailing his arms, but then Rick grabbed him and pulled him down again. Keith's face popped back up in the window, and Jane indicated that she couldn't understand him.

"I can't hear you," she said, pointing to her ears. She turned back around and looked out the front window of the truck. When Keith and Rick realized their parents weren't going to intervene, they rested for a while before setting up the checkerboard again. In the long run, they knew they had to get along or be miserable for the entire trip.

"Rick wasn't hard to get along with," Keith says. "He was a great big brother. He was always good to me and always looked out for me."

The brothers really did seem to have a genuine love for each other. When Rick started walking to school in the first grade, Jane gave him a dime each day so he could stop by the convenience store for a piece of candy on the way home. Rick always stopped, but he wouldn't get just a dime's worth of candy for himself; he'd bring candy home for Keith as well. "He was an unselfish child," Keith says. "And he grew up to be an unselfish man."

Early in school, when a teacher asked the children in her class what they wanted to be when they grew up, Rick was always the first to speak.

"I want to be an astronaut."

The children laughed. Kids in Amarillo dreamed of being a doctor or a rancher or an oil man, but very few dreamed of being an astronaut. When Rick was in first grade, there were only a handful of astronauts in the space program, so it was an unusual goal for a child. Astronauts were in a league of their own. But the laughter never discouraged Rick. If anything, it made him more determined.

Rick's first-grade teacher, Marjorie Roy, remembers Rick as being very studious, even at such a young age. His perfectionist qualities were evident in his handwriting and schoolwork. His favorite subjects all through school were math and science, but when it came to English, he would rather have been run over by a truck than to have to write a theme paper. Rick was born a type A personality and was driven to make A's and do well in school. He was meticulous in his work and took school seriously because he knew it was a means to his goal of becoming an astronaut. Good grades didn't come easily for him, though; he had to work hard for them.

Rick tried different sports as a young boy but never enjoyed them. He was on the softball team his father coached, and he played football in junior high but dreaded each practice. He had to work at keeping his weight down. In the sixth grade he gained his weight before his height, and the kids made fun of him. His parents tried to help him lose weight and made him meat and lettuce sandwiches without the bread. When he told me that story years later, my thought was, *Why even bother calling it a sandwich?* With a lot of work he lost the weight he needed and made the football team in junior high. The team never won a game, but as Rick always said, "The coach yelled all season so at least there was that!" He soon figured out that playing sports wasn't his cup of tea.

He started singing in choir at school and loved it, meeting many of his lifelong friends. Math and science required so much diligent focus that music was a creative change of pace. Even as a young boy, Rick discovered that singing provided great enjoyment and gave him a sense of release. It was a pattern that continued throughout his life. Rick and David Jones sang in choir together and acted in drama club productions of *Fiddler on the Roof, The Man of La Mancha,* and *Carousel.* In *Fiddler on the Roof,* Rick was part of the bottle dance, where the guys danced with a bottle on their heads.

"Rick wanted that dance to be as good as the scene from the movie," David says. "He was determined that the bottles shouldn't be weighted or have Velcro put on them. He was a perfectionist and was going to rehearse that dance for hours so the bottle would stay on his head and it did."

After Rick sprained his ankle during one rehearsal, a fellow cast mate's father, who was a doctor, came by the school and taped Rick's ankle. If it bothered him, he didn't let on; he performed every show with his ankle taped.

He was so active in school that Jane finally sat him down and talked to him. "Rick," she told him, "see if you can get a happy medium, so you're not always pushing yourself so hard." His mother worried that he'd burn himself out. "He was such a perfectionist that everything he did had to be done just right," she says. She was forgetting that the apple doesn't fall far from the tree.

On the phone with her mother-in-law, Floy Husband, Jane said, "I don't know why Rick is such a perfectionist. He just needs to relax."

There was a long pause on the line. Then Floy started laughing. "Gee, I wonder where Rick gets that."

Jane chuckled and realized he got it from her. "There was no room for mistakes with Rick," Jane says. "I thought that would eventually drive him crazy, but it never did." He loved a challenge, and if somebody told him he couldn't do something, he'd work extra hard to prove that he could.

When Rick and Keith were old enough, their father put them to work at the packing plant. "The boys aren't going to just sit around all summer," Doug said to Jane. "They need to work." It wasn't the job Rick had always dreamed of, but it was an early lesson in working with people with totally different economic and ethnic backgrounds and being diligent in your work. Rick and Keith worked primarily in the shipping room, filling meat orders. Rick, Keith, and their cousin, Brian Baker, worked hard but also played hard. Rick laughed to the point of tears when he recalled silly escapades with Keith and Brian, such as the times they'd get on the loudspeaker and page people to the phone.

"Emmett," Rick would say, disguising his voice. "You have a phone call on line one. Emmett, line one." Then they would wait while his poor old grandfather, Emmett, made his way to the office. They'd watch as he picked up the phone and repeatedly said hello to no one on the other end. That was high comedy in Amarillo!

Rick mentioned to his father that he'd like to get a car of his own. One day, Doug drove the family to a car lot and showed Rick a '69 Mustang that had seen better days. Jane saw the look on Rick's face and knew he thought his father was out of his mind. Rick thought there was no way his dad was going to buy that horrible-looking car. But he did.

Rick drove it home, hoping no one he knew would see him, and pulled into the driveway. The family stood back, staring at it. His dad was smiling. Doug went into the garage and pulled out his toolbox.

"What are you doing, Daddy?" Rick asked.

"We're going to tear it apart," Doug said.

Rick groaned inside, but he knew better than to tell his dad that they couldn't tear apart a car. He knew what his father would say: "Can't couldn't do a thing. You can do anything you set your mind to." It was something he repeated often as Rick and Keith were growing up. Rick knew, too, that once his dad started taking apart the car, he'd see it through to the end. Doug and Jane made sure that if the boys started something, they finished it. They weren't allowed to join a sports team and drop out halfway through the semester; they weren't allowed to join a club and then decide they didn't want to participate. Quitting wasn't an option.

The family got to work: fenders came off, then one side panel after another as they stripped down the car to nothing. Jane took the hubcaps into the kitchen and scrubbed them in the sink. They scrubbed and buffed and shined every inch of the car till it sparkled. The neighbors thought they were crazy, but when they finally put the car back together, it was beautiful and Rick was proud to drive it around Amarillo. Even after we married, Rick would spot a Mustang on the road and say,

"That one looks like my car," or "My car looked way better than that one." There was always a soft spot in his heart for that car.

At seventeen Rick started to take flying lessons. Jane and Doug always knew they would give him lessons, but throughout the years they wondered whether Rick would have the patience to wait. "Can I take flying lessons this year?" he asked Jane when he was thirteen.

"No, Honey," she said. "You're too young. You have to wait till you're seventeen." He'd wait a year or more and then ask again: "When can I take flying lessons, Mama?"

Jane knew he was tired of looking at the clouds from the ground and watching planes fly overhead; he wanted to experience that on his own. "Rick, you can't take them until you're seventeen," Jane said.

"Why can't I take them now?"

"Because they won't let you," Jane answered. "You're too young." Jane smiled as Rick walked back into his room; she knew it was just a matter of time before he was in the air.

"When he said he wanted to fly and be an astronaut," Jane recalls, "that's exactly what he meant!"

When he was seventeen, Jane drove Rick to Tradewinds Airport in Amarillo and signed him up for those long-awaited flying lessons. They cost between twelve and fifteen hundred dollars, and Jane and Doug were thrilled to provide Rick with the money. Those lessons were worth every cent. Rick sailed through them with an incredible, natural ability for piloting. It was love at first flight. He worked and studied hard to pass the flying tests, demonstrating the same persistence he had in school, and quickly got his pilot's license. He drove home the day he got his license and found his mother in the kitchen.

"Okay, Mama, let's go!" he said.

"Go where?" Jane asked, knowing what he meant.

"I want to take you flying. I can go solo now."

Jane put down her work and followed Rick out the door. She knew he would want her to fly with him sooner or later, so she swallowed hard and drove with him to the airfield. The two of them pushed a Cessna 152, a little two-seater airplane, out of the hangar.

Jane thought, *Oh, Lord, will this thing even have enough power to get off the ground?* She wasn't afraid of Rick's ability to fly; she knew how conscientious he was. But she was afraid to crawl into something that looked like a toy. However, when Rick took off and she saw that he knew what he was doing, her nerves settled. Rick loved it. He was so proud to be flying his mother. He flew her over Amarillo, and as they landed, Jane knew Rick was happiest when he was in the air. It was what he was meant to do.

Keith was fifteen when he took his first flight with Rick. He took his seat and started laughing because there wasn't room to move, let alone breathe; his shoulders rubbed against Rick's. Keith giggled down the runway and said, "When's this thing ever going to fly?" Rick pulled back and up they went. They laughed when they buzzed cattle and did stalls in the air (something Rick opted not to do with his mother in the plane), they went weightless a few times, and did touch-and-goes, where Rick would come down and land and then take off again without stopping. They laughed the entire time. Both Rick and Keith had such a love for flying that Jane and Doug knew the boys would eventually become pilots.

Rick took his friends up in the plane too. "He got such a kick out of scaring the pants off of me," David Jones says. "He'd do something and I'd yell and he'd laugh at me because I was screaming and that would make me scream louder! One time he pulled in front of a very large transport plane, a huge C-5, on the runway. He didn't mean to do it, but he got a significant chewing out from the tower. They just let him have it! It was pretty quiet in the plane for a while after that, but then we started laughing again. He was comfortable in that pilot's seat. I knew he'd never turn back now."

Both Rick and David shared a similar sense of humor and could make each other laugh by quoting ridiculous lines from the movie *Young Frankenstein*. "I'd start a line and Rick would finish it," David says. "We pretty much had the whole movie memorized since we'd seen it about twenty times." Even when he was grown, Rick claimed his favorite movie was *Young Frankenstein*. I think I watched it once with him and recognized every line from the movie because I'd already heard all the lines a hundred times! Rick and David loved to go to movies on the weekends in Amarillo, always keeping a seat between them so nobody would come to any false conclusions. They'd see *Blazing Saddles*, *Monty Python*, and all the *Pink Panther* movies and then crack each other up repeating lines from the films.

"Rick was a lot of fun," David says. "One of the greatest joys in my life was his friendship. He had a great sense of humor, and everybody

liked hanging around him. He wasn't perfect, but he was a great guy."
The most trouble he and Rick got into in high school was when they
toilet-papered someone's yard. "That was the extent of trouble back
then," he says, laughing.

Rick had the ability to be friends with both guys and girls (a trait that
would carry over as an adult); everyone felt comfortable around him.
One of the friends Rick made in choir was Susan Smith, who was never
a girlfriend (after a few dates they realized it wouldn't work), but they
became very close. They were friends throughout life. A month prior to
Rick's first mission in 1999, Susan got married, and Rick and I were
determined to attend her wedding in Dallas. Susan was in Florida for the
launch of the *Columbia* and was there on February 1 for its scheduled
landing. She would also attend Rick's memorial service in Houston.
When Rick made friends, he made them for life.

Since Rick was a class ahead of me in high school, I knew who he
was and thought he was very cute, but our paths never crossed in
school because he was interested in one set of activities and I was
involved in others. David remembers hearing the girls talk about Rick.

"They liked his bedroom eyes," David says. "Because they were so
big and blue. I wouldn't know," he says, laughing, "I never noticed!
But that's what I was told. He wouldn't have had trouble getting girls
to go out with him. They thought he was tall and good-looking, but
he didn't date a whole lot in high school. He was too busy."

One day, Rick and David came to my house collecting old magazines and phone books. The choir was recycling them to raise money
for a trip to Austria, and choir members scattered throughout the city
making collections. When I saw Rick and David at the door, I ran and
hid in my bedroom because I had curlers in my hair.

"Answer the door," I hollered at my mother from my bedroom.
"See what they want."

"I know what they want," my mother said, moving toward the
door. "They're here to pick up stuff for the choir."

"Don't tell them I'm here! Don't even mention my name!"

My mother rolled her eyes and opened the door. From my bedroom
I could hear her talking to them in the den across the hall for what
seemed like an eternity.

After they left, Mother came to my room and said, "You can come
out now. Boy, you really missed out because they were really cute!"

I wanted to say, *I know, Mother! That's why I was hiding.* There was no way I was going to let two cute guys from school see me with my hair up in curlers. I discovered years later that when Rick was little, his baby-sitter would show up wearing curlers in her hair. One night, she came to the door and he dove into his bed, never to be heard from again. His mother had short hair and never wore curlers so when he saw the baby-sitter, he was terrified, thinking there was something wrong with her head. Little did I know that if I had walked out of my bedroom that day in curlers, I could have brought to an early end my relationship with Rick.

Rick graduated from Amarillo High School with honors in 1975 and headed to Texas Tech in Lubbock to study mechanical engineering. I graduated a year later and also went to Texas Tech to study telecommunications. It was only a two-hour drive, so it was close enough to travel home but far enough away to be on my own.

At the Tech basketball game in 1977, as I went back to my seat in the coliseum, Rick watched me walk all the way up the steps. He joked with me later that he was checking me out. I remember what I was wearing that night, an orange shirt and overalls. When I walked past Rick's seat, I looked over at him. "Hi," I said, waving.

His eyes widened. It startled him because he knew he'd been caught looking at me! Throughout the game he racked his brain trying to remember where he had seen me before. After the game he followed me out of the building, but I didn't know it. I teased him later that if I'd known he was stalking me, I wouldn't have gone out with him. When he got back to his room, he called the Texas Tech operator for a listing of Evelyn Neely (he finally remembered my name). He called me the next day.

"Hello, Kappa Pledge Evelyn," I said.

Rick reeled back in horror, thinking, *I don't want to date a girl in a sorority.* "Hi, this is Rick Husband," he said. "I sat in front of you at the basketball game last night." Rick would later tell me that he was very nervous when he called me because he didn't think I would remember him. He also said he didn't know what we'd talk about on the phone but quickly learned that I am never at a loss for words!

"Oh, yes," I said, excited that he called. "I remember you from high school."

"Would you like to go to dinner and maybe a movie on Friday night?"

I hesitated because I already had a date for Friday night. "I'm busy Friday," I said, hoping it wouldn't discourage him. "But how about Saturday night?" I didn't want to put him off by appearing busy, but it was the truth.

"I'm busy Saturday," he said. "Maybe we can do it another time."

There was no way I was going to let this guy get away. "I'll cancel my date for Friday," I said quickly. I really wanted to go out with Rick. "I'd love to go out with you." That was unusual for me. I had never canceled a date to go out with someone else. In the next few minutes I made plans to go out with my future husband.

Our first date was on January 28, 1977. He picked me up in his 1975 Camaro. (We still have that car. It has more than 200,000 miles on it now. Rick drove it every day to work at Johnson Space Center.) I spent a lot of time getting ready that evening because I knew he was special. My roommate helped me pick out an outfit that would be perfect. The phone rang in my dorm room.

"I'm downstairs," Rick said.

I was nervous as I walked down the stairs. I saw him standing in the lobby, and my heart started beating faster. He was so cute.

"You look great," he said in his Texas drawl. I loved his voice. It was so warm and kind.

He held the door open and he walked me to his Camaro, opening my door. He was a total gentleman. I knew right away that this guy was out of the ordinary. We ate at a restaurant called the Smuggler's Inn. During the meal, he knocked over his water, and a flood came pouring over my side of the table. Rick jumped up and bumped his head on the light as he grabbed for napkins.

"I'm sorry," he said. "Hurry, get out of the way!"

"It's okay," I reassured him. "It didn't get on me."

"I'm so sorry," he said again.

It was love for me at that point. He was able to laugh at himself but was concerned about spilling water on me. I was more than impressed.

Throughout the meal we talked about mutual friends in Amarillo and realized that our parents knew each other. There was never an awkward lull in the conversation, which is unusual for a first date. We really enjoyed each other's company. I'd never met anyone so like-minded to me.

After dinner we slow danced at the restaurant, and he sang softly in my ear. He had a wonderful voice. I thought, *Wow, this is nice!*

Rick had a way of making me feel so comfortable; he had that way with everyone he met. We left the restaurant and went to see a movie called *The Seven Percent Solution*. (I can't remember who was in it or what it was about.) Rick put his arm around me, and I felt totally at ease with him; there were lots of guys I never would have let get that close, but Rick was different.

After the movie we parked by a lake and continued our conversation about growing up in Amarillo and what we wanted to do with our lives.

"So, what do you like to do besides study and sing?" I asked.

He smiled. "I love to fly," Rick said. "I got my pilot's license two years ago. I like to fly every chance I get." I looked at him. For some reason he had the demeanor of a pilot. "I really want to go into the air force, and my lifelong dream is to be an astronaut."

I thought that was an incredible goal. I didn't find it humorous or out of reach; it just seemed to fit Rick. I thought if anybody could make it, he would make it. He had the drive and the personality to be an astronaut.

"What do you have to do to become an astronaut?" I asked.

Before we met, Rick wrote to NASA and asked what qualifications the agency looked for in pilots or mission specialists. He received a letter sometime later stating the specifics, and Rick used that letter as a road map for his future.

"First, I need to get a technical degree in engineering, math, or biological or physical science." Rick was studying mechanical engineering, so I knew he was on his way to meeting the first criterion. "Then, I'll have to become a fighter pilot in the military and get enough hours in the air to even qualify for the space program. But they say that test experience is 'highly desirable,' so I'll need to become a test pilot if I want to be taken seriously."

I shook my head. I was amazed at the amount of work and direction Rick was committed to. It sure seemed Rick had a lot of work ahead of him.

He smiled; he wasn't finished. "After that, I'll have to get a master's degree in mechanical engineering, and *then* I'll be eligible and can apply."

"How long is all that going to take?"

It seemed it would take forever to meet all the criteria, but it didn't seem daunting to Rick. He shrugged his shoulders. "It'll take a while," he said, laughing. "But it's what I want to do."

"I'd love to go flying with you sometime," I said, smiling.

His eyes brightened. "I'd love to take you."

He smiled that big, broad smile of his, and my heart beat faster. We definitely had chemistry, and I knew that Rick was interested.

"I'd love to take you sometime soon."

I didn't think the time would get here soon enough. I wanted to spend as much time with Rick as possible.

Before Rick took me to my dorm, we drove around Lubbock and passed a house that had become something of a legend to college students; it held some sort of mystery that had been exaggerated through the years. Supposedly, a person had gone insane and still lived there, peeking through the curtains from time to time. Rick stopped in front of it, and I looked out the window toward the house, looking for any signs of insanity. I turned to look at Rick, and he leaned over and kissed me. We laughed about it later—he had the opportunity to kiss me in front of a beautiful lake but chose to wait to kiss me in front of the insane person's house. Certainly not the most romantic place, but it was memorable!

I went to my room after he dropped me off, and I knew I was in love with him. He was the most amazingly kind, intelligent, and articulate man I'd ever met, and I was certain I wanted to spend the rest of my life with him. Rick was the only person I had felt such chemistry with. I was attracted to him not only physically but also mentally and spiritually.

We dated on and off through my four years at Tech. One weekend, I took Rick home to meet my parents. My dad grilled steaks and didn't cook Rick's long enough; it was extremely rare. It looked awful, but Rick didn't say anything. He was a slow eater, and my parents and I are speed eaters, so we had already cleaned our plates by the time Rick finished buttering his potato.

It seemed we sat there for an hour watching Rick choke down the rare steak, and the whole time he did, my mother kept mouthing to me, *He's so cute!* Then she smiled and nodded.

I was mortified; I just knew Rick was going to look up and catch her one time. She never let up.

My dad, on the other hand, loved talking with Rick. Daddy loves war stories and always reads books or watches movies about any war.

Rick would take a bite and just chew and chew as my dad talked to him about one battle after another. Rick was a captive audience at that point, so my dad talked his ear off. When Rick *finally* finished eating and got up from the table, my dad pointed to the scraps on Rick's plate and said, "He must really love you because he finished *this* steak."

"We liked Rick right away," my dad says. "He had an easy way with anybody he talked to that was very genuine."

When I met Rick's family, Keith was still in high school. It didn't take long to notice that the two brothers were total opposites, but there was a genuine affection between them. Rick was a straight-A student in school, which could have put pressure on Keith to perform at the same level, but Rick was always the first person to let Keith know that he wasn't "Rick Husband's brother"; he was Keith Husband. Rick always had a great deal of admiration for Keith. He loved his sense of humor and outlook on life. Of course, nothing was ever out of place in Rick's room, and when they were young, Keith would step into that pristine environment and half unmake the bed just to drive Rick crazy. While Rick was always serious and focused, Keith took things in stride, never making mountains out of molehills.

Jane made spare ribs for dinner that night (at Rick's request because they were always his favorite; at Edwards Air Force Base, he was called Ribs), corn on the cob, and every other food that sticks to your teeth. As we talked and laughed, I could feel the corn stuck to my front teeth. I'd try to scrape it away before talking, but it was a losing battle. For some reason, throughout the meal Keith told me how pigs were slaughtered, which he understood all too well because of Doug's meat-packing plant. The whole evening was a comedy of sorts, but Jane and Doug made me feel so at home. They were kind to me from the moment I met them.

Rick and David Jones still maintained their close friendship, and after we had gone out a few times, Rick called David and told him about me. He said, "Do you remember Evelyn Neely from high school?" He described me, but apparently, I didn't have "bedroom eyes" that stood out in David's memory, so he got out the high-school annual and looked me up.

"Sure, I remember Evelyn," David said.

"Well, I'm dating her," Rick said. "And I think she's the one."

Rick and I never talked about marriage specifically, but I think we both knew that we'd eventually come to that point in our relationship. We just weren't sure when it would happen.

It took Rick five years to finish his degree in mechanical engineering, so we both graduated in 1980 from Tech. Rick was in air force ROTC his last two years in college, and on the day of graduation, he was commissioned into the air force as a pilot. I moved to Dallas and, after a long job search, began working for WBAP radio as an account executive. Rick went to Enid, Oklahoma, for pilot training. We would be separated about a year, but Rick knew it was better to go through pilot training as a single man rather than a married one because his hours would be long and demanding.

The days spent training to be a pilot are very stressful. There's much to learn academically, and then you have to turn those lessons around and use them in the cockpit for instruction in the air. A typical day is ten to twelve hours long and consists of a combination of academics, flying, and studying. There's no such thing as a weekend off in pilot training—weekends are meant for more study.

Lots of people are weeded out before that first year of pilot training is over, but Rick *knew* he was going to make it. He had great determination and focus. Pilots need a lot of both during pilot training because instructors put pressure on them to make sure they can handle the strain later on when it really counts. If they can't focus on what they're doing in the air, it won't take long for an instructor to see that they just don't have the abilities necessary to succeed as a pilot.

"If you learn good techniques early on, you stay out of trouble," Rick's friend Steve Schavrien explains. "Rick learned good lessons and techniques early on, so he didn't have trouble in his pilot training. Throughout his career, if Rick made a mistake, he was very honest about it. He was an excellent pilot."

Although we were separated physically during that time, Rick and I continued to date. I'd fly to Oklahoma and spend some time with him when his schedule allowed. I went there one weekend in the summer of 1981, and Rick helped carry my luggage to my hotel room. We sat on the bed and talked about what we would do that weekend.

"We could go to a movie," Rick said, not looking at me.

I noticed he was acting odd. "That'd be great," I said.

"Or maybe we could go to the park," he said, staring at his shoes. He was nervous and fidgety.

"That'd be great too," I said.

He got down beside the bed and sort of buried his head into the side of it. I thought, *What in the world is wrong with him today?*

"Evey," he squeaked out, "will you marry me?" Rick always had a hard time pronouncing the *m* word, so his proposal came as a surprise.

I said yes, but then after I thought about it, I said, "I don't want the story I tell our children for the rest of our lives to be that you proposed to me in some hotel room!" I teased him the rest of the weekend, so every time I turned around, he proposed all over again: in a park, a restaurant, the car, and a movie theater. He was determined to make it up to me.

On Saturday, Rick called me at the hotel. "Do you want to go into Enid and look for wedding rings?" Although I was in love with Rick, it was my time to get nervous about getting married. I called Cherie January, my roommate from college, and asked her if she thought it'd be a good idea to get married.

"Yes, Evelyn," she said, excited for me. "You've been in love with Rick for over five years. I think it will be fine!"

We went to the Zales store in Enid but couldn't find anything we liked. "I want to get you what you'll love," Rick said.

"That might take a while," I said, laughing.

"It doesn't matter," he said, wrapping his arms around me. "I want to get you what you'll love."

I wrapped my arms tighter around him and kissed him. I already had what I loved!

We shopped in Amarillo a few weeks later, and Rick bought me a simple yet beautiful solitaire setting. The moment I put the ring on, I knew it was the one I wanted. It would take several weeks to mount the diamond into the setting we selected. We also found a nice gold band for Rick, and I chose an inscription to go inside the ring. It stated, "All my love to you forever," and included our wedding date. A few weeks later, Rick flew to Dallas with my ring and took me to one of the most expensive restaurants in the city. We had a wonderful evening, and at the end of the meal he presented me with my engagement ring. That special evening more than made up for the marriage proposal! We set the date for February 27, 1982, seven months away. First, Rick would have to go through Land Survival School and Fighter Lead-in School.

It was at land survival training in Spokane, Washington, that Rick and Steve Schavrien met. "We hit it off right away," Steve says. "I think everybody who met Rick hit it off with him right away."

For two weeks, Rick trained in survival, escape, evasion, and interrogation resistance techniques. People dread survival training because there's nothing fun about it. I remember that time clearly because it was over Thanksgiving, and my parents and I wondered if Rick was eating bugs or something. At dinner we prayed extra hard for Rick before we filled up on turkey and dressing and pecan pie.

Rick and the others were given sleeping bags and parachutes and were told to make a tent or lean-to or whatever they could to survive in the woods. There were few rations, roughly one day's worth, but if they were careful, they could survive the three days without getting too hungry. "Some of the guys tried eating greens in the woods," Steve says, "and of course somebody tried eating ants, but Rick and I figured that with the rations we were given, we could make it without resorting to bugs!"

During his time in Land Survival School, Rick had to take part in a mock prisoner-of-war camp where instructors would interrogate the pilots and try to break them down.

"They don't do it long," Steve says, laughing at the memory, "but they do it long enough to give you a taste of what it would be like if you were ever captured. I wanted to get out of Spokane so bad, but I remember looking at Rick on our last day there and he had this big smile on his face. He knew it was one of the steps he needed to take to get closer to his dream, and he was smiling because he had made it through to the end."

After Land Survival School, Rick had three months of Fighter Lead-in School in New Mexico. Pilots selected to fly fighter or attack aircraft go through lead-in training to learn basic fighter skills (gunnery, air-to-air combat maneuvering, weapons delivery) prior to going to specific training for the aircraft they are assigned to. In Rick's case, he was assigned to F-4 training.

He finished the six-week course and flew back to Amarillo for our wedding, which, in typical Southern fashion, was huge. Bridesmaids and groomsmen filled the front of the First Presbyterian Church. It was the church I had grown up in, and the church in which my parents and my maternal grandparents had gotten married. It was a beautiful ceremony, and I remember looking at Rick and feeling deeply in love with him. He was so handsome. I couldn't wait to start the rest of our lives together.

My parents rented a private jet to fly us to Colorado Springs for our honeymoon. We were going to spend three nights at the Broadmoor Resort. We were both so nervous on our way there that we didn't say much to each other. I couldn't think of a thing to say to Rick, and he couldn't think of anything to say either, so he finally got into a good conversation with the pilot, which suited me just fine!

Once the honeymoon was over, we flew back to Amarillo and stayed one night at Rick's parents' house before leaving the next morning for Rick's next assignment in Florida. His mother insisted that we sleep in their bed, which unnerved me to no end. I walked into the room, and Keith smiled at me with an all-knowing smile; I could have just crawled under the bed and stayed there the whole night.

The next morning, since we were newly married and didn't want to spend a minute apart, Rick and his dad hooked the Camaro behind my Cutlass so we could tow it to Florida. We said our good-byes and Rick got behind the wheel, but when he turned the corner at the end of my parents' street, the car started to jackknife. Our two dads watched as they followed us to the edge of town, and they didn't have a great deal of confidence that we'd get to Florida safely. Two days later we drove onto Homestead Air Force Base to look for our new home.

I would soon learn that "home" is where the air force sends you.

3

Desert Times

When God leads through valleys of trouble,
His omnipotent hand we can trace;
For the trials and sorrows He sends us
Are valuable lessons of grace.

—Anonymous

FOR THE NEXT NINE MONTHS, RICK WOULD TRAIN AT HOMESTEAD on the F-4, an all-weather fighter manufactured by McDonnell Douglas that is one of the few airplanes flown by the navy, marines, and air force. The F-4 was the workhorse of the 1960s and 1970s and was used in Vietnam. It could perform air-to-air missions as well as air-to-ground missions. Usually, a plane has air-to-air capability or air-to-ground, but rarely both. In our time at Homestead, Rick would fly the F-4, and when we were later stationed in California, Rick would fly the F-15, also manufactured by McDonnell Douglas. He would count them as two of his favorite planes to fly.

While we were at Homestead, we heard that the space shuttle was going to fly over early one morning. Rick was excited, but when the alarm went off at 3:00 A.M., I was the one waking him! "Come on, get up," I said, nudging him. "We have to see the shuttle." He was a heavy sleeper and could be difficult to wake. "Come on, Rick," I said again. "We're going to miss the shuttle." I couldn't believe *I* was prompting *him*! We got into the car and drove to the end of the street where there weren't any streetlights and waited.

After several minutes, Rick threw his finger in the air. "There it is," he said, spotting it first. "Would you look at that!" We saw a streak of light race across the sky from one end to the other. "Can you believe it's traveling over 17,000 miles an hour and it's almost 200 miles above the earth, yet we can see it so clearly?" He followed the path with his finger till it was out of sight.

I turned to look at him. "Do you think you still want to do that someday?"

He looked at me and smiled. "I sure do," he said. "But first I want to get back to bed. I've got an early flight and I need my beauty sleep!"

I laughed and we went back home. Rick was still seventeen years away from his first space flight, but he had already met NASA's first two criteria by getting a degree in mechanical engineering and becoming a fighter pilot. Slowly but steadily, the dream was getting closer to coming true.

After nine months in Florida, we moved to Moody Air Force Base in Valdosta, Georgia, and bought our first home. We called our parents and told them that the house came installed with trees. In Amarillo, trees were always brought in and planted, but this house had twenty-three pine trees scattered throughout the yard!

Rick pulled into our driveway after his first day in the squadron at Moody. Members of each squadron got a different colored scarf as they reported to their new squadron, and Rick brought his home, beaming. "Look, these are the patches," he said, showing me a patch that would go onto each of his three flight suits.

"Do *I* have to sew those on?" I asked.

"No, they'll sew them on at the base," he said. "You need to meet all the people I met today," he said, putting his things away. "I have a really good feeling about the squadron, Evey. I'm with some really good people. This is going to be a great assignment for both of us." Rick loved flying so much that he could have been assigned anywhere and worked with anybody and been happy, but it truly did seem to be a special group of people.

He was assigned to the same squadron as his old friend Steve Schavrien, and they would fly together a great deal. There were several occasions that they flew on training missions across the country, testing new weapons systems, and performed together what is called Red Flag—they took planes out to the Las Vegas desert and dropped bombs and practiced other military tactics. They flew an advanced version of the F-4, known as the F-4E, at Moody. They both came to Moody as wingmen but rose to flight lead, meaning that if there was a two-ship (two fighter planes flying together) or a four-ship (four fighter planes), Rick was the lead plane.

"He was excellent at what he did," Steve says. "Rick was the best kind of fighter pilot because he had incredible skills, but he didn't have the ego to go with them."

Larry Moore was Rick's wizzo (weapons system operator) on many occasions. "I was thoroughly impressed with his piloting skills," Larry says. "It was obvious he had special talent. Some pilots didn't like a second guy in the airplane, but Rick was never like that—he tried to use the wizzo as essential to the mission. He always made me feel like I was part of his team. He was one of those guys who you instantly liked and was lots of fun to fly with because he was so easygoing, never overbearing."

"Rick was nothing but professional," Steve says. "I was more senior in rank to him, and he and three other men of Rick's rank worked for me in the squadron. We would put together the schedule for seventy-two crewmen every day. It was a job that could drive you crazy juggling that many schedules, but if the stress ever got to Rick, he never showed it. He did his job and flew planes with great ease and grace."

I got my real estate license in Valdosta and worked for a real estate agency there. It started out as a very enjoyable job, but as time went on, I found it to be very stressful and hard to manage. I wanted to do a really good job, especially for military friends, but I couldn't discover how to leave my work at the office—it seemed to follow me home every day. I went for a walk with Rick one particularly stressful evening and cried about the frustrations I had experienced with some clients that day.

"Why don't you just quit, Evelyn?" he asked.

"But I really enjoy it!" I knew it didn't make sense, but I appreciated the fact that Rick never expected me to work or help out financially. His entire focus was on my happiness. Later, I did resign. I discovered I was far too sensitive in my early twenties and took everything personally. I didn't have the thick skin required to work in financial issues with people I knew.

Rick loved his time in the squadron at Moody, and it was a wonderful time in our marriage. A lot of people say that the first few years of marriage, especially the first year, are stressful, but Rick and I had a great time. We loved being with each other.

We loved the people in the community and became very involved with a church there. We'd both been brought up in church, so it was very important to us. I grew up in the Presbyterian church in Amarillo, and Rick and his family were members of the Methodist church. We both liked going to church, but having a deep relationship with Jesus was still in its infancy for us.

Throughout our time in Georgia, Rick continued to reach for his goal of one day becoming an astronaut. He'd pull out that letter he received from NASA when he was in college and read again what he needed to do in order to be qualified for the space program. He knew he'd have to fly a minimum of one thousand hours as a fighter pilot to try to become a test pilot, a crucial stepping-stone to even being considered by NASA.

"He knew he had to have those one thousand hours," Steve says. "But Rick just plodded along, one step at a time. He knew from the time he started flying in '81 that it would take him six, maybe seven years to log that many hours, but he knew that goal was attainable and the best part of being around Rick was that he never stepped on anybody along the way. He did what had to be done, but he did it with honesty and with integrity."

In December of 1985 Rick was transferred to George Air Force Base outside Victorville, California, in the middle of nowhere. We drove across country (in separate cars this time) on I-40 West for days and days. I got strep throat within days of our arrival. I assumed it happened because the air was so dry; we'd been used to high humidity in Georgia and Florida.

In addition to flying, Rick became an instructor at George AFB, teaching pilots and weapons system operators, and he taught German students the basic F-4 course. It was at George that Rick applied to Test Pilot School. He had his minimum of one thousand flying hours, but he knew it was difficult to get into Test Pilot School. Each year, only twenty-five pilots were chosen from the applicants, so the Test Pilot School was highly selective in whom they chose; no one could get in without a recommendation. Rick's squadron commander did everything he could to help, but once the application was turned in, all we could do was wait.

Since it was to a pilot's advantage to have an advanced degree to get into the space program, Rick also began work on his master's degree. He drove an hour through the desert one night a week to Edwards Air Force Base where instructors from Cal State Fresno taught. He studied mechanical engineering with an aeronautical emphasis. He studied for hours, poring over textbooks into the night and on weekends.

I decided against becoming a real estate agent in California. The stress of being an agent just didn't make it seem worthwhile for me to get my license in another state, and I didn't want to deal with the frustrations of the job since we wanted to have children. Rick and I had always adored children and decided it was time to start a family. After months of trying to conceive, I still wasn't pregnant but didn't think anything of it. Since we had never tried to get me pregnant before, we didn't know what a "normal" amount of time should be. For a while, there was no perceived need for alarm.

I had always had an interest in teaching, but my experience was limited to Bible studies. I soon became a substitute teacher in Apple Valley at the junior high school and ended up being hired as the long-time sub for the next year teaching English, speech, and drama to seventh and eighth graders. I'd never had any drama experience before, but I loved it. I looked forward to seeing my students every day, and the busyness kept my mind off my inability to get pregnant.

We went to a church in Apple Valley where Roy Rogers and Dale Evans attended. Each Sunday we made it a point not to sit behind Dale or else we couldn't see around her hair. Rick's parents visited at Thanksgiving, and Jane got the biggest thrill because she was able to shake Dale's hand. Before she did, I said, "Be sure you say 'Happy Thanksgiving,' not 'Happy Trails,'" and Jane giggled the whole time shaking Dale's hand. We enjoyed the church and were active (Rick sang in the choir, and I helped with the youth group), but neither of us was really digging into the Word. We still didn't know what it meant to have a deep, personal relationship with God.

Rick loved his work at George. He had a natural ability as a teacher and was honored with the outstanding academic instructor award. Steve Schavrien was an instructor at George as well. "Rick was always a generous teacher," Steve says. "He was always willing to work with students on the ground or in the air till they understood something. Students really respected him."

Rick also applied at that time to NASA for the first time, but was rejected. The space shuttle *Challenger* had exploded in January of 1986 so NASA put all applications on permanent hold, meaning no one was accepted during that application period. No one was being considered. NASA wouldn't fly again for three years. It was disappointing, but Rick knew he would apply again. In the meantime, he continued to meet all the necessary criteria to be considered for the space program.

One night when Rick came home from work, I was in the kitchen preparing dinner. As he often did, Rick picked up a knife and started helping me chop vegetables for our meal. He had a big grin on his face.

"I've been notified that I'll be going to Edwards Air Force Base to try out for Test Pilot School," he said.

I knew that was big news. "Rick, I am so proud of you," I said, hugging him. "I know you're going to do just great! How long will you be gone?"

"I'll drive there on Monday morning for the week of tests and drive back on Friday night. I hope I do a really good job." He didn't have to worry. Rick always did a great job. "I'm so glad we live close to Edwards so that I'm already familiar with the airspace."

Putting my arms around his neck, I kissed his face. "Rick, I'm going to pray hard this week that you'll do your very best."

"I can't afford to screw up this week," he said. "This is really important." Both of us knew that he had to be accepted into Test Pilot School if he was going to be considered for the space program.

Rick was evaluated at Edwards every day while performing different flight test maneuvers and techniques. He'd take a plane up for check climbs, which determine the best rate of climb for a particular aircraft, and he'd perform level accelerations—he'd stabilize at a relatively low air speed to near stall and then accelerate to as fast as the aircraft would go to assess the aircraft's performance. Instructors also had him perform trim shots, check descents, and windup turns. These various maneuvers test a pilot's basic flying abilities along with precision flying skill and aptitude.

Pat Daily was another exceptional pilot who was called to Edwards for test pilot tryouts. Rick met Pat at George and found a kindred spirit; Pat also wanted to be an astronaut. "There's a lot of precision required at those tryouts," Pat says. "They're looking for pilots who have more than just a basic flying skill. Test pilots have to be very precise and controlled in their flying, and a big part of that is in a pilot's personality so they look for someone who is precise, yet can get along with others, someone who doesn't goof around in the cockpit."

One evening during the tryouts, Pat asked Rick to see the movie that was playing on base, and Rick stopped what he was doing. "You'll have plenty of chances to see that movie," he said, looking at Pat. "But this may be the only chance you get to try out for Test Pilot School. Isn't it worth spending two extra hours to get ready for it?"

"He'd spend time at night studying the maneuvers," Pat recalls. "He'd read about how they were supposed to be performed and how to execute them in a particular aircraft. People have asked me what made Rick such a great test pilot, and I always say, 'The better question is what made Rick the best pilot I've ever met.' It wasn't Rick's basic stick-and-rudder skills; it was the fact that he put a phenomenal amount of effort into everything he did in an airplane. He was always prepared when he went up. He did everything with excellent preparation, and instructors recognized that."

At the end of the week, Rick drove back home and waited for word. If he passed, he would be accepted into Test Pilot School.

Rick's squadron commander at George, Col. Gene Patton, brought him into the office at the beginning of the week. "Rick, I need to see you for a minute," he said. Rick sat in a chair, and Colonel Patton smiled. "You're going to be moving soon. You've been accepted into Test Pilot School at Edwards Air Force Base." Rick leaped out of his chair, he was so excited. He pumped Colonel Patton's hand up and down.

He ran out of the office and called me right away. "Evey, I've got wonderful news! I just found out that I'll be going to Test Pilot School. We'll be moving to Edwards in December!"

"I knew you'd make it," I said. I was thrilled for Rick and I could tell he was beside himself with excitement, but my mind immediately started thinking of all the things we'd need to do to prepare for our move and all the friends we'd be leaving. The most difficult part of the military for me was the good-byes we had to say each time we picked up and moved.

"Thanks for always supporting me, Evey," Rick said. "This is going to be a great year for us. Thanks for always praying for me. I couldn't do this without you." Rick always made me feel that this was *our* life, not just his. He made me feel that we were in it together.

Whereas George AFB was at least in a town in the desert, Edwards was right *in* the desert. The closest town was forty-five minutes away. I didn't know it then, but God had taken us out to the desert so we could find Him. It seems we had to have a wilderness experience to learn about God's true love and grace.

We had a house on Sharon Drive at Edwards, a street where all the test pilot students lived. We opened the front door and got to work. We'd seen our share of drab, colorless housing, and every time we moved into a new place, we worked hard to turn it into a home. We unpacked our stereo and listened to Christmas music while Rick carpeted the entire house. I got to work unpacking and hanging curtains, and in three days we had everything finished and our belongings unpacked. Looking back, I don't know where we got all that energy; I'm not so sure I could do that again.

Rick threw himself into Test Pilot School. After all, it was a crucial step in getting accepted at NASA, and Rick was one of only twenty-five pilots chosen that year for training, so it was important that he prove himself. (His class had twenty-three members and was broken down between pilots and engineers. Another test pilot class would take place in six months and would have roughly the same breakdown, bringing a total of twenty-five pilots per year.) While at Edwards, Rick learned how to fly about thirty different airplanes. He learned how to test their performance, handling qualities, weapons systems, and engines. Throughout his career in the air force, Rick learned to fly more than forty types of aircraft.

Pat Daily was also accepted into Test Pilot School, and he and Rick became close friends. "You'd think that since we both knew how hard it was to become an astronaut, we would have been competitive, but I never felt any sense of competition from Rick. He was more than happy to help you if you needed help with anything. He'd sacrifice his own time to help you. Often, pilots have an ego that can get in the way of a friendship, but Rick was never like that."

Rick's hours were brutal during that year. We still desired to have a family, but nothing was happening. We could see others around us easily getting pregnant and having children, and the stress of trying was starting to get to me.

Rick remained upbeat and steady. "Everything will happen in God's time, Evey," he'd say to me. "We just have to be patient."

I knew he was right, but sometimes God's timing doesn't work into our schedules. I thought maybe it was the stress of Rick's hours that was responsible for my still not being pregnant. His first flight brief took place at six-thirty each morning. He'd fly in the morning and go to class in the afternoon. He'd leave around five-thirty that afternoon and come home to work on a project throughout the night or stay at the school to work as part of a team of three or four. I couldn't imagine that the stress was helping our efforts.

"There's a lot of pressure at that time," Pat says, "because our instructors could say, 'Be ready to fly the A-7 tomorrow,' but we wouldn't have flown that aircraft yet. We'd have to go home and study throughout the night to familiarize ourselves with that plane, learning how it operated before we took it up."

It was a year of intense study, yet Rick was never too busy for me. He knew I was having trouble dealing with our infertility, and he was always so gentle with me, bringing out the best in our situation. Sometimes, when he knew I was blue, Rick would come up from behind me and pick me up, swirling me around until I started laughing. He came home one day after work and could tell I had had a particularly bad day.

"Is anything wrong, Evey?" he asked.

I shook my head. "Not really," I said. "Just a little down, I guess."

He looked at me in all seriousness. "Am I gonna need to pick you up?"

I held my hand out to keep him away. "No, please don't pick me up. I'm too heavy."

"Don't make me pick you up," he said, grinning.

I backed away. "Rick! Do not pick me up. I'm not in the mood."

He threw his hands in the air. "That's it! You leave me no other choice. I have to pick you up." He bolted for me and I ran, but he caught me, swinging me around, making me laugh.

Please, just let me feel light, I thought.

During that time we could not conceive, I really started to dig through the Bible. I was hurting so much that I searched the Scriptures for comfort. We attended chapel on base, and the chaplain taught the Bible in a simple yet personal and meaningful way. For the first time in my life I really wanted the kind of relationship with God that the chaplain told us about—a relationship that was close, dynamic, and real.

Rick and I decided that we wanted to be baptized in the base pool. Both of us had been baptized as babies but never publicly proclaimed our belief in Jesus, and we felt compelled to do that. Church wasn't just church anymore; we were discovering that it was a way to get closer to the Lord, and I felt myself growing spiritually by leaps and bounds. This desert time became a huge turning point for me. I was going through the hurt of infertility but was understanding that God was going through it with me. He was becoming personal to me in a way I'd never grasped before. As a child, I had learned that God loved me and that He was good and kind and all-knowing, but I'd never realized that God desires a relationship with us more than anything else. He wanted a relationship with *me*.

Although I was growing in a way I hadn't experienced before, I wasn't so sure that Rick was growing at the same pace. Pat Daily recognized Rick's struggles in school. "When Rick arrived on base, he was a basic air force Christian," he says. "He loved God and attended chapel, but that's where his faith ended." But sometimes, what we think is the end of our faith is really just the beginning.

Before Rick graduated, he applied to NASA the second time. Again he was rejected. He didn't get past the initial air force screening. It was a process that drove Rick crazy, especially since he knew the navy didn't have that same procedure. A panel of air force personnel, who were neither astronauts nor affiliated with NASA, reviewed each application and determined whose application would be forwarded for consideration in the space program. For whatever reason, Rick's application was not forwarded. What aggravated Rick more than anything was that people who weren't involved with NASA were deciding his future. Looking back, I know it was God's perfect timing, but at that time it was frustrating.

In January of 1989, only a few weeks after Rick's graduation from Test Pilot School, I found out I was pregnant, and we were ecstatic. Rick joked that it had required *all* of his brain cells to make it through Test Pilot School and that he could finally concentrate on other things. At last, we were going to have a baby!

After Rick graduated, we moved off Sharon Drive since only test pilot students lived on that street. Once they graduated, they moved to other housing on base. We moved into our new base house in April. I was eleven weeks pregnant, but I felt as if something was terribly wrong with the pregnancy. I was spotting and cramping and knew it wasn't going well. I miscarried during that move, and it ushered in a dark, depressing time. Of course, I felt that it was my fault, that the move had caused the miscarriage. I cringed every time I heard a clichéd comment such as, "These things happen for a reason." No one ever wants to hear, "These things happen for a reason," when she has already been childless for many years. Comments that I didn't want to hear would upset me, but Rick was always encouraging. "God has a plan for us, Evey," he said. "I just know it." He'd hold me, I'd cry, and he'd always speak gently to me.

I became pregnant again later that year, and I was overjoyed. That joy soon faded when I miscarried again. I had to have a D and C and stay in the hospital. I met with a staff member at the base hospital in charge of referring patients off base and asked to be sent to an infertility specialist in the town of Lancaster, outside Edwards AFB. She sat at her desk and very coldly informed me, "It's not classified as infertility until you have miscarried at least three times." I couldn't believe it.

"These are babies to me, not events," I said. "There's something wrong, and I need a specialist." Fortunately, I eventually found a human side to this woman, and she started the ball rolling for me to have off-base care with a wonderful infertility specialist, Dr. William Jack Copeland.

I started to go to counseling to help me through the pain. I'd heard the heartbeats of the babies; I knew they were real and growing inside me, and I mourned losing them. Rick and I went through a series of invasive fertility tests, but he joked through them, making them easier. Rick and I always relied on humor, especially during stressful times. He'd quote ridiculous lines from movies like *Young Frankenstein* or any of the Monty Python films, making me laugh, or he'd talk in a high-pitched voice with a German accent as if he were one of the nurses. He always remained upbeat. "We just need to have faith and ride out this process," he said, wrapping his arms around me in the waiting room. "We need to maintain hope because I know God has an incredible plan for us." He had much more faith than I did during that time, helping me through my lowest moments.

Dr. Copeland finally determined I had low progesterone levels, so he put me on medication to see whether that would help maintain a pregnancy if I became pregnant again. I kept going to counseling, and one day the counselor talked about laying all my burdens at the foot of the cross. I got to the point where I saw myself handing my babies over to Jesus and seeing Him holding and taking care of them. That image gave me a tremendous feeling of peace because I knew I'd see those babies again, but for now Jesus would watch over them. That thought took a great deal of the pain away.

Rick supported me through counseling and never wavered from his belief that God would bless us with children. "Our blessing is coming, Evey," he'd say whenever I was down. "I just know God is going to bless us."

At the end of January 1990, one year from my first miscarriage, I became pregnant again, and that pregnancy went very well. Dr. Copeland prescribed progesterone up to the fifth month of pregnancy, and I passed the eleventh and twelfth weeks without incident. When I was five months pregnant, Rick finished his master's degree in mechanical engineering. We drove to Cal State Fresno in central California for the graduation ceremony and realized on the way there that it would be Rick's first time on campus!

I remained healthy throughout my pregnancy, and on October 5, 1990, Rick drove me to the hospital in Lancaster, California. I had Laura naturally and was in tremendous pain, but Rick was right there with me. "Doing great, Evey," he said. "You're doing just great!" When he saw Laura being born, he was overwhelmed by it all. "The baby's coming, Evey! The baby's coming!" The doctor allowed Rick to cut the cord, and he was beaming. He was a father!

Rick wrote this in Laura's baby book:

Evelyn did a great job in delivery. As Laura was being born, I could see her face first and the first thing I noticed was her chubby cheeks— they were so cute. It was so amazing to see face-to-face the wonderful little baby we had waited so long for. Then as the doctor was handing her to the nurse, I kept looking, trying to see if it was a girl or a boy. "It's a girl!" Dr. Copeland said. Evelyn and I were thrilled to death. Little Laura Marie was here!

Rick was so happy. We both were. Laura was such a good baby; neither of us could get enough of her. Rick came home every day for lunch so he could play with her. One time we put our David Winter decorative cottages on the floor. Rick grabbed the video camera and lay on his stomach, instructing me to move Laura around as if she was this giant baby stomping through a town. "Make it look like she's stomping on the castle," he said, holding the camera just right. "Okay, now make it look like she's crushing the village." Laura giggled and laughed. Time with Daddy was guaranteed fun.

When he came home from work, Rick took her to the park and walked with her or chased her around as she screamed and giggled. He'd peek around a tree and say, "Where's Laura?" That game was popular inside the house too. He'd sneak through the living room, saying, "Where's Laura? Where's Laura?" and then run up on her, making her shriek. I'd try to cook in the kitchen and Rick would sit with Laura on the floor, putting pots and pans on their heads. He was a hands-on daddy from the moment Laura was born, and every single day he told her that he loved her and that she was beautiful. She was Daddy's little girl.

Laura's birth added to Rick's spiritual growth, but he still wasn't as strong as he wanted or needed to be. We still had more days of wandering in the wilderness before either of us would get to the point of desiring a relationship with God above everything else.

Rick's goal of being an astronaut was still part of his dreams. In March of 1991 he filled out the application to NASA again. He sat in our study for hours, answering each question, and came across one that simply asked if he'd ever worn hard contacts (since hard contacts can change the shape of the cornea, neither the air force nor NASA allows them). Rick had worn them for a brief time to help correct his vision, but he knew the answer NASA was looking for was "no," so that's the answer he wrote down. It wasn't honest, but he told them what they wanted to hear. He reasoned that others had worn hard contacts to improve their vision with good results and had answered the question the same way he had. He thought that since he wasn't currently wearing hard contacts, there wasn't a problem. Rick didn't talk with me about answering the question the way he did; he kept it to himself.

Years later, he wrote in his journal about lying on the application:

My false justification at the time was that I had seen someone else do it successfully who was chosen for the space program. My selfish desire to be an astronaut overrode my integrity and I lied on my NASA application about wearing hard contacts.

I essentially had no clue what it meant to "trust in the Lord with all your heart and do not lean on your own understanding" (Proverbs 3:5). Also, even though I thought all of this was relatively minor, it was still dishonest—not something I had thought of myself as being. I thought, "Well, I'm a pretty good guy and this is no big deal. Besides, I know other people are doing it." I was mired in a worldly way of thinking, not trusting God in my life . . . I was definitely *not* glorifying God by these actions in my life.

He mailed the application and hoped it would get past the air force screening. After months of waiting, he got a call from someone in the astronaut's office at NASA. They wanted to interview him for the space program. Pat Daily got the same call and interviewed as well.

"It was like spending an entire week under a microscope," Pat says. "Every part of your body was poked and prodded." Rick, Pat, and the other applicants went through a series of medical tests, which included being hooked to a twenty-four-hour EKG. Doctors performed an EEG—an ultrasound of the applicants' hearts and other organs—and did a twenty-four-hour urinalysis. "They gave us what looked like a large thermos and asked that we collect every drop for twenty-four hours," Pat says. The urinalysis test was mild compared to other, more intrusive tests. "The proctoscopic exam was the most discomforting," Pat remembers. "They gave us a tray full of enema packs, instructions, and told us to tell them when 'everything was clear.' Once through that minor indignity, we got to meet Dr. Hind. [Yes, that was his actual name and the subject of many jokes among the applicants.] Dr. Hind used the proctoscope to explore the last two feet of our large intestine. The discomfort and indignity were somewhat mitigated by being able to view parts of our body normally unseen!"

When Rick returned to California, he told me about one of the psychological exams. At one point, he wore a heart monitor and was ushered inside a pitch-black, three-foot-diameter ball, with several hoses attached to supply fresh air, and left alone. The only thing he could do was lie in a fetal position.

"Why do they put you in there?" I asked.

"They want to see how long you can last without freaking out," he said.

"How long did you last?"

"I don't know," he said. "I fell asleep."

I didn't know how he could curl all six feet two inches of his body into a ball and fall asleep.

He saw the look on my face. "What was I supposed to do?" he asked.

"NASA claimed this test was to help them analyze the viability of a prototype shuttle escape system," Pat says. "They wired us up to an EKG, took away our watch, and told us that we would be there for an undetermined length of time. Most of us did just fall asleep, but some folks got a little upset and asked to be let out. I don't think they passed," he says, laughing.

Rick and Pat went through other mental and psychological exams, including a variety of IQ tests, psychology questionnaires, and interviews with astronauts and doctors of all types, but those tests didn't cause the anxiety associated with the eye exam. NASA requires visual acuity of 20/70 or better uncorrected, correctable to 20/20, for each eye. "The eye exams were what had both Rick and me most nervous as we knew we were borderline," Pat says. "We could pass the air force required tests easily enough, but NASA had both more stringent requirements and more exotic exams—ones you couldn't bluff your way through. I remember that Rick sweated the eye test." Pat didn't know the real truth of why Rick sweated that test; he didn't know that Rick was nervous because he had lied on the application and feared the truth would be discovered. "I thought he was afraid that he was a little myopic," Pat says.

"After the eye exam, the rest of our time there was a breeze," Pat continues. "We had to go through a panel interview: one applicant being interviewed by eleven NASA personnel. Rick's up-front humility, demeanor, and sense of humor saw him through the panel interview with ease."

Scott Parazynski, our family escort and backup CACO for the STS-107 mission, remembers his astronaut interview. "After all the tests," he says, "it basically comes down to that ninety-minute interview. That's the make-or-break event. They're looking for well-rounded people who get along well with others, have a caring attitude, a sense of humor, and compassion. I'm sure in Rick's interview that rang true the first minute he walked into the room because it was one of the first things you discovered when you met Rick. His empathy and concern for other people were probably greater than for himself. It was an amazing quality."

During his time in Houston, one of the astronauts Rick met was Jean Claude Nicollier, with the European Space Agency, who was training for a mission. Rick got to sit in on training in a flight simulator and sat next to Jean Claude. Rick talked with him and enjoyed hearing about what the European Space Agency was doing. Rick finished up the training session and said good-bye to Jean Claude, moving on to the next test that NASA had scheduled that day. He flew back to California and eventually received a phone call from an astronaut at NASA. He gently let Rick know that he had not been accepted into the space program but encouraged him to try again. Pat was not accepted either.

Rick was disappointed, but he didn't dwell on it. More than a year later, he would look back on that interview and see that things don't happen by chance in our lives—God weaves people in and out of our lives for a reason.

"I just knew Rick was going to make it someday," Pat says. "He was one of the hardest-working, most determined guys I'd ever met. He truly believed that the harder you worked, the better you were. There were a whole lot of guys who thought things were just good enough, but not Rick. He was always trying to get better and be better, and he had an amazing effect on people around him. He set an example and made us want to get better, not only as a military leader but as a human being. He was an example for people, and I knew that NASA would recognize that someday." But that day seemed so far away for Rick.

After Laura was born, I had an even deeper desire to grow close to God. Once you have a baby, you begin to understand God's love for us: it is totally unconditional. Laura was my child, and I would love her regardless of what she did. In the same way, I knew that God loved me with a love that was indescribable, and that love was powerful and real. The Bible was becoming a daily, hands-on tool for me.

In the summer of 1991 I was learning more than I ever had in Bible study, and each day I shared with Rick what I had learned. But he never responded; he never really wanted to talk about it. One day I told him about something and got the same lack of response. I was becoming frustrated because for the first time in my life, I was energized and excited about the relationship I was developing with the Lord. I wanted Rick to share that excitement with me.

"What in the world is going on, Rick?" I asked. "I keep sharing with you, but you act like you're not interested. What's going on?" A look came over his face, and I knew something was terribly wrong. Laura was eight months old at the time and was in bed for the evening. I gave Rick my full attention.

"Evelyn," he said. His voice was quiet. He looked at me, and I could tell that there was something serious on his mind.

"What is it?" I asked, holding him.

Rick began to explain some things he'd been keeping from me for years, things he'd kept bottled up, hoping they'd just go away or take care of themselves.

"Why are you telling me all this now?"

His face was somber. "Because of the messages we heard at church."

Dave Prather, our pastor at Central Christian Church in Lancaster, had preached a two-week message about overcoming guilt and how Satan uses secrets in our lives to bind us from growing in the Lord, holding us hostage by our past. That's exactly what Satan had done with Rick. He had convinced Rick that some lies are too big to make right, and as a result, Rick was miserable. He was bound by the cords of his past, but he had convinced himself that the guilt was coming from God; he didn't realize the guilt was being driven by Satan. After those messages, God really worked in Rick's life, and he knew he had to share his burdens with me.

At the same time, God had been strengthening me in my spiritual walk so I could handle the information, and when Rick told me, my first reaction was to fall into God. I'm thankful that my own relationship with the Lord was stronger than it had ever been because it gave me the strength I needed to help Rick and to take him off the pedestal where I had been keeping him for years and to put God there instead. In other words, I put God first in my life and not Rick. No human should ever have the kind of pressure of trying to stay on someone else's pedestal; it's an impossible expectation. I had so much love and admiration for Rick, but I realized I had to put God first. It was a lesson that Rick would learn too.

Rick wrote this in his journal:

Circumstances and choices—sins in our lives start to take their toll on us. Our lives get messed up and our vessels end up cracked and broken. How many of us worry more about breaking a vase with a hammer than they would about ruining their lives with the choices they make?

In the late 1990s, a church asked Rick to give his testimony, and he titled it "The Devil Loves a Secret." He talked about how from childhood we keep those little things secret that we don't want our parents or friends to know about, but as we grow we continue to keep secrets—bigger secrets. Although Rick had grown up in church and by everyone's account (even his own), he was a good person, an all-around great guy whom everybody loved, he didn't know what it meant to have a relationship with Christ. Rick asked Jesus into his heart when he was in college, but he kept that a secret, afraid of what people might think. When he and I married, he kept things from me, but Rick said in his testimony, "God was working in my life. He is very patient." Satan loves for us to carry baggage through life because it keeps us from drawing close to God. Satan convinces us that we're no good or not acceptable to God, but that's a lie and Rick was learning that.

In his journal, Rick wrote,

Lots of folks live as discards when they don't have to.

Rick knew that the baggage he had been carrying was forcing him to live as a discard, but he realized that God wanted so much more for his life . . . for our lives together. It was Satan, not God, who wanted him to feel small and worthless. God wanted to lift Rick up and bless him. He wanted to bless us. Rick knew that if he wanted to get closer to God, he was going to have to change his thinking—those thoughts that Satan had so easily persuaded him to believe over the years.

We met with Pastor Prather, and he encouraged us to get with people who would help us grow spiritually and hold us accountable. Rick jumped in and started studying the Bible in a brand-new way. He was determined to really get close to God this time. We counseled with another couple, and the man led Rick through a book titled *Point Man* by Steven Farrar. *Point man* is a military term referring to a small ground force on patrol. One member is on "point," or in the lead. This person should spot trouble or an ambush first, but it's also the most dangerous position to be in. The book delved into being a spiritual leader or point man in the home. It became a huge part of Rick's spiritual journey that helped change his life. He was learning how to be a man of God and how that required more than just going to church and being good and kind. It required a close relationship, and a relationship always requires communication and getting to know the other person. Rick dug into Bible study, and the more he read through the Scriptures, the more thankful he became. When he realized the magnitude of what Jesus had done in his own life, he wanted to get busy and serve God however he could.

He wrote in his journal:

It is necessary for *movement* to take place if we are going to draw close in the presence of God. *We* have to *move* near to God. *Nothing* can compare to the presence of God.

Rick was experiencing a freedom he had never known, and it was obvious.

"Rick got to the point where he really started to strengthen his faith," Pat Daily says. "He went through a time of self-study that turned him to the Scriptures. It was a steady journey along a path that helped him get stronger every day."

That summer of 1991 became a defining moment for Rick. He was tired of wandering around in the desert. He wanted to get into a love relationship with the God who kept pursuing him, the God who wouldn't let him run away, the God who loved him no matter what he did, and he wanted to give his all to that God. But he had no idea that God would take him across the sea in order to do that.

4

Leap of Faith

God lets us endure pressure we can't handle on our own—
to help us realize we can't live without Him.

—From Rick's journal

THE U.S. AIR FORCE HAS HAD A LONG-STANDING ARRANGEMENT
with the British Royal Air Force where a Royal Air Force test pilot
spends three years at Edwards Air Force Base in California and one
USAF test pilot goes to (what was then called) the Aircraft and
Armament Evaluation Establishment in Boscombe Down, Wiltshire,
England. Wiltshire is about eighty miles southwest of London and,
we would soon discover, a wonderful part of the English countryside
in which to live. The exchange programs are very popular and give
men and women an opportunity to experience the operational and
flying regimes of Allies. In 1992, Rick was chosen as the only USAF
test pilot to go to England.

"I've been selected as the Exchange Test Pilot for England," Rick
said one day.

I knew it was an honor to be selected. I put down my work and hugged
him. "Congratulations," I said. "I know this is a huge honor for you."

He sat me down and held on to my hand. "This is going to be a
great opportunity for us, Evey," he said. "I just know that God is
going to do an amazing work in our lives."

I smiled. God was already doing an amazing work in Rick's life.

In June we would leave the desert for Boscombe Down. I was thrilled
at the prospect of living in a new place, but I was also heartsick. I hated
moving away from my friends and the church we had grown to love.
Yet it was as if God was saying, "You don't need all those things,

Evelyn. You've got Me." He was telling me that my comfort came from Him if I would simply rely on Him. It wasn't just a United States Air Force assignment this time; this was a God assignment.

Day by day, God was teaching me how to forgive, and Rick was enjoying his newfound freedom in Christ, learning more and more about God's grace and forgiveness. He was also taking on the role of spiritual leader in our home for the first time: praying with me, for Laura, and for our lives together. Looking back, I know that if Rick had made it into the space program any earlier than he did, we would have been thrown into a rigorous lifestyle, a lifestyle that would not have given us as much time for communication and healing. God knew that. He knew that we needed to be in England for three years, far away from familiar surroundings, family, and friends, in order to grow.

Rick was disappointed that he hadn't made it into the space program, but at that point he had turned it over to God. He was learning in a real way what it meant to be in God's will.

He wrote in his journal:

I've finally come to the point where I've put God's will ahead of my desire to become an astronaut. Don't get me wrong—I still want very badly to be an astronaut, but only if it is God's will. I wish I had come to this point earlier, but better late than never.

"I don't want to do it my way anymore," Rick said to me one day before our move. "I want to do it God's way this time."

"God has great things for you, Rick," I said. "Just look at everything He's done in your life already. Look what He's doing for us now." God was leading me every day, helping me love Rick in a brand-new way. He was so gracious to us at that time.

"If I became an astronaut and lost you or Laura," he said, "it wouldn't be worth it. And I know that if I had done things my way and become an astronaut, I very well may have lost you." Becoming an astronaut was no longer Rick's greatest desire. His love for God and for us was surpassing his dream of flying in space.

Before we flew to England, Rick's dad flew out to California so they could drive the Camaro back to Texas; his parents were going to take care of it for us. It was a three-day drive, and Rick was so excited to have that time with Doug.

"I thought I knew Jesus," Rick said to his father during the drive, "but I didn't. I knew that He was God's Son and that was always enough for me, but there's so much more to Him than that and now I know it. I realized I couldn't just believe He was the Son of God. I had to believe *in* Him and believe that He was real and alive. For the first time in my life, Daddy, I have a relationship with Jesus, and it's no longer academic; it's heartfelt."

Rick loved that drive with his father. Since joining the air force, he hadn't been able to spend a lot of one-on-one time with Doug, and he couldn't stop talking about it, commenting that he felt so blessed to have three days alone in the car with his father.

Laura and I flew to Amarillo, and once Rick and Doug got there, we celebrated Rick's parents' thirty-ninth wedding anniversary. We decided to spend time together as a family and invited my parents to join us at Lake Meredith in Texas, north of Amarillo. Doug had hand-built a cabin near the lake, and Rick had helped with it whenever he could throughout the years. We had an incredible time and said our good-byes amid a lot of tears.

In June of 1992 we flew to England, where we moved into a nine-hundred-square-foot home that was beige. Granted, the largest home we'd ever lived in was twelve hundred square feet, not huge by any means, but nine hundred square feet was tiny! We decorated it as we always did with colorful curtains. It would be quite some time before our personal household goods would arrive on a ship, so in the meantime, we used functional RAF furniture. Someone lent us a little black-and-white television set, and if we held the antenna just right and stuck out our tongues just so, we could watch Wimbledon. Unfortunately, right in the middle of an all-important play we'd lose the signal and have to contort our bodies in order to get the signal back. By then it was too late; we missed seeing the shot.

I felt very detached and out of place in England. It was all so different from what we were used to: our appliances were plugged into transformers, I had to walk to a nearby village to buy fruits and vegetables, and we were charged for making local calls! I couldn't for the life of me figure out how to call my mother in America from a call box (pay phone). The food took a bit of adjusting to; it was somewhat bland, but then again one of our favorite places in Texas was a fast-food restaurant called Whataburger where we savored every fat gram. The sun set at 11:00 P.M. in the summer and rose at four in the morning, at which time Laura proclaimed, "It's a beautiful day."

I'd yell, "No, it's not yet. Go back to sleep!" That was one of the hardest adjustments to make. Thank the Lord, Sears made blackout window shades, and we received one in the mail before the summer was over.

Rick wasn't sure what to expect professionally other than he'd be test-flying with the RAF. He learned after our arrival that he would be assigned to an organization called Fixed Wing Test Squadron (FWTS). It was an unusual mix of people, a Noah's ark of aircrew: two Tornado pilots, two Buccaneer pilots, two Tornado navigators, two Hercules flight engineers, and so on. The squadron commander was Wing Commander Nigel Wood, who had previously been the RAF exchange pilot at Edwards and selected as Britain's first man to go into space a few years earlier. He flew to Houston for training, but the *Challenger* accident occurred and that brought an end to his chance to fly in space.

A reception was held in our honor at a neighbor's house, a gathering for the RAF members to welcome the American exchange officer. Rick's predecessor had crashed an RAF plane, so there was more than just a little curiosity involved in meeting the new guy. We met a couple named Angus and Carole Hogg, and Rick and I felt our uneasiness about living in England lift at that time. Both Angus and Carole were from Glasgow, Scotland, so they had a beautiful Scottish brogue. The trouble was, I couldn't understand a word they were saying. I could see their mouths moving, but I would think, *What in the world are they saying?*

"Did ya av a fen treep ova?" Angus asked.

My mind tried to process what he said, but nothing was connecting.

"Did we have a fine trip over?" Rick translated, nodding at me.

"Yes," I said loudly. "It was really fine!"

"And yur mecking yur adjoostments, then?"

A blank look crossed my face. How in the world did these people understand each other?

"And you're adjusting well?" Rick said, nodding again.

"Yes! I'm adjusting very well," I answered more loudly. I watched Angus's and Carole's lips for months before I could ever really understand anything, but they were very patient.

Angus was a tall, strapping Scotsman who always had a smile on his face, and he and Carole didn't have an ounce of pretense about them. They were genuine and warm, and we discovered they were people who shared our faith. We knew that night Angus and Carole were going to be good friends. Rick took to Angus immediately that evening, though I can't imagine anyone who can't relate to Angus; like Rick, he has been gifted with an incredible ability to put others at ease. There's no presumptuousness to him at all.

"Rick was very gentle and funny," Angus says. "He had a wonderful sense of humor and was very considerate. I remember him asking questions about our family. He was a great listener. Test pilots are normally very assertive and are not the slightest apprehensive about coming forward, but he was the opposite of that. There was no bravado about Rick. I knew right away that he was going to be an easy guy to get along with."

My dad had an absurd statement he always made when Rick and I were dating, and Rick picked up on it, thinking it was funny. So, early in our marriage, Rick started saying, "I feel more like I do now than when I first got here," and it would leave people confused and for good reason: it didn't make any sense. He'd say it with a straight face, and I could see the wheels spinning inside someone's head, trying to decipher what it meant. When Rick said it in England for the first time, the Brits were very polite, but I could see the looks on their faces and knew they chalked it up as another strange American saying. Angus thought it was a hoot, but he and Rick could always make each other laugh with very little effort.

Rick had to learn to fly RAF aircraft prior to joining the FWTS squadron, so he went through a low-level flying and tactics course at the Tactical Weapons Unit at RAF Chivenor in Devon, located in the southwestern portion of England. Low-level flying is a tactic used to get "below" enemy air defenses such as search radars. At low altitudes (300 feet or below at speeds in excess of 600 miles per hour), this type of flying is extremely challenging and dangerous since it puts pilots at extreme risk from small arms fire. While there, Rick learned to fly the Hawk two-seat trainer aircraft, the Brit equivalent of the T-38. A lot of the flying involved operating at low level (about 250 feet above the ground) around England and Wales. Rick loved it but realized the tricky part of flying in Britain is the weather. Days of rain, low clouds, poor visibility, and mountains make flying at low level a demanding environment.

When Rick learned the basics of RAF flying, he was sent to the Trinational Tornado Training Establishment at RAF Cottesmore in Leicestershire to learn to fly the Tornado GR1, a two-seat, all-weather ground attack aircraft flown by the Brits, Germans, and Italians. After intense training, Rick returned to Boscombe Down to start flying with the squadron and begin his job of testing aircraft systems and weapons on planes such as the Buccaneer, the Tornado GR1, the Tornado GR4, and several other aircraft.

Rick wore a waterproof suit over his uniform each day because of all the rain. I'd open the window, and Laura would yell, "Bye, Daddy," as we watched him ride his bike toward work in a misty drizzle. Every now and then he'd fly a noisy, bright-yellow, single-engine piston plane called a Harvard over our house. When I'd hear it, I'd grab Laura and run into the yard.

"Here comes Daddy," I'd say. Laura would lift her little head and look up to see Rick rocking the wings back and forth. She'd jump up and down and wave, squealing when she saw the bright-yellow plane. She got a kick out of knowing her daddy was in the sky. Out of the dozens of airplane pictures we own, my very favorite is a photograph of Rick flying the Harvard over Salisbury Cathedral. It was presented to him when we left England, and he hung it front and center behind his desk at NASA.

In England Rick was making consistent strides in his spiritual walk. He continued his Bible study and became accountable to Angus. "A light was coming on," Angus says, "and he knew there was a slackness in his spiritual life; it was still flabby." Rick worked hard to develop a close relationship with God. Most of his life he'd kept God in a box marked "loving and good," something that is taught in Sunday school, but now he wanted to move beyond that and do away with any stereotypical thoughts he had about God and discover His heart.

Rick wrote in his journal:

Don't be satisfied with technique, form, or tradition—have a *heart* relationship with *God*.

Rick and Angus flew together quite often—Angus was Rick's navigator on their flights, equivalent to the wizzo (weapons system officer) in U.S. terms. At times, they left the squadron for days and flew to West Freugh, a test-flying base in the middle of nowhere near the southwest coast of Scotland. They performed flair (a British test) and air-to-air refueling trials and did lots of low-level flying to test the systems and boards on various planes. Since they spent a lot of time together in the squadron and in the air, Rick became comfortable articulating his fears, dreams, and spiritual walk with Angus. "There were no walls between us," Angus says.

"Angus," Rick said one day, "I need to tell you everything Evelyn and I have been through over the last couple of years because I need the accountability in my life." Over the next hour, Rick told Angus about the "baggage" he had been dragging around for years.

"Rick," Angus said, "we serve a wonderful God of forgiveness, and I know that God's desire is to heal your heart." Rick nodded. He knew that was true, but it was so nice to hear Angus say it. "Many people in the Bible suffered consequences from their sinful choices, yet if they repented, God would restore them and trust them with much." Angus leaned closer to Rick, making sure Rick heard him. "I believe that God wants to fully forgive you and trust *you* with much."

Rick immediately recognized God's provision in this newfound friend. He could discuss his deepest spiritual thoughts without fear of ridicule or rejection. It was a two-way street because Angus was totally at ease discussing everything with Rick.

"Rick was incredibly open and shared his most intimate of details," Angus says. "He shared totally from his heart how he was feeling. There was a great openness in this hurting man that revealed a true desire to get closer to God. I felt honored and privileged that he felt he could share such personal things with me. We could talk at any level; nothing was barred from our conversations. It was yet another building block in a very close friendship. It is a rare thing to find a man whom you can share that deeply with. We became soul mates as Christian brothers." Someone once said that we're blessed to have two or three close friends by the end of our lives—Angus and Rick were such friends to each other.

As Angus and Rick were developing their friendship, I was spending time with Carole. Angus and Carole's children, Douglas and Alison, played with Laura as Carole ministered into my life in a gentle, loving way. She was teaching me about forgiveness and helping me to learn to trust God in everything through prayer. She taught me how to fill my head with God's words and not my own and to rely on those words whenever I was anxious or upset. She'd pray with me, as Angus would pray with Rick. It was an incredible time with these friends who loved us for who we were. There were no fronts; everything was stripped away. It was a true blessing to have friends of that depth, and time and again, Rick and I reminded each other that we had been brought to England for a reason.

"There's more going on here than just an officer exchange program," Rick said one evening as we were lying in bed. "God brought us here for a purpose."

"I know," I said, looking at him. It was a conversation we had had several times.

"He is *always* at work in our lives, Evey. Always! I just wonder how many times I missed seeing that throughout my life."

I held his hand. "We see it now, Rick," I said. "We see it, and we know how amazing it is to be walking in God's will."

He leaned over and kissed me good night, and we fell asleep. It's incredible how well you sleep when you're following God with all your heart.

Our marriage blossomed in England. Both Rick and I were building a stronger relationship with God and learning to develop an even stronger love for each other. I had never thought a deeper love was possible between us because we already loved each other so much, but God blessed us with that kind of love. It is the kind of love that sacrifices regardless of the cost, the kind that automatically thinks of the other person's needs first.

Rick began to obey not perfectly—but as he never had before—Philippians 2:3, which states, "Do nothing out of selfish ambition or vain conceit, but in humility consider others better than yourselves." Both of us began to experience a level of our marriage that we had never known—we put God right in the center, and everything else fell into place.

"Rick's marriage and spiritual walk were awakening," Angus says. "His time in England was a great time of reflection. He was out of the mainstream American culture in a quiet place, and he was becoming very disciplined in his walk with God, focusing on what was most important—his family. He became very grateful for his life. He knew he wanted to honor God and be a better Christian man of integrity."

In his journal Rick wrote,

> Our society is full of quick cures for putting our lives back together again. But *only* the master potter Jesus can fix our lives.

Day by day, step-by-step, Rick was letting Jesus fix his life. He was learning to give the Lord control of his career and his dream of becoming an astronaut. Rick had plotted out his course for becoming an astronaut early on and had followed that plan with discipline, but he was realizing that it was *his* plan, not God's plan. If God wanted him to become an astronaut, he knew that it had to be done in God's time and in His way.

While we were in England we received word that Rick's father wasn't feeling well. He'd had open-heart surgery two years earlier, and everything went well with that operation; his heart was fine, but for whatever reason, Doug never felt like himself again. He went through tests and doctors couldn't find anything wrong with him, but Rick was concerned. He adored his parents and hated being so far away from them when his father was ill. Doug was admitted to the hospital on October 5, Laura's birthday. After twenty days, doctors were stumped; they didn't know what was wrong. When Doug's health began to deteriorate, doctors moved him to another hospital where it was discovered that he had kidney cancer.

"I told the doctors that I had a son in England," Jane says, "and they told me to get him back here right away."

Doug was diagnosed on a Sunday, and with the help of the Red Cross, we flew out immediately. Rick was beside himself; he loved his father very much, and this diagnosis came out of the blue. For months doctors hadn't found anything and now this. It was devastating.

"I can't believe this," Rick said to me on the plane. "I can't believe my dad is dying." His voice was faint. "I want to see him, Evey. I want to spend as much time with him as I can." He stopped and looked at me. "I don't want to have to say good-bye to Daddy." He wiped tears out of his eyes, and I grabbed his hand. "I love him so much. I am so thankful for that drive to Amarillo last summer."

"He knows you love him, Rick." He nodded. "He knows how much you and Keith both love him."

"He always believed in us," Rick said. "He always made me believe that I could be whatever I wanted." He wiped tears away again and leaned his head against the seat. I jostled Laura on my lap and kissed her. "I want to be a good father for Laura. I want her to know that with God's help, she can do whatever she wants, and I always want her to know that I believe in her." He leaned down and kissed Laura. "Your Pop-pop loves you so much," he said, kissing her head. He closed his eyes, holding on to Laura's hand, and I prayed that we would arrive in time for him to tell Doug good-bye. The flight seemed to last an eternity. Would we ever get to Texas?

We landed and drove straight to the hospital. When we walked into the hospital room, I could see that Doug was losing strength and was uncomfortable, yet his face lit up immediately when he saw Rick.

Rick leaned down and hugged him. "I love you, Daddy," he said.

Doug smiled, and I could see tears in his eyes. "I love you, too, son." He patted Rick's hand. "I'm really proud of you, Rick. I'm so glad you're here." I could see Rick's shoulders give in; there was no greater praise than hearing those words from the father he adored.

"You are such a wonderful dad," Rick said. "I couldn't do anything without your love and support."

Doug motioned for Rick to come closer. He had something to say. "I want you to know that I've made peace with God," he said, holding Rick's hand. Rick clasped his hand around his father's. "I don't have any regrets in this life," he said, "except one." He looked at two-year-old Laura in my arms. "I won't get to see Laura grow up, and I'd give anything to do that."

I know it killed Rick to hear him say it. Before we had children, he commented about the incredible grandfather his dad would be to our children and was looking forward to our kids spending time with him and Jane in Amarillo. Now our daughter would never get to know him.

We spent as long as we could talking with Doug and told him how much we loved him. It was a bittersweet time because we were all waiting for the inevitable, but Rick used that time to share with his dad everything he had always meant to him. When it was apparent that Doug was slipping farther away, Rick told him to let go.

"It's okay, Daddy," Rick said, holding his hand. "You don't have to hold on anymore. You can let go now. We'll be fine. I promise to take care of Mama."

Doug died on a Wednesday just after midnight; it was only three days after his diagnosis. "I think he waited till Rick got there before he died," Jane says. "He wasn't going to leave without saying good-bye to Rick." Funeral arrangements were made right away: Doug's cousin Joe Bement would give the eulogy, and Rick's dear friend David Jones would sing "How Great Thou Art."

After Doug's funeral in Amarillo, Rick talked with Jane in the cemetery. "I want to buy plots for Evelyn and me in this section," he said. "I want to be buried near Daddy."

"There aren't any left," Jane replied. "This little section of plots is full."

"I'm going to go inside the office and ask anyway," Rick said. He went to the office, and someone happened to be in there who wanted to sell four plots back to the cemetery.

"He bought those four plots that day," Jane says, "and they're three rows back and down from his dad's."

When we returned to England, I finally felt settled. Carole and I had tea every day; it was a much more laid-back atmosphere than what I'd been used to in the States. Since local calls weren't free, I'd often get a note on my door from someone and I'd drop by her house or she'd drop by mine and we'd talk for hours. Carole and I started a women's seeker group, and I loved being around the women. Angus and Carole and Rick and I also started a couples' program that we had in our home once a month. Angus and another friend named Colin taught, as Rick and I were hosts. We served a formal dinner, and the Brits have a way of balancing a plate on their laps and eating with a knife and a fork without the plate ever going topsy-turvy. I was never quite as poised; my napkin would fall off my lap, and when I'd reach for it, my plate would start to topple. I'd grab it, but then the knife and fork would fall clanging to the floor. I'm sure it was difficult to pick out the American in the room! Those evenings of fellowship were such sweet times of teaching and learning. God was growing us in profound ways.

Although Rick had surrendered his dream to be an astronaut to the Lord, he still struggled with the desire in his heart. He wasn't sure if it was just what he wanted or if God wanted it for him as well. A friend of ours in the States had recently told Rick about an opportunity he had to fly a plane he'd always wanted to fly—it was something our friend had worked toward all his life, but the opportunity fell through and he wasn't able to move forward with his career as he had hoped. Yet he realized what he was longing for was his dream, not necessarily God's plan for his life. He shared a passage with Rick from the book of Psalms that was giving him peace as he learned to trust God's purpose for him: "Delight yourself in the LORD and he will give you the desires of your heart" (37:4).

Rick thought about that verse for a long time; it was on his mind day and night. Before the launch of the shuttle *Columbia,* Rick talked in an interview about what that verse came to mean to him during those days. He said,

> So I got to looking at that and it was almost like God asked me, "Okay, so what really are the desires of your heart?" And so initially the first thing I kind of brought to mind was, "Well, I want to be an astronaut." But it's like God said, "No, no, no. Think about it for a little while and then tell Me what really is the desire of your heart," because that was just kind of an automatic response and had been up to that point.
>
> And I got to thinking about it and thought, "Well, if I ended up at the end of my life having been an astronaut but having sacrificed my family along the way or living my life in a way that didn't glorify God, then I would look back on it with great regret, and having become an astronaut would not really have mattered all that much." And I finally came to realize that what really meant the most to me was to try and live my life the way God wanted me to. And to try

and be a good husband to Evelyn and to be a good father to my children and to do everything I possibly could to make sure that they knew who Jesus was and that they had every opportunity to make a choice themselves for Jesus. And it was like a light came on all of a sudden, where I finally realized that this thing about being an astronaut was not as important as I thought it was, and I finally came to the point where I said, "Okay, Lord, I don't care what I do or where You send me; I just want to try to do those things: I want to be somebody that lives a life that glorifies You; I want to be a good husband; I want to be a good father; and come what may as far as the rest of it goes."

Rick prayed that if being an astronaut wasn't God's will, He would take the desire from him. He didn't want to pursue it unless God's hand was covering him. During his Bible study one day, he came across Proverbs 3:5–6, which became his life's motto:

> Trust in the LORD with all your heart
> And do not lean on your own understanding.
> In all your ways acknowledge Him,
> And He will make your paths straight. (NASB)

We carried on with our lives in England and kept growing in our faith, waiting to see what God would do with us next. Throughout that time, the space program was always in the back of Rick's mind. It was clear that God was not taking the desire from him.

In March of 1992, Rick decided to apply a fourth time to NASA. I remember that he sat at our dining room table and answered every question again, but this time he had a problem. He came across the question about whether he had ever worn hard contact lenses. It was very emotional for him to type *yes*, indicating that he had worn them. He just knew he was removing any possibility of ever being selected by NASA, but he felt as if God was saying, *Trust Me. You've done it your way. Do it My way this time.*

He finished the application and drove nearly two hours to mail it at an American air base. That meant God had another two hours to encourage him, but Rick was arguing with Him; he was very uptight.

He recalled that drive years later in an interview:

The whole time I'm talking back and forth to God, saying, "How's this going to work? Oh, man, they'll look at it and know I lied the last time and say, 'What a scumbag this guy is,' and toss the application." That's the kind of situation where you can say the devil loves a secret because if he knows you've got something you're trying to hide, he can use it against you in such a huge way. So I just dropped the thing in the mail and said, "Okay, Lord. Let's just see what happens."

In his journal he wrote,

Trusting God *completely* is tough when you are not used to doing it on a regular basis.

That four-hour-round-trip drive was the beginning of Rick's trusting God on a regular basis.
He wrote,

We just have to face the mountains that loom in our lives with *faith* in God that *He* can overcome those obstacles if we will just trust Him.

Rick was trusting God to get him over a huge mountain. "He laid it all on the line and trusted God because he wanted to get his life right," Angus says. "The reality was, he could have been facing disaster by telling NASA the truth; his lifelong ambition could come crashing down around him. The enemy stepped in right away to let him know that by honoring God and telling the truth, he would amount to nothing, but Rick took that chance because he had to do what was right in the eyes of God."
In his journal Rick wrote,

Proverbs 3:5–6: "Trust in the Lord with all your heart and do not lean on your own understanding. In all your ways acknowledge Him, and He will make your paths straight." That, to me, was a very comforting reminder that God is in control and He has my best interests in mind. It has been a real big mental adjustment for me to realize that I may very well not become an astronaut even though it is what I have seen as my destiny for such a long time. It is very comforting to know, though, that God loves me and He has blessed me beyond anything I could imagine throughout my life and I have every reason to believe that everything would work out for the best here. Romans 8:28 [NASB] says, "And we know that God causes all things to work together for good to those who love God, to those who are called according to His purpose."

Rick returned from mailing the application and came through the door looking exhausted, yet relieved. "That was one of the hardest things I've ever had to do," he said. "But it feels so right to tell the truth and to leave it in God's hands and not mine. It'll be interesting to see what happens."

"We'll just have to hide and watch," I said. Whenever we wanted to see what God would do in our lives, Rick and I would say, "Let's hide and watch." It was basically letting God be God without our manipulating the situation. Rick had done everything possible to get accepted by NASA; he had achieved every goal, met every criterion. Now, there really was nothing to do but hide and watch.

The day after Rick mailed the application he was sure that he had said good-bye to the space program. Then during the weather briefing at the squadron, it was announced that there would be a space shuttle briefing for anyone who wanted to attend. Rick's mouth dropped open; he couldn't believe it! Was it a coincidence that someone from the space program was at the squadron in England, or was God trying to tell him that no, he wasn't saying good-bye to his dream? Rick went to the discussion and was amazed at whom he saw there.

In his journal he wrote,

It turns out the guy giving the briefing was Jean Claude Nicollier, an ESA astronaut working at NASA. During my interview in January '92 I got to sit in a shuttle launch simulation with a crew preparing for a future mission. Jean Claude Nicollier is who I sat next to! And now I'm in a briefing a little over a year later watching him tell about the mission they flew. It was extremely interesting and I had the same strong desire to be an astronaut . . . almost as if God was saying, "Don't give up hope, trust Me!"

Jean Claude's talk that day was just the encouragement Rick needed, but we ended up waiting over a year without any word.

He wrote in his journal:

Today (4 June '93) is the day the USAF astronaut nomination list *should* come out. I say should because there is no set date. This is the first hurdle to getting selected. If my name is on the list then I will have at least made the USAF cut. NASA will then review the lists from the USAF, Army, Navy, Marines, and the civilian world and pick interviewees. I am anxious to see what God's answer is for all this.

Rick *was* on the USAF list, but he had to wait to see if NASA was interested. Just when he would get discouraged, something would happen that let him know that NASA was checking him out. The phone rang at David Jones's house one day and his daughter, Caite, answered it.

"Dad, it's for you," she said.

"Take a number and ask if I can call them back," David said.

"No, Daddy, you better take it. It's the FBI asking about Rick."

David jumped up and answered questions for about forty-five minutes.

"I'm sure they didn't believe that Rick could be how I described him," David says. "I knew they didn't think that anyone could be that nice, be that exceptional, but he was. Rick was unique and I wanted to convince them of that."

When someone from NASA talked with Rick's superior officer in England, we knew the agency was getting serious about the inquiries.

He eventually received a phone call from NASA; the agency wanted him to fly to Houston again for an interview.

"I made it, Evey," Rick said in our kitchen. "They've called me for an interview at NASA."

I gave him a huge hug. "I knew you'd make it," I said. "I can't believe you get to go back to the States . . . especially Texas! I'm so jealous. You can do anything you want while you're there, except go to Whataburger."

He laughed. "Don't worry about that! I've got to start exercising like crazy so I'm in good shape for the interview. I can't eat anything fattening." I looked at his face; he was glowing. In three short years he had become a changed man.

"Rick, do you realize that God has vindicated you and is giving you a second chance at your dream of becoming an astronaut?"

He nodded. Rick had reset his priorities in England, and I felt God was honoring him with his desire of getting into the space program. I believed with all my heart that he would be accepted.

"Even if I'm not selected as an astronaut," he said, "God has given me every desire of my heart, Evey. My greatest desire is to be a good husband and father, and God is helping me every day to do that." He smiled; he was content. "I have everything I need."

Rick had trusted God by telling the truth on his application, but now was the time when the rubber was going to meet the road. He'd be seeing people face-to-face who would have his application in hand. He knew there was the possibility that he'd have to explain why he had written that he hadn't worn contacts, but Rick was ready to tell the truth. He'd rather have everything out in the open than get into the program by lying.

At the interview in Houston, Rick had to go through the same written, psychological, and medical tests again, but this time he knew what to expect. "It's a thorough process," Scott Parazynksi says. "They perform every kind of test imaginable and do an in-depth search of your work record and personal life because they're going to spend a lot of money to train you. They want to be sure to get the right folks."

Rick again met some unbelievable people who were all at the top of their fields, just as he had done at the interview in 1992. "You meet all these qualified people and think, *Wow, any one of these could be an astronaut*," Scott says. "They're fighter test pilots, scientists, engineers, and doctors. You don't go in thinking you have any sort of edge because everyone there is more than qualified."

Rick went through the many psychological exams so they could assess what kind of personality and temperament he had. The bottom line was: they were looking for someone who was a team player and whom, as Steve Lindsey says, "they could spend sixteen days with in something the size of a Winnebago."

After a day of testing, Rick was told he would take the eye exam the next morning. This is how he described it in an interview:

> I went in the first morning to take the eye test, and I flunked it. And I thought, *Oh my goodness, Lord, to come this far! Even if I don't get hired . . . I'd really like to pass that test.* I called Evelyn who was back in England and told her, and she alerted the prayer chain and two very good Christian men in the squadron with me—Angus Hogg and Chris

Huckstep—and those two fasted and prayed until I got through the test. Evelyn brought to mind this verse, "Vindicate me, O Lord, for I have walked in my integrity."

The NASA eye exam wasn't the typical eye test that we have at an optometrist with the big *E* chart in front of us. It was something called a Landolt C test: the letter *C* appears on a screen, and you grab a joystick and move it in whatever direction the *C* is pointed. If Rick didn't pass the Landolt test, he wouldn't be eligible for selection. I contacted Angus and Chris Huckstep in the squadron at Boscombe and told them what was happening.

The next day, at three o'clock in the afternoon, our phone rang at home in England. I answered it and was thrilled to hear Rick's voice on the other end.

"How did the eye test go?" I asked.

"I passed it," he said excitedly. "I even improved a *whole level* on both eyes. I prayed so hard before I went in and it wasn't even difficult, Evey."

"Angus and Chris fasted with me," I said. "But they broke their fast with a biscuit in the squadron because they just knew that you passed it. They knew that God would be faithful."

In an interview this is how Rick described what happened:

It was a vigil preparing and looking forward to the next test. This was the absolute moment of truth. So I walked in and took the test and I passed! Both eyes had improved one level! Angus and Chris didn't even wait to hear. They went down to the crew room in the squadron and broke the fast because they just knew that I had passed. That was a great testament to their faith. It's always amazing how we can take a look where we are now and wonder, "How is God going to work this out?" I've learned over the years that if I just trust God, I don't have a clue *how* it's going to work out, but at some point when I look back, it'll all fall into place so perfectly and in a way that I can never imagine.

Rick stepped out in faith and put his reputation on the line to tell the truth, and God blessed him in ways Rick had never fathomed. It didn't matter if he wasn't accepted into the astronaut program at that point; God had vindicated him, and Rick and I were so thankful.

He wrote this in his journal years later:

Faith doesn't give us the power to change things—it gives us the ability to cope with the tough things that come our way. God lets us endure pressure we can't handle on our own—to help us realize we can't live without Him. You have to give God control of your life and let *Him* rain [this was Rick's play on words for the word *reign;* we must let God "rain," or drench us with His overwhelming presence and love] in your life the way *He* wants to—not the way you want Him to. Don't be afraid to get muddy!

Rick had gotten muddy and come out clean before God.

He finished the next few days of the interview process, but before flying back to England, he did something that was out of character for him: he rented a car so he could drive to Whataburger. He spent who knows what on the rental car to be able to buy a hamburger and chocolate milk shake! Rick's cholesterol was high and he was always battling to keep it in normal range, but his cholesterol didn't matter that day. I couldn't believe it. Rick had long been very frugal: at that point he was still using the same comb he had in junior high and would actually sew up his socks instead of throwing them away. It got to be a joke in our family because his mother would buy him J. C. Penney underwear for Christmas. (I think she was afraid he'd start mending his old ones!) He would use every square inch of a piece of paper when he wrote notes. At the bottom of one full note card he wrote: PMPP (Poor Man's Palm Pilot). We would never trade in a car for another one; we always drove cars until they fell apart. At one point we had a Chevy Celebrity that had almost 190,000 miles on it; the engine bolts blew as we sat in a Subway drive-through.

When we moved into our home in Houston, Rick went from one home under construction in our neighborhood to another and asked the carpenters for wood they weren't going to use. Over time, he gathered a large pile of it, spent six dollars for hardware, and built floor-to-ceiling shelves in our garage. Of course, the absolute testament to his frugality is that we still own the same car he drove in high school! Many people are under the impression that astronauts make a lot of money. The truth is, they are paid according to their military ranks, or if they're civilians, their pay is set in accordance with their academic achievements and experience. We've never owned an expensive stereo system or television. Rick never bought any "toys" that some men are known for, but then again he didn't have to—he got to fly jets and airplanes for a living. He never bought anything for himself at all, so that's why I was shocked when he actually rented a car to buy a hamburger!

Rick flew back to England, and we waited months before we heard anything. During the same week of December 1994, Rick was promoted to lieutenant colonel in the air force, I found out I was pregnant, and he got *the* call from NASA.

I was upstairs when the phone rang and was half listening to try to tell who had called. I thought it was someone local because I heard a lot of, "Uh-huh, hmm, okay." It was driving me crazy so I went downstairs and stood next to him. He looked at me and raised his eyebrows up and down with a big grin, giving me a thumbs-up. I still couldn't identify the caller but had my suspicions. He hung up the phone, gave me a hug, and said, "They picked me to be an astronaut! Whoo hoo!" His dream had come true, and we were ecstatic. He picked me up and swung me around.

"I'm so proud of you," I said. He sat me down and hugged me tight.

"This wouldn't have happened without your prayers and encouragement, Evey. I love you so much!" He hugged me tighter and let out another whoop in celebration.

Four-year-old Laura came running down the stairs. "What is it, Daddy?" she asked.

"Daddy gets to be an astronaut," Rick said, leaning down to look at her. "We get to move to Texas. Let's call Nannie, so you can tell her the news." We called Jane, and Laura told her grandmother that her older son had achieved his lifelong dream. Out of 3,000 applications and 120 interviews, Rick had been selected as one of 19 astronauts. We were on our way to Texas!

We had a difficult time leaving England. We had established many close friendships, and our hearts were breaking at the thought of moving away from Angus and Carole. They had loved us and ministered to us at the time of our greatest need, and we knew it was going to be hard to leave them behind. We were given another reception, this one to say good-bye to the American exchange officer.

"I remember the night he left," Angus says. "I just felt so sad to see him go. It was the end of an era for both of us. I can't emphasize enough how easy he was to be with. He showed a rare balance of leadership and grace. Some people are good leaders but are difficult to be around. Rick was a good leader and was easy to be around. There was a natural humility to his leadership. He wasn't there to prove anything. For me personally it was very sad, but my professional life felt very empty after he left as we had had such a great relationship. Somehow I hoped that this time would never end."

We said our good-byes amid a great deal of tears again and flew to Houston for the next chapter God had written for our lives. Rick had been dreaming of the stars since he was a boy, and now he was finally going to reach them.

5

NASA at Last

I have heard of You by the hearing of the ear;
But now my eye sees You.

—Job 42:5 NASB

MOVING BACK TO TEXAS WAS A SHOCK TO OUR SYSTEMS. IT WAS
only February, and it was already hot in Houston. Since I was pregnant, I was extremely uncomfortable. I had a sinus block from flying,
but I couldn't take any medication and I was so sick. We moved into
an apartment and made an appointment with a Realtor for help in
locating a home. We walked into the Realtor's office and met a couple
named Michael and Sandy Anderson, who were also moving to
Houston. They were the first people we met in our new city, and we
discovered that Rick and Mike were going to be in the same astronaut
candidate class! We had no idea that day that Rick and Mike would
eventually end up on the same mission together.

Thankfully, we found a home in six days, but it was in the building process so we'd have to live in the apartment for a while until it
was finished. Mike and Sandy ended up buying a home in the same
neighborhood, a block away from us, and we felt such a bond with
them from the beginning. Mike was also an air force pilot but was
training as a mission specialist at NASA. He was laid-back and warm
and easy to be around. He and Sandy had a way of making you feel
comfortable, and we loved getting to know them. Throughout the
years, Sandy became like a sister to me. We would eventually attend
the same church, Grace Community Church in Clear Lake, just a few
minutes from our homes. A private school was associated with the
church, and when we interviewed with the principal, we knew that's
where we wanted Laura to attend once she started school.

Though it felt as if we were off to a good start in Houston, I wasn't sure how I felt about being back in Texas. My first impression was that it was very fast paced. I had gotten used to having tea with Carole every afternoon as Laura played with Douglas and Alison. England was so relaxing; everybody in Houston came across as busy and loud.

We moved into our home two months after our meeting with the Realtor, and every time I went up and down the stairs I had Braxton Hicks contractions. There were many times I thought I was going to have the baby while lugging a box marked "bathroom" up the stairs. Since I was little to no help and Rick was moving at full speed in classes at NASA, Jane and Keith took mercy on us and came to help.

I unpacked boxes during the day while Rick dug into ASCAN—astronaut candidate classes. There are two types of astronauts in the space program: pilots and mission specialists. Rick was one of ten pilots in his class, along with nine mission specialists. (Steve Lindsey was also one of the ten pilots. Steve would eventually pilot STS-87, and in 1998 he was the pilot on STS-95 with former astronaut John Glenn, who at the age of seventy-seven was the oldest person ever to go to space. Steve was also commander of STS-104 in July 2001.) In addition to Mike Anderson, Kalpana Chawla, another crew mate on the *Columbia,* was in the class, training as a mission specialist. For the next fourteen months they would learn all of the shuttle systems and take classes in all the sciences such as geology, climatology, oceanography, and astronomy. They toured all of the NASA centers and had an introduction to the plans for the International Space Station, which was in the process of being built on the ground at the time (the first element of the space station wouldn't launch until 1998, a year before Rick's first flight). Rick was extremely busy.

"I can't believe I'm in that class with such amazing people," Rick said one evening. "It's an honor to sit there and learn with them, and I know what Angus means when he says that somebody has the brain the size of a planet because my classmates do! They're top-notch in every way." Rick never thought of himself as being one of those top-notch people. He was simply grateful that he could learn beside them.

"This is what you've wanted since you were a little boy," I said, lowering my pregnant belly down on the couch next to him. "I'm so glad you're in a class with people who are making it so interesting for you."

"How many people get to live their dream, Evey? I mean *really* live it? I am so blessed because I'm living out my desire of being a good husband and father." I looked up at him and he grinned. "Oh, yeah, and I get to be an astronaut too!"

I made it through the Houston heat and gave birth to Matthew Douglas Husband the morning of August 3, 1995. Rick came home so tired the night before Matthew was born; he was exhausted because he'd been up since the early-morning hours and had to stay for a late-night training session. When he walked through the door, I knew he was whipped, but I also knew that it wouldn't be long before I had the baby.

"This is the most tired I've ever been," he said, dragging himself upstairs to our bedroom.

I told him to sleep well, but I just knew that I was going to have that baby very soon. I thought I should do something to distract myself. Even in my extreme pregnant state, I was rational enough to know that 1:00 A.M. was not a good time to phone anyone but realized everyone would be waking up in England, so I called Jo Czaja, a dear friend, and was talking with her when my water broke.

"I need to call you back, Jo, because I'm going into labor now, if you can believe it!" I'm sure I unnerved her to no end, but I was calm. I hated to do it, but I climbed the stairs and went into our bedroom where Rick was sound asleep. I tapped him on the arm. "I'm really sorry to wake you," I said, "but I'm in labor."

He bolted out of bed and we got Laura up. Through sleepy eyes, she very sweetly said, "This is a very important moment, and I will never forget it!" We dropped her off at the home of our friends Joe (a flight surgeon at NASA) and Holly Ortega. At the hospital they put me in a room with a big chair next to the bed. Rick sat down and kept nodding off.

"I'm awake," he'd say before falling asleep again. His naps didn't last long.

Matthew came quickly, all nine pounds and ten ounces of him! (I had too many Whataburgers when we moved back to Texas.)

Rick came home each evening with a stack of books, but he never opened them until Laura and Matthew were in bed. He never once came home and sat down; he helped me in the kitchen or played with the kids. Although he was now living his dream, Rick wasn't going to jeopardize his family for it. He'd put the kids to bed and read to

Laura or sing to Matthew before opening his books, studying for the next few hours.

Rick and his classmates learned emergency egress (how to get out of the orbiter quickly) at Johnson Space Center. They had to practice again and again because if there ever was an emergency, they would have to rely on that basic training to help them out of it. The class spent a great deal of time learning how to operate the robotic arm. They also had sessions in the space shuttle flight simulator where students learned how to operate the shuttle during ascent, on-orbit, and entry. Instructors input multiple failures, sometimes up to ten to twelve malfunctions during a single eight-and-a-half-minute ascent, to teach the crews and Mission Control how to work as a team and exercise their systems knowledge during stressful situations. NASA requires intense training on the simulators because when they're operating a 120-ton spacecraft in a very unforgiving environment, the pilots and mission specialists must understand all the systems backward and forward so that they'll know what to do in case something unexpected occurs. A crew that can handle multiple malfunctions in a simulated environment can probably handle the unknowns that occur during the stress of real space flight. The shuttle simulator is unique among aircraft simulators in that it rotates 90 degrees into the vertical to simulate ascent.

"The first time the simulator rotated on me," Steve Lindsey says, "I felt like my IQ dropped 50 points. The first time I was rotated into the vertical, because I was now on my back, all of the switches and cockpit displays looked 'different.' I had trained often in the horizontal, but it was very strange in the vertical—much different than flying an airplane."

Rick told me the experience was unbelievable. "Just when you think you know something, you realize you don't," he said.

In addition to his classroom work, Rick and the other pilots trained in a T-38 aircraft to keep their flying currency and often flew to El Paso for training in the Shuttle Training Aircraft (STA). The STA is essentially a Gulfstream business jet modified to fly like the space shuttle. Inside the aircraft, the left half of the cockpit is identical to the space shuttle cockpit. During a "dive," the right-seat instructor pilot flies the STA up to about 35,000 feet or so and engages the shuttle simulation. The shuttle pilot in the left seat takes control of the aircraft and flies the "shuttle" to a simulated touchdown on the runway. In order to achieve the same flight characteristics as the space shuttle (a high-speed, high-drag glider), the instructor lowers the landing gear on each dive and puts the engines in reverse prior to engaging the simulation. "When all engines fail on airplanes, they turn into a glider," Steve Lindsey says. "How far they glide depends upon a number of factors, but they *can* glide without engines. The STA also glides, but because the STA's drag is so much less than the shuttle, it glides 'too well' and too far. So to simulate the shuttle, instructors make it 'more draggy' by putting the engines in reverse. This forces a steeper glide angle to make the aircraft fly at the correct speed. At that point, it more closely emulates the shuttle flying and handling characteristics." Shuttle pilots and commanders complete approximately ten dives per two-hour training session, and before qualifying as commander, a pilot must have completed a minimum of one thousand dives.

That time was one of the busiest of our lives: Laura started kindergarten and took ballet, Matthew was a newborn, Rick was going through his training, and we were worn out all the time.

Rick wrote in his journal:

Dear God, I am in bondage to exhaustion! *Exhaustion* is robbing me of a right relationship with You and my family.

Rick became frustrated with himself because he wanted to spend his quiet time with the Lord in the mornings before he left for school, but sometimes it was hard. He had a difficult time trying to balance that part of his life, and it drove him crazy.

In another entry he wrote,

Even God *rested* after making the heavens and the earth.
We need to rest *also* and honor God on the Sabbath.
Sabbath means "day of rest."
Sabbatical comes from *Sabbath*.
Lord, help me to get the rest I need. I want to honor You on the
    Sabbath and not profane it or make it common.

Although Rick was exhausted, he never wanted to think of Sunday as a catch-up day for sleep, and he was consistent in making sure that we went to church as a family.

Many times, it felt as if we were burning the candle at both ends, but Rick always made sure that we spent time together. Even if he was tired, he was ready to be with us when he walked through the door at night. As I made dinner, he rolled around with the kids on the floor and let them jump all over him. Laura crawled up on his lap, and he read a book to her, playing with her hair and kissing her. Laura adored time with her daddy. Matthew shrieked and giggled at anything Rick did. Rick loved to pick him up and zoom him through the house like an airplane. Matthew kicked his legs and laughed at every dip.

We had learned in a parenting class before Laura was born to have couch time as a couple, where we were supposed to sit down and share for ten minutes about what happened in each of our days. We tried to do it, but every time we sat down, the kids wiggled their way between us. Rick made sure we talked in the kitchen or somewhere else. There were some days that we'd see each other only a few minutes, but Rick made sure we took the time to be together.

In a PBS special, Rick said,

> I try to be the best husband and father I possibly can. And it doesn't mean I get to spend as much time with my family as I'd like, but I do the best I can. Even if you do get to be an astronaut and get to go and do a lot of interesting things, at some point that will come to an end. If in the process you shortchange your family or compromise your values along the way, when you get through on the other side, it won't really be worth it. At least not to me.

It was tough during those fourteen months of classes, but we made it through. I know Rick dealt with a lot of guilty feelings because he felt he wasn't spending as much time with us as he'd like, but he did the best he could and I knew that. I told him that everything was okay and not to stress about it. Yet I know it bothered him.

"I just can't juggle everything the way I'd like," he said after dinner one day.

I knew he was frustrated. "Rick, there are only so many hours in the day, and I think you do a great job handling everything."

"I can't keep up with everything, Evey. Just when I think I'm getting caught up at work, something happens that puts me behind again. Just when I think things are rolling along here at home, something breaks and needs fixing. I feel that I'm always behind, and that you, Laura, and Matthew are suffering because of it." He stood up and grabbed our empty dinner plates off the table, rinsing them in the sink. I scraped the rest of the casserole into a smaller dish.

"Rick, do you know how happy Laura and Matthew are? They think you're the greatest dad in the world. You play with them; you love them; you pray for them every single day. Rick, they have so much more than some children will ever have. They're doing great. I'm doing great. God has blessed us with so much. Don't convince yourself that you're neglecting us or that we're not happy because it's just not true." I could tell he was still down. "Do I need to pick you up? Huh? Do I need to pick you up?"

He threw his head back and laughed. "No! But I'd love to see you try!"

It's an amazing gift that God gives to married couples: when one is down, the other is able to pick that one up. It was something that Rick and I had often experienced in our marriage, and I was always so thankful for his bright spirit when I was low and I was grateful that I could help pull him up when he needed it.

Before Rick graduated, he was still digging deeper into the Bible. He strove every day to get closer to God—that was more important than any graduation or space flight assignment.

In his journal at that time he wrote,

Today, I was thankful for:

1. Church and the opportunity to worship God and know that He is in control and that He loves us.

2. Getting to know the men in choir a little better.

3. Richard and Janetta Curtis and their ministry to help people with their finances. We have enjoyed getting to know them and appreciate their help. [The Curtises are sweet people from our church who helped Rick and me finally get on a budget!]

4. Getting to take Laura to buy a baseball glove and then playing catch with her in the backyard. She is such a sweetheart and it is so much fun to see her excited about playing "coach pitch."

5. Reading to Matthew and hearing him talk so much—with all of his facial expressions. His big smile that we saw when we picked him up from Sunday school was priceless!

6. Praying with Evelyn.

> God, thank You for all my many blessings. Please help me to have self-confidence and to work with focus and diligence. Please help me to cope with work, family, and get Air War College finished before I'm assigned to a flight. [Air War College is a course that air force officers take as part of their career development. Rick took it by correspondence when he was a lieutenant colonel.]
> In Jesus' name, amen.

All of Rick's entries reflect where his heart was at that time. Each entry names friends or family members as blessings. Even when he was at work, I knew that his heart was with us. Rick had learned to leave his work at work. He knew there was no way to get everything done so he left work behind and came home to us. Somehow, in the middle of his hectic schedule, Rick managed to take on yet another activity.

In the spring of 1998 he wrote,

> Today began with Matthew's sweet voice saying, "Daddy, I wake up!" at about 6:40 A.M. I was very tired! But it doesn't take a rocket scientist to figure out that you'll be tired after 5½ hours sleep! Matthew stayed at the Cottens' while Laura and I went to baseball practice. The practice went well although I feel a little out of place, never having coached before. Everyone has his first time! I am thankful, though, to be able to do this with and for Laura because I know how much it meant to me when my dad coached my softball team in 3rd grade.

He was honored to coach Laura's third-grade softball team but was so nervous.

"Rick, you made it as an astronaut," I said, amazed that he could fly more than forty aircrafts, yet was anxious about coaching eight-year-olds!

"That's easier," he said, worried he'd let the team down.

I remember praying for him before every game. (I think I prayed more for him than I did for Laura!)

Laura, Matthew, Jane, and I attended Rick's graduation ceremony from astronaut school, and on a NASA video he is seen putting his arm around Mike Anderson and patting his back. Throughout the fourteen months of training, Mike and Rick had become prayer partners and good friends. We didn't know then that God was preparing them for their future mission together.

From the time a new class starts training at NASA, it usually takes two and a half years before participants get their first space assignment. Rick ended up being the last pilot of his class of ten to get assigned a flight, but then again, so was Neil Armstrong! He was excited when he finally got his flight assignment in 1998 because it meant he could park by building Four South at Johnson Space Center—before that he had to park in the boonies. His classmates gave him a party, and the cake was in the shape of a parking space. It was as if he'd finally arrived!

Rick was selected to be the pilot of Space Transportation System-96, or STS-96 as it is known in NASA lingo, on the space shuttle *Discovery*. He would sit in the right-hand seat in the shuttle, backing up the commander, Kent Rominger, and was responsible for the shuttle's electrical systems, the auxiliary power units, the orbital maneuvering system engines, the attitude control jets, and the shuttle main engines on ascent. He would train for the next nine months for his mission. His would be the second shuttle crew to board the uninhabited International Space Station, which launched a year earlier, but the first space shuttle to actually dock with it. (The first shuttle crew, STS-88, used a mechanical arm to board the station so they didn't actually lock down and dock.) The crew would transfer supplies to the space station, and a couple of the astronauts would do a space walk so they could do some installation and repair work. (If either of the two primary space walkers couldn't do it in space, Rick was trained as a backup.) They were scheduled to be in space for ten days, and Rick was beyond excited.

In his journal he wrote,

God has appointed me to be the pilot on the Space Shuttle. Lord, help me to be strong and courageous and move on in Your plan for my life. Help me not to dwell on the past but to look to the future that You have for me. Help me to *glorify You* in the way I perform in my job and the way I live my life as a husband and father. In Jesus' name, amen!

Regardless of the assignment, Rick wanted to bring glory to God's name. At the bottom of one journal entry he wrote,

Let everything I do be to the glory of God!

That was Rick's most important mission. It meant everything in the world to him.

6

Reaching the Stars

Don't die before you're dead!!
Don't let anything stand in the way of God's appointed purpose for your life.
—From Rick's journal

RICK ROLLED UP HIS SLEEVES AND PREPARED FOR THE NEXT NINE months of training with the STS-96 crew that included Ellen Ochoa, Tammy Jernigan, Dan Barry, Julie Payette, Valery Tokarev (a Russian cosmonaut), and Kent Rominger as the commander.

"We had a great experience preparing for that mission, and Rick was a large part of that," Kent says. "He was the kind of guy people would flock around because he was so unselfish. He was a compassionate, caring guy with a great sense of humor. He had the funniest sayings. He'd say, 'You can't swing a dead cat without hitting an engineer around here,' or 'I feel more like I do now than when I first got here,' and make me laugh every time. He was hysterical in a very down-home way. He was never mean or sarcastic in his humor. Our crew bonded into a very close-knit group, and I was proud of how the crew performed as a cohesive team. I really hoped our mission would get slipped because we had such a good time training together. I didn't want our time to end." (Whenever a launch date is moved, NASA refers to it as a slip. Less than four years later, Rick would experience slips time and again with the *Columbia* crew.)

In nine months, Rick would develop some close friendships with the STS-96 crew. He always said that the best part of training is bonding with people. "We were a very tight-knit crew," Dan Barry says. "Training for space flight is always fantastic because over a course of the year you develop six new, really close friends. We took a two-week trip to Russia. We flew T-38s and did intense simulator

training. By the end of training and in being together every day, you
start to know what the other people on the crew are thinking before
they say anything; you become completely confident in trusting your
life to these six other people. Rick, in particular, brought a sense of
humor and was the glue that stuck us together. You could talk to him
about anything. In a tense situation, Rick was always calm and
patient. He was the perfect choice for the pilot of our mission."

As part of the training for STS-96, Rick often went to El Paso,
Cape Canaveral, or Edwards Air Force Base in California to fly the
STA, the shuttle training aircraft, to practice landing, or he went to
Ellington Field in Houston to fly a T-38. Dan Barry was with Rick
for many of those flights. "We flew in T-38s a lot together," he says.
"Rick was one of the world's greatest pilots. He really improved my
flying skills while we trained for the mission. He was like my big
brother in the sky when he taught me to fly. He was a natural teacher.
He could teach in a way that made me feel good about myself. He
didn't get upset or frustrated. He was very patient, always had a
warm demeanor. You couldn't upset the guy. He would correct me,
but I wasn't afraid that he'd throw me out. The worst I'd hear is, 'I've
got it,' and he'd step in and take over. He always taught with humor
and grace and with an eye to help me, or anyone who was flying with
him, improve. It was never part of his nature to demean or put anyone down. Rick made you feel like you were part of a team when you
flew with him. I always looked forward to flying with him, and now
every time I fly, I use the lessons I learned from him."

Rick routinely worked in the flight simulators and trained at the
neutral buoyancy lab, which is a huge swimming pool, to be prepared
for the space walk. (This pool is the largest in the world at 40 feet
deep, 100 feet wide, and 200 feet long—the cargo bay of the space
shuttle can be put inside it.) The two space walkers, Dan and Tammy
Jernigan, and Rick, who was the backup EVA (extra vehicular activity or space walker), put on space suits along with weights and
trained in the pool so they could be neutrally buoyant, meaning they
wouldn't sink or rise. Astronauts adjust weighting so they can stay at
the same depth in the pool. This is the closest astronauts can get to
simulating zero gravity (0g) besides the "vomit comet," but they can't
do space walk training there since they get only twenty to thirty seconds of 0g at a time. (The vomit comet is a KC-135—an Air Force

version of the Boeing 707. The back of the aircraft has all of the seats taken out, replaced by padding and test instrumentation. The pilot pulls the nose 45 degrees high, then pushes the aircraft over until about 45 degrees nose low. This gives 20 to 30 seconds of zero gravity for the astronauts in training.)

Rick was also the backup robotic arm operator, so he had to train on that as well. It was a lot of work and required a lot of hours; he was busy all the time. Rick was thrilled he could be a part of all that training, but at times he felt snowed under. "The first thing that happens before your first flight is the sense of being totally overwhelmed," Scott Parazynski says. "The stakes are high. Everyone is watching. An incredible intensity sets upon you that you have to learn everything and be ready. You have a year or more to get ready, but as you're coming up to speed on all the payloads [payload is what each shuttle mission carries to space; if a shuttle crew is flying equipment for the International Space Station, that equipment is the payload] and the unique tasks on your mission, it can be stressful because you feel as if you're just not going to be prepared. It's only a month or two before the mission that you really start to savor the experience and feel like you're ready to go."

Rick had to study very hard for the mission, and once the kids went to bed at night he stayed up late, studying and preparing. It was a running theme in our life: put the kids to bed, study, put the kids to bed, study. One night, after Rick had an exhausting day, we sat on the couch and caught up with each other around 11:00 P.M.

"How's training going?" I asked.

"I don't feel like I know the systems very well. Rommel [Rick's nickname for Kent Rominger] has been very encouraging but says I need to know the systems a lot better. I'm not at the right proficiency level as the pilot. I need to do a lot more studying, but I just don't know where to fit it in. I need to do a really good job, Evey."

I knew Rick was exhausted, trying to juggle training and us.

"The main thing I want is to do the best job I can and to hopefully glorify God in the way I do it, but I know I'm not."

I grabbed hold of his hand. "Okay, we need to come up with a plan that works for you so that you're not always so tired," I said. We knew that staying up late wasn't the answer, but we just couldn't get everything done during the day. "We need to go to bed early so you can get up early and start studying when you're not so tired. We just really need to pray that you can get both your work and studying done."

Even if things like doing laundry or paying bills wasn't done before ten o'clock, we disciplined ourselves to go to bed anyway. What wasn't done would just have to wait till the next day. That way, Rick could get up between 4:30 and 5:00 to study with at least six hours of sleep under his belt.

Several weeks later, Rick came home from class and said, "Rommel says I'm doing much better on the systems."

When we adjusted our schedules, Rick became much more proficient in his work. We simply asked Him, and God blessed us with time we didn't even know we had. Rick was thrilled with the results. His greatest concern was doing his job with excellence because he didn't want to let any of the crew members down, and he knew that how he performed his job and how he conducted himself reflected God.

Six months prior to launch, Rick was asked to speak at Crockett Middle School, his former school in Amarillo. He was like a kid going back that day; he always loved talking with students because he felt their dreams were important and they needed someone in addition to their families to encourage them. He wore his flight suit and stood in the auditorium, telling the student body about his upcoming mission.

At the end of his scheduled time with them he said,

> If you set high goals for yourself and work hard in school and do the best job you can at everything you do, you'll be able to accomplish just about anything you set your mind to.

After he finished with the kids, Rick sat down with the local PBS affiliate and spoke about his time at the school. In a television special that would air before the launch he said,

> Kids need to know that they can get excited about something and set a goal and they can work hard toward achieving that goal. Along the way there are lots of things they can learn and there's a lot of fun they can have . . . the *whole journey* is the worthwhile experience in getting

wherever it is they want to go. I just wanted to try and tell them how important it is to try to set some goals for themselves.

Rick loved talking with students because he was well aware that their dreams and goals would pave the way for our future. He wanted them to know that there are no easy ways to achieving any goal; any dream will require lots of hard work and perseverance, but it can be achieved. Just like Rick's. He persevered through four NASA applications and finally made it. He was going to space!

In January of 1999 Rick and I attended a Steve Green concert in Houston. Steve had long been one of our favorite singers. At the end of the concert we walked to the front where people were standing in line to meet Steve. We wanted to invite him and his family to Rick's launch in May. We finally reached the front of the stage, and Rick told Steve that he had always loved his music and that he had even sung some of his songs in church. But he didn't say he was an astronaut. I knew there were people who still wanted to meet Steve, and if we wanted to invite him to the launch, we had to keep things moving. "He's an astronaut," I said, leaning into Steve. His eyes widened.

"The little boy in me came to life," Steve says. "One of my dreams has always been to fly, and here was a real, live astronaut! I told everyone who was left in the auditorium that Rick was an astronaut, and the line shifted behind him so people could get his autograph. Rick's humility made an impact on me that night and during the next few years. We tend to get our sense of worth and significance from what we do, and you just wouldn't have known what Rick did unless someone told you. A lot of people have an air of importance; they want to be noticed; they want to be important, but I would talk to Rick and realize he was incredibly brilliant but so humble. Another thing about Rick is that he was very disciplined—you have to be to reach the level of his career. He was particularly disciplined in the areas of his spiritual walk and with his speech. He chose his words carefully. He was so gentle and controlled in his speech. I was impressed with his simple but quiet witness. How people handle their faith in the marketplace is always interesting to me, and Rick did it with tremendous grace."

We didn't get around to inviting Steve to the launch that night, but I contacted his office in Nashville and made the arrangements that way. I even stepped out on a limb and asked if Steve would sing at a reception I was having the day before the launch in Florida and was delighted that he agreed.

The shuttle mission was scheduled for May 27 through June 6. In the days leading up to it, Rick and I sat down and went through our finances. He wrote down anything of significance so I would have names and phone numbers in case anything happened. In the back of my mind, I knew what he did was risky. Since the *Challenger* exploded at launch, I knew that tragedy could strike, but I never wanted to think about it. We talked through important issues and made sure a will was in place, but we never talked specifically about anything happening— we simply took the precautions that all married couples should take.

Rick had to gather items he would take into space for different people and organizations. (Flying something on the shuttle is a way to honor those who have done something for the betterment of mankind.) The astronauts can also take personal items from family members with them, and I decided to give Rick my wedding band. He'd have his wedding band, and I thought that keeping mine close by would somehow, in the figurative sense, keep us joined together. NASA needed to gather all the items and specially seal them, so I gave it to Rick months before the launch.

"Please bring this back to me," I said, handing it to him. It was emotional for me to give it to him because it had been on my hand since the day we were married.

"I absolutely will," he said.

Before any shuttle launch, the crew has to go into quarantine for the week beforehand. Quarantine begins in Texas in crew quarters at Johnson Space Center but finishes at Kennedy Space Center in Florida. Spouses are given a physical, and if we pass, we can see our spouses in quarantine. Children under eighteen are not allowed in at all, so Laura and Matthew weren't able to see Rick that entire week. At one dinner in quarantine, crew members were witnessing with a signature each other's last will and testament, and the whole procedure unnerved me to no end. They weren't flippant about what they were doing; it was something they had to think about and take care of before launch, but I didn't want to hear them talking about what to do in the event of tragedy.

Crew quarters are unusual because there are no windows except in the dining room, and the ceiling is filled with lights so that the astronauts get light therapy. Since they often sleep shift in crew quarters, many times they wake up at night when it is dark outside. Bright lights are used to simulate day and try to force their bodies to adjust accordingly. There is an exercise room, and laptops and computer workstations are set up so they can get work done. The only people allowed to see the crew must have passed a physical and must have authorization. They can't be around anyone who hasn't been cleared for contact.

I was amazed to find that this sterile environment was the junk-food capital of the world. You expect to see a quarantined world of health, but there's every junk food under the sun: candy bars, potato chips, and bowls of peanuts and M&Ms. The astronauts were sleep shifting during Rick's time there, so their hours were all mixed up. When I'd get there around 6:00 P.M., they'd be serving pancakes and sausage because the astronauts would have just gotten up and were ready for breakfast. Everyone would cheerfully exclaim, "Good morning!" but I would be thinking, It's 6:00 P.M.! One evening Rick looked out the dining room windows and said, "Well, lookie there, the sun has decided to come up in the wrong place!"

After dinner one night in crew quarters, I received a phone call from the baby-sitter at our home. She couldn't get three-year-old Matthew to go to sleep, and he felt feverish. I had waited all day for this tiny, allotted time with Rick and was very frustrated. I had just gotten there and hated to leave. Rick didn't want me to leave either, so he slipped into the car with me. I drove to the house and Rick hid on the floor of the car, so Laura wouldn't see him. We knew that if she caught sight of him, she'd run out to the car, but he wouldn't be able to hold her and that would cause another set of problems altogether. It was a risk Rick couldn't take. I went inside and realized that Matthew didn't have a fever; he was just hot from being wrapped in a blanket. We didn't have time for illness, and I was thankful that he was okay. When I drove Rick back to crew quarters, I tried to talk him into going to Sonic, but he wouldn't do it.

"It's just a slushy," I said.

"I can't eat anything NASA hasn't prepared," he said. All I could think about was that table full of junk food back at crew quarters. "If something happened, it'd be my fault." That was Rick; he was very diligent about following the rules.

Rick and the crew flew to Kennedy Space Center to finish up quarantine there. He called me the night he arrived and said, "We're here, Evey."

I had had an unbelievably stressful day and told him I wasn't going to fly in on the NASA plane the next day because I couldn't get everything done on time. "We'll fly in on a commercial plane on Tuesday," I said.

He was quiet. "You need to be on that NASA plane tomorrow," he said.

"I just can't do it," I said, upset. "I haven't even started packing."

"Evelyn, you and the kids have to be on that plane!"

Rick needed to get to crew quarters, so he hung up the phone and said he'd call me later. I looked at eight-year-old Laura and three-year-old Matthew and said, "You can go to bed right now, so we can get on the NASA plane tomorrow, or we can stay home and watch Daddy's launch on TV." For the first time in my children's lives, they put themselves to bed, and I stayed up and packed till three o'clock in the morning.

On the morning of launch-1 day (launch, minus one day), I said good-bye to Rick at the beach house on the property of Kennedy Space Center. It had been renovated years earlier and was like a conference center. I held tight to Rick because, although I was excited, I was also very anxious. As the days dwindled down to flight day, I couldn't distinguish whether I was nervous or excited because I was feeling every possible emotion.

"I love you," he said. "You mean more to me than you'll ever know." He kissed me and I held on tighter.

"I'll miss you very much," I said. "We'll pray every day. I hope everything goes really well because I know it's everything you've ever wanted." He kissed me again. "Take time to enjoy the view up there, and come back to me when you're finished." I started to walk away.

"You're a beautiful woman, Evelyn Husband," he said, smiling.

I turned to look at him. It was the same smile I'd fallen in love with twenty-two years earlier when he spilled water on me.

"I'll be praying for you and the kids every single day."

I knew he would; he always kept his word.

"There are a couple of really tough things that we have to do before a launch," Scott Parazynski says. "It's very hard to say good-bye to your kids when you go into quarantine about a week before launch because there is that underlying sense of 'what if something happens?' And the last thing we do that is emotionally draining is when we say good-bye to our spouses the day before launch. It's a tough moment. You try not to dwell on implications of what might happen, but it's certainly a palpable undercurrent."

I'm sure Rick and I both had thoughts that swirled through our minds the day we said good-bye, but we didn't talk about the what-ifs. When I left him at the beach house that day, we left each other in God's hands.

That afternoon I hosted a reception at nearby Calvary Chapel for four hundred of our family and friends, and Steve Green sang. Steve and his son, Josiah, flew to Florida for the launch, and he sang beautifully at the reception. It was a great time to thank God for Rick and his faith. He was now one day away from living his dream.

I went to our hotel that evening, ordered pizza for Laura, Matthew, and myself, and then went swimming before I put them to bed. I was so tired that my lips were numb, but I had to stay up and pack our things; we had to be ready to go at 2:00 A.M. for the launch at 6:48 A.M.

It is a tradition at Kennedy Space Center for a dry marker board to be set in one of the offices of the Launch Control Center for the children of the astronauts to draw space themes on during those last few hours of preparation. Once they're finished, it's covered with Plexiglas and hung in the hallway as a permanent reminder of that day. Laura and Matthew relished their time away from adults as they drew on the board with the other crew children, and the activity kept me from worrying about them. Rick and the crew were strapped into the orbiter around four o'clock that morning, before we even got to Kennedy Space Center. We would be taken to the top of the Launch Control Center to watch the launch once the last of the holds, called the nine-minute hold, was over. At that point, Rick and the crew would be ready to fly. I wondered what was going through Rick's mind as he waited for launch because this was it: he was experiencing his lifelong dream.

"When you're finally strapped in," Scott Parazynski says, "you just can't believe that you're physically there and that you're going to space. You're trying to concentrate on all the systems in front of you and are very focused. The main thing you don't want to do is mess up—lots of people are counting on you. There are also brief periods of time when the count is progressing, but there's not a lot for the crew to do, so we'll start joking around to diffuse any tension. All we can do is wait."

We had invited more than four hundred guests to Cape Canaveral, but only the immediate crew families, which included Laura, Matthew, and me, were allowed on top of the Launch Control Center to watch the launch. Extended family members and friends were taken to bleachers outside the Saturn 5 Building. I was so busy leading up to the launch that I never had a chance to get nervous about it. But when the nine-minute hold was over and I walked to the top of the Launch Control Center, it hit me: I was nervous! But for the astronauts inside the orbiter, it's an entirely different feeling.

"Once L-minus nine minutes is over," Scott says, "the train is on the track and you get very focused. We've been on our backs for over two hours waiting for launch and fluid has shifted to our upper bodies, we've been wearing an eighty-pound space suit that doesn't have perfect cooling, there's pressure on our bladder, and we're getting uncomfortable. When it's time for launch, we just want to go do it. We don't want to repeat it again the next day."

"The events that occur are pretty familiar because you've trained for so long," Dan Barry explains. "But there's no way to describe the sense of excitement and anticipation or the sense of joy that you're finally living your dream and it's coming true. That sensation and emotion is unequaled. The launch is loud and the orbiter shakes and we get slammed back in our seat, but the emotional sensation is greater. It's the feeling of, *This thing I've waited for my whole life is happening right now!*"

Everybody knows that launch is risky, and those fears have intensified since the *Challenger* explosion. There is a significant chance of something bad happening on launch because of the dynamic nature of powered flight and the incredible energy involved. A fully fueled shuttle sitting on the launchpad weighs 4.5 million pounds—the vast majority of that weight is highly explosive and volatile rocket propellant. Together, the shuttle's solid rocket boosters and main engines provide 7.5 million pounds of thrust, which accelerate the vehicle from 0 to 17,500 miles per hour in just eight and a half minutes. The shuttle main engines burn liquid hydrogen and liquid oxygen so quickly that a single shuttle fuel pump could suck an Olympic-size swimming pool dry in thirty seconds. The solid rocket boosters are like enormous Roman candles; they have to work perfectly because once they're lit, you can't shut them down.

Rick understood the risks going into his job. All the astronauts do. Mike Anderson said, "I take the risk because I think what we're doing is really important. For me, it's the fact that what I'm doing can have great consequences and great benefits for everyone, for mankind." It is a thought that most of us never have to think about in our jobs, but astronauts must think about the danger prior to any flight.

"One of the things you have to understand as an astronaut is what that risk is and whether you are willing to take that risk for yourself and your family and whether you think the gain is worth the risk," Steve Lindsey says. "Everybody has to go through that process and needs to think about that before they make the decision to fly. Rick always thought that the gain of what we do in space is worth the risk."

I stood on top of the building that day and looked at the shuttle in the distance and knew I couldn't change what was going to happen. I started praying that God would give me peace. Rick's mother was in the bleachers out in front of the Saturn 5 Building and was feeling the same emotions.

"I can't remember being any more nervous than I was waiting for that launch," Jane says. "I wasn't nervous about what Rick was doing because he had worked so long and hard for it, but that wait was horrible."

All of the crew families were quiet on top of the Launch Control Center, and I just kept praying silently that God would give me peace. About ninety seconds before launch, Joe Tanner, another astronaut, came over and prayed for me, which made me cry.

The countdown began, and I picked up Matthew and held on to Laura's hand. The moment Rick dreamed about was here.

"It's an amazing sensation at ten seconds before launch," Scott says. "Inside the orbiter we feel the vibration from the water deluge system." Thousands of gallons of water flow beneath the shuttle so that the tiles won't vibrate off; the water also protects the launch tower itself. "At six seconds before launch, the main engines ignite and the orbiter starts to sway a little and we can feel that vibration," Scott continues. "At T-minus-zero the solid rocket boosters ignite and the force pushes you back into your seat. During the course of the launch we experience up to 3 g's, which is like three times your body weight plus the weight of your suit. A lot of people have said it's like a gorilla sitting on your chest."

"The g's are directed from the front of your chest to the back of your chest," Dan Barry says. "If you pull too many g's in a jet, you might gray out, but on the shuttle, the g's don't push down through your head to your toes as in a jet. We experience only 3 g's, which is not much compared to a fighter jet, but it's still an interesting sensation. You definitely know something is happening!"

When the shuttle launched, I could feel my heart beating; it was pounding hard inside my chest. Launch is an awesome, powerful, and overwhelming thing to watch. Matthew, Laura, and I watched the shuttle go up in silence through a thin layer of clouds and then a shadow, a straight plume, shot out across the sky and it looked like a cross. At first I thought I was just seeing something, but some of the astronauts standing behind me commented on the shape of the cross. That was an answer to prayer for me because it gave me peace. I watched the shuttle go up, up, up and thought, *Go, Rick! Go!*

"You can't believe that anything can possibly accelerate that long and that fast," Scott says. "At 3 g's, in order to breathe, we have to take a deep breath and hold it and then forcefully exhale. It's a lot more work than normal breathing, but we know our mild discomfort won't last long. We blast into space in no time at all."

I held my breath and strained to see the shuttle climb. At the Saturn 5 Building, Jane watched as the *Discovery* rocketed higher and higher. "When that thing lifted off, I started crying," she says. "I just kept thinking, *My son is on that thing and there's nothing I can do about it.*"

At two minutes into the flight, I waited for the solid rocket boosters to break away. Laura was very quiet. Matthew kept holding on to me, but when the solid rocket boosters broke away, Matthew felt free to break away as well. He squirmed out of my arms and started weaving in and out of the astronauts' legs who were standing behind us. He managed to run back down the stairs of the launch tower building at an alarmingly fast speed. I started running after him, the shuttle launch forgotten at that point. One of the astronauts who saw me dragging Laura behind me took chase after Matthew. He finally caught him, and I'm certain it was before Matthew could find the switches linking NASA to the International Space Station.

After the eight-and-a-half-minute ride to orbit was complete, an astronaut found Jane and Keith and handed each a letter. Jane opened hers. It was from Rick.

Dear Mama,

Well, I made it! I love you very much and want to thank you for all the love and encouragement you've given me throughout my life.

You never tried to dissuade me from flying or going in the air force or becoming an astronaut. You just always told me I could do it—and for that I am ever thankful. I hope Evelyn and I can do as well for Laura and Matthew.

I thank God every day for blessing me with you for a mother. I will pray for you every day while I'm gone—even as I do now.

I love you very much and will see you on landing day!

Love, Rick

Jane smiled through her tears, finishing the note, as Keith read his.

Dear Keith,

Well, I made it! I hope you enjoyed the launch. You can bet your paycheck that I did!

I just want to tell you how much I love you. I thank God every day for blessing me with you as my brother. Thank you for being such a wonderful brother to me, son to Mama, brother-in-law to Evelyn, and uncle to Laura and Matthew.

Hope you have a wonderful 39th Birthday. Now you've caught up to Mama. I'll be praying for you every day. Take care and I'll see you on landing day.

Love, Rick

He had taken time to write letters to Laura, Matthew, and me as well, and once everything calmed down I was able to read them. He told us that he loved us and that his life wouldn't be complete without us and thanked us for the months of support and sacrifice we made during his training. Rick had a way with words that could make me cry before I even finished a letter. I always felt his love for us, no matter how short the note. I finished reading and could only imagine what Rick was doing at that moment.

"In eight and a half minutes we watched as the sky turned from blue to black," Dan says. "Kent and Rick had amazing views from in front where they could see everything as we burst through the clouds. The really special moment came when we unbuckled and floated through the orbiter. We floated right up to the windows and put our noses up to the windowpane and drank up the earth from space. No film ever brings back the beauty of the earth. It just doesn't reproduce the colors or the contrasts of the earth, and Rick was enthralled. We all were."

After the launch, it is customary for the crew families to meet with the director of NASA, and Matthew chose that time to talk a blue streak, telling the director how happy he was that his daddy was an astronaut. A couple of the secretaries thought it would be a good idea to give Matthew truck stickers to play with to occupy his time. There is another custom that once the shuttle is in space, NASA officials affix a patch sticker from that mission onto a particular door. There are several patches on one side of the door, leading up to the *Challenger,* but after the *Challenger,* the door is empty; to honor the crew members, it was the last patch placed on that side of the door.

Matthew was standing near the door for the ceremony, and I could see what he was thinking as he held on to the truck stickers. I was standing several people away from him; stuck in the back of the full room, I couldn't very well call his name or lunge for him. The NASA officials were talking about the shuttle mission, but I couldn't hear what they were saying because all my focus was on Matthew and whether he was going to place his truck stickers on the door. I thought, *Please, Lord, don't let him do it. Don't let him do it!*

When the officials were ready to stick the patch on the door, something distracted Matthew, and he turned to look behind him. I let out a huge sigh: another disaster diverted in the nick of time.

We moved to another room where it's customary to eat brown beans after a launch. I have no idea how that tradition started, but it seems to me that someone along the way should have changed it to something more appetizing for those early-morning launches. But tradition at NASA is very important. I couldn't stomach the idea of eating beans at seven o'clock in the morning, so I ate one bean.

NASA flew us back to Houston later that morning. It was a whirlwind day, and I was exhausted from being up since two o'clock. Every time I would doze off on the plane Matthew would say, "Mommy, you sleeping?" I dragged our luggage back into the house, and at seven o'clock that evening I put Matthew and Laura in bed.

"But I'm not sleepy," Laura said.

"You will be if you just close your eyes," I said.

"No, I won't."

I was too exhausted to play the "no, I won't/yes, you will" game.

"Then read a book for a little while," I suggested.

Laura picked up a book and was asleep thirty seconds later.

I fell into my bed and thanked the Lord for a beautiful launch and fell asleep.

7

Man with a Mission

Let everything I do be to the glory of God.

—From Rick's journal

FOR THE NEXT TEN DAYS OF RICK'S MISSION I WAS ABLE TO TURN on the NASA channel and watch Rick day or night. The kids loved staring at the television screen and waiting to see their dad, or at least part of him, float into view.

"Look, there's Daddy's ear," Laura would say.

"There's his watch," I'd say.

"That's Daddy's nose," Matthew would say, laughing.

I could hear Rick and the others talking, and it was a great comfort to hear his voice. He was having a ball.

"Rick was in his glory," Dan Barry says. "We had a great time as a crew on that mission. One time I was on the mid-deck and Rick was on the flight deck working. He said, 'Hey, Dr. Dan, come on up here.' I floated up, and he had all the lights out on the flight deck. He pulled me over to the window and pointed to an amazing view of the southern lights—an incredible eight-hundred-mile snake of glowing atmosphere off the southern tip of South America. We spent a minute experiencing it together, and it was absolutely beautiful. Then it was back to work. Rick always had a great balance of work and play."

My mother came to visit during Rick's mission, and that enabled me to go to Mission Control and watch what was happening. It was fascinating, and I was so happy for Rick. After years of reaching for his goal and persevering through four applications, he had made it. He was living his dream, and I could hear the excitement in his voice; I could tell by watching his face that he couldn't believe he was in space.

"He was confident in his skills," Dan says, "and I think that stemmed from his faith; it gave him an aura of confidence. He had this reassuring quality in everything he did—whether it was in the simulator or inside a T-38 or piloting to space. He was confident in his work, yet was never overbearing, and he was always encouraging. He could see where someone was gifted or skilled and could encourage us in the simplest ways. It's great to work with someone like that."

Many times, as I watched Rick at Mission Control, I felt tears in my eyes because I was overcome with the feelings of happiness and was aware of how greatly God had blessed us. I was overwhelmed by the goodness of God.

For each of the ten days that Rick was in space, my mother sneaked downstairs in the middle of the night for a bite of ice cream. She didn't even bother to get a bowl; she just took a couple of bites out of the container and headed back to bed. One night, she slipped on our stairs and tumbled down the last few steps, and her shoulder went through the drywall.

I got up the next morning and discovered a gaping hole in the wall. I couldn't figure out how in the world it happened.

"Why is there a hole in the wall?" I asked.

My mother sheepishly told me the story.

Laura and Matthew call my mother Grammy, and they started calling it "the Grammy Hole" in honor of my mother. Some astronauts came to our house the next day and took a digital picture of the kids by the hole and sent it to Rick in space, which he found very humorous. He loved my mother and couldn't wait to tease her about the Grammy Hole she left in our wall.

I worried that Mother hurt her foot in the fall because she kept complaining about it; I thought maybe she chipped a small bone or something. I called one of the doctors at NASA named Chris Flynn, who is actually a psychiatrist, and he said he'd have her foot x-rayed.

Several hours later she returned home and kept commenting on Chris. "He's one of the nicest men I've ever met," she said. "I've never met anybody before that would just let me talk and talk and talk, but he did. All he did was listen. He never interrupted!"

"That's because he's a psychiatrist," I said, laughing. "And I'm sure he found you fascinating."

Rick got the biggest kick out of that story and never let my mother live it down.

The *Discovery* was scheduled to land on June 6, 1999, at two-thirty in the morning. Laura had a ballet recital, so she was unable to go, and because of the early hour, I decided that Matthew would stay behind too.

There is a totally different feel on landing day; there's no nervousness at all, and the spouses are excited. There's an energy because the mission has been a success and the crew is coming back. NASA flew us to Florida the day prior to landing, and that night all the families got together and went out for a meal. We laughed and talked and laughed some more. I'm sure the wait staff was happy to see us go, but we couldn't contain our excitement because our spouses were coming home!

We were picked up at the hotel a little after midnight to get to the landing by two-thirty.

My mother had gotten up to watch the landing, and Matthew happened to get up to use the bathroom and sneaked downstairs. Together, they watched the landing, which was smooth and uneventful, before Matthew crept back up the stairs to his room. His daddy was safe; he could sleep through the night.

Once the shuttle landed, the other spouses and I were taken to the building where the astronauts are brought after they walk off the shuttle. When I saw Rick, my heart melted. I can't remember a time I was more overcome with joy in reuniting with him. I was so happy to be able to touch and hug him. He was safe and sound and back on earth again; now we could get our lives back to normal. I laughed because he couldn't walk straight; he was wobbly because his equilibrium was off, but I couldn't stop hugging him.

After his physical, we got in the car, and I stopped at Subway to get him a sandwich. He kept talking about how great the bread smelled. "This is the best thing I've ever smelled," he said. I couldn't smell it at all. "This is unbelievable! I can't stop smelling it." He had been used to eating food that didn't have an aroma, so he thought the bread was like something baked by a French chef. I had purchased a regular cup of Coke, but he drank it down immediately. When we got to our hotel and saw Jane and Keith and a few others, Rick kept ordering one Coke after another. Finally, a kind waitress brought him a huge pitcher of Coke, and we watched in amazement as he drank the entire thing. Rick loved sodas, especially the caffeine. Coke tasted exceptionally wonderful that day to him (especially when the caffeine started kicking in!).

He told story after story, and his eyes lit up as he talked with excitement about the mission. He had just come back from the greatest experience of his life, and he couldn't wait to share every last detail with us.

I don't remember what time we fell into bed that morning; all I know is that it felt great to have Rick's arm around me again. "Was it everything you dreamed it would be?" I asked.

"It was so much more, Evey," he said. "I can't even describe the beauty of the earth. It's just absolutely beautiful and amazing, and I can't believe that just a few hours ago I was in space looking at it!"

"Do you want to go back?" I knew the answer.

"I can't wait to go back," he said. "I can't wait to do that all over again." He wrapped his arm around me and fell asleep.

Before I fell asleep, I thanked God he was home. I had missed him so much.

Rick and I woke up in the afternoon and got ready to go out to eat that night. We drove to a beautiful spot and sat on the terrace of a restaurant overlooking the ocean. The sun was setting, and it was so romantic; I loved being with him. I watched the sun go down and looked at him.

"That must look pretty boring to you now," I said.

"The sun rises and sets in the blink of an eye in space," he said. (Astronauts can watch them every forty-five minutes in space.) "God created sunsets on earth that are nice and slow, giving us time to really enjoy them here."

Many people, reporters especially, have questioned Rick concerning the argument of science versus religion. When he came back from the *Discovery* mission, he was more than ready to answer their questions.

In a taped interview Rick said,

> Even if you look out at the universe and all the stars, our solar system—all the order that is there, and the fact that the planets orbit around the sun, and the way that the different galaxies behave, all the different interactions that are there . . . I don't believe that's something that just happened by chance.
>
> Nobody can explain where everything came from and how it all got here. You just take a look around and you see the complexity in so many

things and the detail in so many small things; how the simplest cell works, up to a tree, the human being; just the miracle of seeing our children born; and you say, "This just didn't happen by chance." If you even take a look at a system like the space shuttle—that is the most complicated and complex flying machine in the world and it didn't happen by chance and it doesn't approach the complexity of a human being. It took a lot of people a lot of time to sit down and think and put together that space shuttle and the entire system. Then to sit and think that the entire universe could have happened just by accident, it doesn't make sense to me.

It'd almost seem you have to have more faith to accept that it happened by chance than to accept that God created the universe.

In an interview before the *Columbia* launch he was questioned about watching the sunrise and sunset in space during the *Discovery* mission. He said,

I felt quite humbled by the whole thing . . . but God's presence in creation is just as much in evidence here on earth as it is two hundred miles above the earth. And then just taking a look at every single person that you pass every day—after seeing our kids being born and realizing what a miracle each and every human being is and the beauty we see in God's creation here on earth—there's every bit as much evidence here as while you're up in orbit.

For Rick, there was never a conflict of interest; to him, science only deepened his appreciation for God's handiwork. To him, God was the ultimate Scientist: He created cells and knew how each of them operated; He put knowledge in men and women that enabled them to find cures for diseases and invent something as complex as the space shuttle; He hung the stars and placed the moon in orbit, telling it when to come out at night. God was the inventor of physics and math and science, so Rick considered what he did to be a blip on the radar screen compared to God's greatness.

The next day, we flew into Ellington Field in Houston, and a huge celebration awaited the astronauts. For the next few months they would be busy traveling and speaking. They visited the schools that had sent something into space with the shuttle and talked with the kids about their mission. They toured all of Canada because of their Canadian crew member, Julie Payette, and had a blast meeting different people there. They were busy, but at least it felt like Rick was home. Things were feeling normal again.

We went on a long vacation that summer, driving to Destin (Florida), Atlanta, Chattanooga, and Nashville, where we visited with Steve Green and his family, who were becoming dear friends to us, before Rick went back to work. The kids had a ball. In the same way, when we went on vacation, he was on vacation. He worked hard, but he played harder.

Usually, once an astronaut returns from a mission, there is a two-year wait before he'll fly again. When Rick returned to work, he was given a technical assignment as the safety officer for upcoming missions, monitoring the safety issues of each flight. He also kept up his training so he wouldn't get lax on any of his skills.

That period was a wonderful time for our family. We played games and instituted "Family Night" every Friday where we'd make pizza and rent a movie. Laura and Matthew loved it when we moved all the furniture out of the way in the living room and put sheets over their heads. They'd have to try to find Rick and me, and they'd shriek with laughter. We did scavenger hunts and even played softball in the backyard in our pajamas (I'm more than grateful for our privacy fence).

Rick started to compile everything the kids had ever given him in a book and wrote down some of the funny things they said. One day, Laura said, "Heaven is behind the black in space; it's not just in space," but the next day she changed her mind and said, "Space is behind the blue; heaven is *behind* the black." Rick filled the book with stickers and playing cards and construction paper crafts. He taped down a leaf that Matthew had given him during a picnic at the Houston Zoo. When he taped down a rock, I thought he'd officially lost it! But then I read what he had written beside it:

> Matthew gave this rock to me when he and I walked Laura to school. He handed it to me and said, "Here, Dad, keep this to remember me by." What a sweet little guy!

One day after school, Laura brought home football player cards for Rick. He taped them into the book and wrote,

She could have gotten a sucker or something else for herself, but got this for me. What a sweet blessing from God!

Rick took the time to tape a tiny splinter into the book that we got out of Matthew's thumb. It took a grand total of five hours to finally get it out (we started extracting it on Friday night and tried again on Saturday). Rick wanted to document it so we'd never forget it. We haven't!

At some point during this period, Rick and I thought it would be a good idea to do some sort of family devotions together, although I'm not sure how clearly either one of us was thinking, considering we had a four-year-old at the time. We wanted to do something that would incorporate God's Word into Laura's and Matthew's lives, but we wanted to make it fun for the whole family. We started out with the best of intentions, yet each devotional time quickly turned into a comedy of errors.

Rick would read one or two sentences out of the book before Matthew or Laura started talking.

"Shh. Listen to Daddy," I'd say.

Rick would read another sentence or two, and then they'd start talking again.

"Daddy's trying to read us something," I'd say, my voice carrying more weight this time.

Rick would go back to the book and read again. Matthew would get up and walk around.

"Matthew, come back here! Daddy is trying to teach us something!"

I'm not sure who was crazier: Rick, for thinking he could hold the attention of a four-year-old, or me, for trying to persuade a four-year-old to sit down.

We managed to stumble our way through a devotion, and then we had to answer questions from the book we were using as a family. One of the questions asked what we enjoyed doing most as a family.

"Sleeping," I said.

"Hitting Matthew," Laura said.

We were hopeless. At the end of our time we prayed that we'd do better at obeying and not interrupting, but I had my doubts.

We tried the devotional time on and off that summer. Right after Matthew turned five, he brought several "prizes" to our devotional time. He laid out a medal that looked like something an Olympian would win and a few pieces of gum and candy.

"What are these?" Rick asked.

"These are for everybody who can keep quiet," Matthew replied.

Rick was impressed; maybe Matthew was learning something after all. But as soon as Rick started to read, Matthew started to talk.

"Shh, be quiet, Matthew," he said.

He read some more, and Matthew continued the conversation with himself.

"Matthew, I'm reading," Rick said.

He went back to the book, and Matthew chattered away.

"Matthew, sit down. Be quiet and listen, or you won't get a medal."

"I don't need a medal," Matthew said, looking at him. "I'm the judge."

We thought maybe a change of venue would help, so we decided to go to Piccadilly Cafeteria one day, or "Pickle Dilly," as Matthew called it. We started to eat and noticed that Matthew wasn't eating any of his vegetables. I kept encouraging him to eat them, telling him the ever popular "they'll help you grow big and strong." He wouldn't touch them.

"I don't want to eat vegetables," he said. "I just eat dessert."

When we started the devotion, we could see that our brilliant plan of changing venue wasn't so brilliant after all.

Rick wrote in the margin of the devotional book:

At one point Matthew and I had to go to the bathroom for counseling because he was being very disruptive. He was much better afterward.

Our family devotions weren't producing the fruit we had hoped. The biggest question Matthew had during that time was, "How come we say 'almond' at the end of prayers?" It probably wouldn't go down as our most spiritually enlightening time as a family, but we had fun. The kids loved the activities at the end of each lesson: we played circus in the backyard, and Laura wrote skits that she and Matthew starred in, giving us handmade invitations to the shows. It was a wonderful time of growing together, and Rick loved it.

In his journal he wrote,

> I have been given a place of influence in my son's life and it is my
> responsibility to do everything I can to make sure he knows Jesus as his
> Lord. Lord, please let it be that Matthew will come to know You.

He had already prayed with Laura and explained that Jesus died
on the cross for all of us. When she was four years old, Laura asked
Jesus into her heart so she could have a close, personal relationship
with Him, and Rick wanted Matthew to accept Him as well.

Rick used the time between shuttle missions to memorize Scripture
and continue his steady walk with the Lord. He got up each morning
and studied the Bible and spent time in prayer before leaving for
work. On the days he was unable to do that, he felt a great deal of
frustration. If he didn't spend that early-morning time with God, he
felt his whole day was off. An interviewer asked him how important
it was for him to stay in Bible study, and he said,

> It's almost like exercise. If you don't continue to exercise, your body
> doesn't stay physically fit. If you don't continue to study the Bible, you
> don't stay spiritually fit. I have to review, continuously remind myself
> of what God says to us in the Bible. Jesus went through all the things
> that we go through. He has felt all the pain; He's been tempted in every
> way possible. He's gone through that and has victory over that.
> Everything that He has to say is very helpful, very motivational. You
> have to continually feed yourself with it. You don't want to go on a
> diet from that kind of stuff. That's what's necessary to keep you grow-
> ing spiritually. You need that to carry you through the days, especially
> with all you see that goes on in the world today—it's comforting to go
> back to the Bible and know that God is in control.

God had always been faithful to Rick, and he wanted to remain
faithful to his calling of being a man who followed God and who was
a good husband and father.

I remember that as a time of great undergirding—it felt as if God
was preparing both of us for something that was going to happen. I
had experienced the same feelings in California when I was active in

working on my relationship with the Lord and Rick talked with me about the baggage in his life that had been troubling him for years. We didn't know what was going to happen but felt we were being strengthened physically, mentally, emotionally, and spiritually for something that we would face.

8

The Columbia and Her Final Crew

The future doesn't belong to the fainthearted—it belongs to the brave.

—President Ronald Reagan in an address to the nation
following the space shuttle *Challenger* tragedy

In September of 2000, fifteen months after Rick's first mission, the science crew of the *Columbia* was announced: Michael Anderson, a lieutenant colonel and pilot in the air force, was assigned as payload commander. It was hard to believe that Mike and Sandy were the first people we met in Houston, and now he and Rick would be on the same mission together. David Brown, a navy pilot and flight surgeon, was assigned as mission specialist, as was India-born Kalpana Chawla (or K. C. as everyone called her), who held a Ph.D. in aerospace engineering. Laurel Clark, a commander in the U.S. Navy and a naval submarine medical officer and naval flight surgeon, was assigned as a mission specialist, and Ilan Ramon (pronounced E-Lan), a decorated colonel in the Israeli Air Force, who would be the first Israeli in space, was assigned as payload specialist.

The flight crew, consisting of the commander and pilot, was announced three months later, in December of 2000, and that's when Rick was assigned his second mission, chosen as the commander. Willie McCool, a navy test pilot who graduated second in his class of one thousand at the U.S. Naval Academy, was selected as pilot.

Typically, pilots have to fly two shuttle missions, sometimes three, before being considered as commander. Rick was named commander after one flight, something that hadn't been done at NASA in years.

"Rick was a very gifted pilot," Kent Rominger says. "He was very natural, which is a lot of the reason he had been assigned commander after one mission. He was very professional and clearly demonstrated the ability to step up to the plate and be a commander after only one flight. Not all pilots can do that, but Rick was extremely skilled."

Rick was never one to focus on honors; he never got caught up in them but remained focused on what had to be done.

I was well aware that this was very unusual. "Isn't this a really big deal that you have been chosen as commander after only one flight?" I asked.

He didn't think anything of it. "I was just at the right place at the right time," he said. "Rommel was such a great commander that I learned everything from his leadership skills."

"Rick, you're going to have to give yourself some credit for this. You did an incredible job on your first flight."

But Rick wouldn't hear any of it. He was always the first to put the compliment on someone else, which at times frustrated me.

"I just owe everything to Rommel," he said. "I was sitting in the seat next to him. He taught me what I needed to know." Rick was self-effacing, but others recognized his leadership abilities and skills.

In *Sixteen Days: Columbia's Final Mission,* a TV special on the Discovery Channel, Robert Hanley, the crew mission lead on the training team, said, "In my history, I've worked with about fifty-five different crews over time . . . and I've learned that the commander will set the tone for a crew in how you work with them, in how they work with each other and how they interface with everybody. It was going to be a very high-profile flight, having an Israeli astronaut on board, and they chose Rick because they knew of anybody, he could handle the stress, he could handle every aspect of a long mission and all the science and organizing everything, and he would have the right attitude about it. He was the perfect choice for STS-107 commander."

Beth Vann, a crew trainer, said, "He was just a very kind, very good man. Not to mention he was just America. He'd walk in the room and you wanted to say the Pledge of Allegiance. I mean he was Texas and apple pie!"

Dr. Angel Abbud-Madrid, lead scientist for one of the combustion experiments, remembered a conversation he had with K. C. during training: "I told K. C. that it was really a pleasure working with this crew . . . they were all very helpful, they were really acting as a team, and she responded, 'It's all because of Rick.' I didn't understand then, but when later on I heard the stories about how he kept that crew together and was very well focused, then I understood the importance of his role."

Rick would have been embarrassed to hear the comments on the Discovery special because more than anything, he was humbled to be selected as the commander of a crew for which he had so much respect. He told me several times that there wasn't a weak link in the entire group. They were all incredibly strong, talented, intelligent, and very humble. (I think it's difficult to find a stuck-up astronaut; they're all down-to-earth and unassuming concerning their abilities.) Egos didn't get in the way with the crew of STS-107—I don't think any of them had any egos to speak of. Rick looked for ways each individual could be his best because he wanted all of them to shine. From day one, he knew the mission wasn't about him as the commander; it was about the entire crew and team effort. Rick loved every minute he spent with the crew.

When Angus referred to someone's intelligence in England, he said, "He's got a brain the size of a planet." Rick quickly surmised that K. C. had a brain the size of a planet. She had flown in space once before, aboard the *Columbia,* and for the STS-107 mission she would sit in the seat behind Rick and Willie, watching over them and making sure all the systems were running smoothly. K. C., age forty-one, was a gifted woman in many ways, but her personality was always consistent. I never saw her grouchy or frustrated; she was very even tempered, and she had one of the most beautiful smiles I've ever seen—the world lit up when she smiled. Even though she was beyond intelligent, she was easy to talk with, and when you spoke with her, she made you feel as though you were the only person in the world that she wanted to talk to at that moment. She had a natural way with the crew children and always had a loving attitude toward them.

On one particular evening, she and her husband, J. P., had us over for dinner, and they served the most delicious Indian food. Afterward, she dressed all the children in gorgeous Indian clothing and jewelry, and they held a fashion show for us. K. C. introduced each of them as King this or Queen that. I'm not sure who enjoyed it more, the kids or K. C.

Mike, age forty-three, had also flown in space before, so he was considered a veteran for the *Columbia* flight. Mike was always very

Christmas 1958—Rick's early training for the military.

Jane Husband with her three-year-old son Rick.

Rick (center) with friends Carl Lorey and David Jones, taken outside of Crocket Junior High School, Amarillo, Texas, in 1972.

Rick, a senior in high school, flying with Aunt Josie in 1975.

Rick Husband and Evelyn Neely at a 1979 ROTC dance at Texas Tech.

Christmas 1981, Rick Husband and Evelyn Neely . . . engaged!

Evelyn and Rick married at First Presbyterian of Amarillo, Texas, on February 27, 1982.

Evelyn and Rick's mom, Jane, "pinning" Rick at graduation from Texas Tech when he was commissioned into the Air Force (his father, Doug, and brother, Keith, look on).

Evelyn pinning wings on Rick at his graduation from pilot school training in December 1981.

Evelyn welcoming Rick home with a kiss in 1983 at Moody Air Force Base.

Rick and Evelyn celebrating her birthday on September 18, 1990; Laura would be born the next month.

Captain "Ribs" Husband (nicknamed after his favorite food) at Edwards Air Force Base in 1990.

Rick, pilot for STS-96 mission, arriving in Florida, May 1999.

Rick with baby Laura in 1990 at Edwards Air Force Base.

Chuck Yeager and Rick at Edwards Air Force Base, where they flew together one afternoon in 1990.

1995 Husband family Christmas photo ("All males in photo are wearing diapers," says Evelyn).

Matthew visiting his daddy in 2001 during Rick's training for STS-107.

Angus Hogg and Rick in the Husband's back yard in Houston, Texas.

Rick, Evelyn, Laura, and Matthew in their front yard.

Rick with lifelong friend (since fourth grade) David Jones.

Columbia crew, after crossing the Continental Divide, reaches the summit of 13,192-foot Wind River Peak in Wyoming.

The insignia for *Columbia*'s STS-107 mission of multidiscipline microgravity and Earth science research.

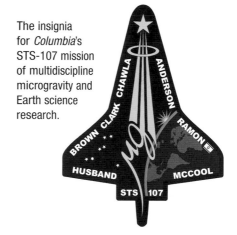

Evelyn and Rick stand in front of the *Columbia* Space Shuttle during a pad tour on January 14, 2003, at Kennedy Space Center.

Matthew and Laura with Rick after he returned from his NOLS (National Outdoor Leadership School) course in August 2001.

From left to right at January 14, 2003, pad tour at Kennedy Space Center: Ilan Ramon, J. P. Harrison (crew member Kalpana Chawla's husband), Rona Ramon, NASA Mission Specialist Clay Anderson, Rick, Evelyn, and USAF Colonel Steve Lindsey.

The *Columbia*'s team departure, January 16, 2003 (NASA photo).

Columbia blasts off, January 16, 2003 (NASA photo).

Rick's family photo in his command book, which was on a roll of film recovered from a debris field in east Texas (NASA photo).

The *Columbia* team in space, a photo also from the recovered roll of film (NASA photo).

Rick and Evelyn renewed their wedding vows in August 2002.

Husband family photo, September 11, 2002.

Above: Laura, Evelyn, and Matthew on February 1, 2003, at the countdown clock, not knowing that *Columbia* had already come apart.

Left: Florida Today / USA Today political cartoonist Jeff Parker honored the *Columbia* crew.

Evelyn and the Reverend Billy Graham in San Diego on Mother's Day 2003.

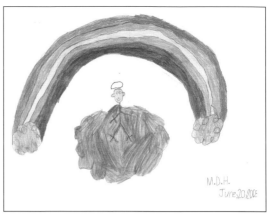

Matthew's artwork, remembering his daddy.

Sean and Lani McCool, Laura and President George W. Bush, Evelyn, Laura, Evelyn's father, Dan Neely, and Matthew at the NASA memorial service, February 4, 2003 (White House photo).

Evelyn, Laura, and Matthew with former President George H. W. Bush.

Matthew, with the other *Columbia* crew's children, threw out the first pitch at the Houston Astro's 2003 home opener.

Evelyn, Laura, and Matthew in Colorado near 13,980-foot Columbia Point.

soft-spoken, very much a gentleman. He had an incredible smile and a tender, sweet spirit about him. Rick felt a strong bond with Mike from the moment we met him and Sandy at the Realtor's office; he was thrilled when he learned Mike was on this crew. Mike loved computers and could tear them apart and put them back together again with little effort. He upgraded his computer every year and upgraded ours before the launch of the *Columbia*. Mike was the payload commander of the crew (again, payload is what the shuttle carries—in the *Columbia*'s case, the payload was the science experiments) and was very driven to make sure the payload was exactly right. He had dreams at night of not being where he was supposed to be and everything going haywire, but of course, that never happened.

Mike loved his wife and their two girls, Sydney and Kaycee, more than anything, and he was a wonderful husband and father. Mike and Rick actually started a Bible study together, and Mike joined a prayer group called Dads in the Gap that Rick started, where dads got together and prayed for their kids. An amusing thing about Mike is that he always looked well groomed. If the others had taken off their helmets after a rigorous training session and looked a mess, Mike looked great. When the crew climbed a mountain in Wyoming and looked tired and haggard, Mike looked great.

Willie McCool, age forty-one, had the perfect name for a navy test pilot! He would be going on his first flight with the *Columbia,* and he was beyond excited. Rick loved the incredible energy that Willie brought to the team. Always upbeat, he approached every day with enthusiasm and zeal. Willie was extremely organized: if someone asked him to do something, he'd have it done before the words were out of the person's mouth. He was a great father and devoted to his wife. The first time I met him and Lani, I could see how incredibly loving they were as a couple and toward their three boys. He was a runner and could outrun anybody. Willie enjoyed athletics of any kind. He loved the thrill of competition. Rick was more than excited to have Willie by his side in space.

Dave Brown, age forty-six, would be making his first flight into space on the *Columbia,* and everybody at NASA knew how excited he was about that. Dave was the only single person on the mission, and Rick considered him a Renaissance man. When he was in college, Dave had performed with the Circus Kingdom; he owned two planes, a Piper

Cub and a Bonanza, and actually lived on a runway in Houston (the hangar was right behind his house); he loved photography; and he was a navy pilot and flight surgeon. He was very close to his parents and always spoke of them with high regard and respect. Dave was quiet and kind of shy but very personable and witty once you got to know him. When they were training for the STS-107 mission, Dave would look at Rick and say, "This is so exciting. This is so cool." He had the enthusiasm of a kid, and it was contagious. He could not believe he was going to be flying in space.

Rick adored Ilan Ramon because he was a very warm, genuine person. He had tremendous pride in his country, and that was just one of the things that drew Rick's respect. Ilan, age forty-eight, enjoyed being here in the States, but when he and his wife, Rona, talked about Israel, you knew it was their home. He was a national hero in Israel, but you would never know that if you met Ilan; he was very humble and didn't like to talk about himself. His mother was a Holocaust survivor. During his time in the States, Ilan was called to speak to many groups around the country about his mother. He always told his four children how much he loved them, and it was obvious the children adored their father. Rick felt it was an incredible blessing to have Ilan in the crew and considered it an honor to get to know him. Ilan jumped in with both feet during the training and couldn't wait for his first mission to space.

Laurel Clark, age forty-one, was one of the most compassionate and caring people I'd ever met. She absolutely adored her eight-year-old son, Iain, and wanted to be involved in everything he did. Her husband, Jon, works as a flight surgeon at NASA. (Flight surgeons are trained in the field of aerospace medicine. Each mission crew usually has a primary and a backup flight surgeon. The flight surgeons track all crew medical issues during training, flight, and postflight.) Laurel loved working so close to Jon. Rick thought Laurel was unbelievably talented and capable, and he loved her personality. When they would train, she'd say, "This is so much fun. I'm so glad you're my commander." She was always uplifting. Laurel's claim to fame was that she bought a complete ensemble of STS-107 shirts, earrings, pins, and necklaces, and anytime you'd see her, she'd be wearing them. She just couldn't hide her enthusiasm about her first flight.

"This team is remarkable," Rick said one evening as we prepared for bed. "I just can't get over how brilliant they are and that I was chosen to command them." I pulled the covers back on the bed and crawled in beside him. "I am blessed to work with these people, Evelyn. It doesn't feel like work at all when we're together."

"So the dream just keeps getting bigger and better, doesn't it?"

He shook his head and smiled, looking up at the ceiling. "I just pray that Laura and Matthew will be able to grow up and discover what the Lord has for them to do because I want them to be content and blessed in their work like I am."

I smiled. Rick had always been content with his job. He absolutely loved flying and working with people.

He looked at me. "I don't want to let this crew down, Evey."

"You won't, Rick. I know that you'll lead with nothing but integrity and character."

"Pray for me, Evey. Pray that I will be a good leader because I don't want to let them or NASA or the Lord down. He put me in the role of commander for a reason, and I just want to lead in a way that will bring glory to Him in all that I do. I don't want people to see me. I want them to see how God has worked in my life."

I put my arm around him, and we talked for several minutes until Rick fell asleep. Before I fell asleep I lay my hand on his chest and prayed, as it says in the Psalms, that he would lead the crew with integrity of heart.

The crew's flight was the 113th for the shuttle program. The sixteen-day mission would focus on research in life, space, and physical sciences, and the crew would work twenty-four hours a day in two alternating shifts (Red Team and Blue Team) to carry out more than eighty experiments aboard the space shuttle *Columbia*.

It would be the twenty-eighth flight of the *Columbia*; its first journey was in 1981. Half a million people stood on beaches and rooftops and along roadsides near Kennedy Space Center in anticipation of that first launch of the shuttle program.

In July of 1972, NASA contracted with North American Rockwell Corporation for the shuttle to be designed and built. During the Mercury, Gemini, and Apollo programs, spacecraft were protected on entry by a covering of material that slowly burned away when it entered the earth's atmosphere, but those vehicles were designed for only one trip to space, not several. The shuttle needed to make repeated trips. After years of extensive testing, NASA decided to use foamed silica (sand) tiles coated with borosilicate glass, a breakthrough in space technology, developed by Lockheed Missiles and Space Company. The tiles weighed only nine pounds per cubic foot but could remarkably protect the shuttle from temperatures up to 3,000 degrees Fahrenheit on entry. The tiles would take time to manufacture, lots of it: each was made specifically for its location on the *Columbia*, meaning it was slightly different from the one next to it, and then there was the time-consuming and daunting task of attaching nearly 25,000 tiles.

Finally, on April 12, 1981, fifty-year-old John Young took the commander's seat and forty-three-year-old Robert Crippen was strapped into the pilot's seat for a two-day mission to space. Eleven minutes from launch, President Ronald Reagan delivered a message to the crew inside the orbiter:

> We are the first and we are the best. We are so because we are free. As you hurtle from Earth in a craft unlike any other ever constructed, you will do so in a feat of American technology and will. As you embark on this daring enterprise, the hopes and prayers of all Americans are with you. May God bless you and bring you home safely.

When the *Columbia* launched, there was a deafening chorus of cheers and shouts as it climbed into space. It was the maiden flight of the U.S. shuttle program, and it was a brilliant beginning.

9

Climbing Mountains

Rick's faith was as much a part of him as his sense of humor.
—John Kanengieter, National Outdoor Leadership
School Professional Training Director

THE STS-107 MISSION WAS SLATED FOR THE SUMMER OF 2001, giving Rick and the crew plenty of time for training, but problems and delays began immediately. Extra wiring inspections and delays in repairs while the *Columbia* was in California for a $70 million tune-up threw a wrench in everyone's plans, slipping the launch from July. Rick wasn't concerned. He knew the crew would fly when the timing was right.

When the *Columbia* was returned to Florida in March of 2001, more work needed to be done, but NASA had two missions for the shuttle: the STS-107 research mission that Rick was on, and the STS-109 Hubble Space Telescope servicing mission (they needed to swap out a major camera on the Hubble and work on its control systems). The servicing needs of the telescope took precedence over the science mission, so NASA selected the Hubble mission first.

During the delays, Rick had an idea. He had heard other astronauts talk about taking an NOLS (National Outdoor Leadership School) course and thought it would be perfect for the crew.

When NASA started working with the Russian Space Agency and began sending people to the Mir Space Station, they realized astronauts would be on a whole new playing field, being in space six months as opposed to ten days for the typical mission. It was maintained that if the U.S., Russia, and other countries were going to build the International Space Station together, we would need to learn how to be a team for long durations. NASA has been concerned about long-duration flights—that's why the agency takes great effort in astronaut selection. An individual's personality is a factor on each mission, and NASA's leaders have to be sure they're selecting people who can work and cohabit with someone who may come from a different ethnic, racial, or religious background.

An astronaut had taken an NOLS course in his youth and told someone at NASA about it. In 1999 NASA sent to a test course in Wyoming a few astronauts including Shannon Lucid, who had been on the Mir Space Station. The program, which was created to build leadership and cooperation, was a success, so NASA signed up other astronauts who were scheduled to be on the International Space Station.

The NOLS expedition followed a leadership model similar to the one at NASA, focusing on competence, expedition behavior, communication, tolerance for adversity and uncertainty, judgment and decision making, self-awareness, and vision and action. Rick was fascinated with the program and wanted the *Columbia* crew to go for the training. An entire mission crew had never been sent before, but management at NASA agreed that it would be a crucial element in their leadership and teamwork training; the request was approved. The crew would fly to Wyoming in August of 2001 for a ten-day outdoor expedition. They started wearing heavy backpacks at NASA, then climbing bleachers and stairs to prepare for the trip. Houston isn't known for rolling hills, but you can find bayou hills, small mounds of earth that would never win any sort of "hill" competition. Nevertheless, NASA provided Rick with an expensive pair of boots and he went out in search of them to get used to wearing his boots and carrying a pack.

Rick was excited about this trip; the crew members were already close, but he knew that the NOLS experience would only draw them closer, helping them to learn about one another's quirks and idiosyncrasies and how to pull all those individual traits into a cohesive team. He knew the course would help him become a better leader of this group of incredibly intelligent, gifted, driven, best-in-their-field, type A personalities.

As Rick caught the plane for Wyoming, Matthew was preparing for the first day of his own wilderness called kindergarten, with a teacher appropriately named Mrs. Flowers. But the men in the family weren't the only ones entering their own wilderness; Laura and I would be going through the uncharted land called homeschooling. A close friend was homeschooling her children and often described the off-the-wall fun ways they learned about science, history, and even math. I was intrigued and knew Laura would enjoy a change of pace for our year of homeschooling. We would be very busy during Rick's absence.

Cell phones wouldn't work in the Wyoming mountains. If there was any sort of injury, Rick and the crew would have to look to one another for help. NOLS Instructor and Leadership Consultant Andrew Cline and NOLS Professional Training Director John Kanengieter met them at the airport.

"I remember reading their bios before we got to the airport," John says, "and I was so impressed. They all had such extensive backgrounds. At first I wasn't sure how easy it would be to get along with a group who was obviously so intelligent in different medical and scientific fields, but then I met them and all my perceptions changed. Rick had this big, beaming smile and was so easygoing. Willie was a top gun pilot, but he was like an adult Opie Taylor, just so friendly."

Andy wasn't sure what to think of Willie when he first met him, however. "John and I were in the restaurant in the airport, and Willie was the first of the team I met. He said something right off the bat that made me think I'd have to put up with this Tom Cruise/Top Gun guy for two weeks, but then I looked in his eyes. They were amazingly gentle and kind, just like Willie. That's how the entire crew was: they were all such gentle, kind, friendly people."

The crew spent the night in a hotel, but the next day they traveled two and a half hours to the trailhead of the rugged, glacier-carved Wind River Mountains Range in west-central Wyoming. For the next ten days they would learn how to bring outdoor survival skills to space as they crossed the Continental Divide and summited to the top of Wind River Peak, which at 13,192 feet is one of the highest mountains in the state.

A couple of the crew members made comments to Andy that referred to Rick as their commander. "Not in a bad way," Andy says. "They all had great respect for Rick and were letting us know that there was a structure in place, but I was getting this feeling that they were going to be looking to Rick to lead the next two weeks. But Rick didn't know anything about the terrain or what they were up against. I took a few minutes to talk to the entire crew and let them know what was ahead of them and that they had to look to John and me as the leaders in the wilderness, not Rick. Rick's authority as commander of the crew was a given. I felt awkward saying it, but when I finished, Rick made a comment to the crew that let me and them know that John and I were the leaders while on this wilderness expedition. In one statement, he took any sense of tension away, and it was never an issue for the rest of the trip."

They hiked one and a half miles to their campsite, and John and Andy taught them how to cook, camp, and live in the outdoors as a team. It wasn't every man for himself; they had to do things together.

"We taught the importance of eating and drinking," John says, "because even if you don't feel thirsty, you could be getting dehydrated." They tried to teach them that it was crucial to eat breakfast every morning.

"I don't eat breakfast," Ilan said.

"Well, even if you're not hungry, the food helps sustain your energy level throughout the day," Andy said.

"I never eat breakfast," Ilan said. "I drink coffee."

Andy and John didn't argue. "We knew it would work itself out," John says. "We'd done enough climbs to know that you need food in your system!"

The next day the crew got up and, with the exception of Ilan, ate breakfast as they discussed the subject matter of how they would characterize themselves as a team. It was part of the NOLS training that would help focus their efforts as a group. They weren't just individuals; they were individuals who made up a team and had to discuss how they wanted to portray themselves: Were they a collaborative team, or did they fall in line behind the commander and have him make all the decisions? Were they a team that had two members doing one thing while others were doing something else?

"Mike led the two-hour discussion," Andy says. "And he did it with such skill. He had to be a participant and a facilitator at the same time but was so graceful in how he handled both roles."

"It was a great discussion," John recalls. "Everyone got involved, and I could see that Rick was a great leader for that group. He was very authentic: what he said was what he meant; there were no hidden agendas. He'd love to see his teammates succeed ahead of him. He was the quintessential leader because he was able to create a collaborative feel; that was important to him."

"Rick was one of the most amazing leaders I've ever seen around a team of people," Andy says. "He edified his crew by making room for them to lead within the group whenever possible. He was always on the lookout for opportunities where between them they could build trust, and Rick knew how to create that environment. Even better, he knew on this mountain expedition that we could let nature be that teacher and create that environment for us."

Rick took along a journal for his time on the expedition, and before he left, we had agreed to read a chapter a day from the Psalms, starting with chapter 1. He documented his readings every day, and although I'm sure I got the days mixed up and confused, Rick stayed on course reading a psalm a day. At the top of the page for the second day he wrote, "Read Psalm 2." He was always looking for ways to further educate himself, and at the end of that morning's discussion with the crew, after his Psalm 2 note, he wrote,

Leadership: It's not only about what you do, but what you do next.

On the next page he wrote,

We need to have a high threshold of tolerance for: uncertainty and diversity.

As I read through Rick's journal, I knew he had written those words pertaining to survival in the wilderness but realized they easily apply to life: *life* is a wilderness marked by uncertainty and diversity. I knew that, but in eighteen months it would become all too real.

The crew came to the conclusion at the end of their discussion that morning that they were a collaborative team; each person was as vital as the next one. At one point in the discussion, Rick said, "We've never talked like this before as a group." He was pumped; Rick loved any sort of breakthrough in a relationship that made it stronger and better. In his experience with the group, he was confident that this conversation would help all of them grow closer together as a team.

Once the discussion was over and everything was packed and

ready to go, Willie and K. C. acted as group leaders (each day, two team members acted as navigators for the group) and led the team toward the next camp. It was going to be a long day, traveling five miles at fourteen hundred feet with sixty-pound packs. They made a slight navigational error, and John and Andy stood off to the side observing as they worked through the problem and eventually found their spot for the night, at the end of a beautiful river valley.

"We learned so much about them on the hikes," Andy says. "The whole crew was mischievous but so focused on what they were doing. They were always doing things in service to the person next to them, not for their own self-service. It is the essence of why they were so amazing with one another."

"We'd be hiking and they'd give each other a hard time, joking around with each other," John says. "They were in great spirits throughout the hikes."

In his journal Rick wrote,

Ilan and I cooked dinner: refried beans, rice, cheese—on flour tortillas. Mm, mm! My favorite! I love it! Thank you!

Rick had told everyone a story of being on board a ship one day for a campout with Laura. It was a special campout through the YMCA Indian Guides/Princesses on board the USS *Lexington,* which is permanently docked in Corpus Christi.

"Rick was a true storyteller," John says. "He had more funny anecdotes than anyone, and we always looked forward to what he was going to tell us."

While on board the ship, Rick said that the captain had drilled it into everyone at mealtime to say, "Mm, mm! My favorite! I love it! Thank you!"

"Of course, the crew started yelling that at every meal," John says. That evening, Rick wrote,

The weather was gorgeous all day. I am praying like crazy for good weather the whole trip, for my family, for me and my crew, and the instructors.

Early the next morning, Laurel got up and took a picture of a tree that was grossly contorted every which way. "She said she felt sorry for the tree because it had arthritis," John recalls. "She said she empathized with it because she felt the same way after two days of hiking and climbing. It was like Laurel to do that. She was always taking pictures of something because she absolutely loved the outdoors."

Rick got up that morning with altitude sickness. He was nauseous and had a pounding headache with chills. His pack load was redistributed throughout the team, so he wouldn't have to carry as much weight that day. He told me he was out of it that day, just going through the motions to get to the next campsite, but on the hike he was moved by the beauty of his surroundings and started singing. He wrote,

Along the way, I was singing "Amazing Grace" and got teary at the point I was singing, "'twas grace that brought me safe thus far . . ."

Rick was always aware of and extremely grateful for the grace of God.

Once camp was set up, Rick went to his tent and lay down. The crew crouched around the entrance of the tent during the day's debriefing so that Rick could listen and participate in the discussion. He wrote,

I am very blessed with the people I have on my crew. They are all caring, helpful, and willing to pull more than their fair share. They are also all very enjoyable to be around. "It just don't get no better 'n that!"

After the debriefing, Rick tried to sleep, hoping he'd feel better for the next day's events. "It's miserable to get sick, but it's common," John says. "Rick made light of the situation. He had the best Eeyore impersonation of anyone I've ever heard—a deep 'don't worry 'bout me, I'll manage somehow,' voice. You immediately knew he read in that voice to his kids many, many times. He kept up with us that day, but he was out of it that night. He went to bed right away, but when he got up the next morning, he was excited about the day."

On that day Ilan finally admitted he was tired but still refused to eat breakfast. "Nothing was going to change his mind," John says, laughing. "When he said he didn't eat breakfast; he meant it."

"A twinkle was always in Ilan's eye," Andy says. "They were so bright and intense. When we were in the field, the Israeli and Palestinian conflict was heating up again. I became more curious to hear his viewpoint. I had a conversation one day with him about Israel, and he was so thoughtful about his answers. I knew he had been intimately involved with the Israeli military. He told me that before Israel was a nation, Jewish and Palestinian people lived in the same geographical area in peace, and he believed it could and should happen again. He was a tremendous ambassador for his culture."

They hiked four miles and camped beside an unnamed lake, which they immediately named Lake 107 (NOLS has kept that name). K. C. and Dave made pizzas for the crew, although Dave protested, saying he wasn't a cook.

Andy and John said he'd have to be if he was going to be part of a team. "He never complained, though," John says. "He dove into it."

"If he knew he had to learn a skill," Andy says, "he jumped in with both feet and learned it, whether it be cooking or fly-fishing. He went full bore."

"Dave was very inquisitive," John says. "He had a very dry, wry sense of humor that made him a lot of fun to be around—unless he had his video camera, that is."

Rick said that Dave was married to the video camera. He documented everything the crew did on hours of videotape.

"He was always coming up with scenes he wanted to tape," Andy says, "but he would erase over it if there was any chance that someone could misinterpret it. Every one of them was always looking at something like, 'Is this in service to the crew and what we're doing?' It's really what made the crew exceptional. They were always looking at things from the perspective of, 'Is this strengthening the group? Is this helping what we're going to do as a team?'"

Dave fumbled his way through the pizza-making process as best he could, and when he served it that night and the crew saw it, they teased him that maybe it would be a good idea if they didn't eat his cooking. Yet every bite was devoured. After dinner, Willie pulled out one of his passions, a cribbage board game.

"He loved to play cribbage," John says. "He was competitive but in a good, fun way. He thought he was unbeatable, but Andy and I kept beating him and it was driving him crazy. As soon as we'd end a game, he'd say, 'Let's play again.'"

At one point, Laurel came up to John and Andy and asked, "What kind of scat am I holding?"

Andy looked into her hand. "Moose," he said.

Laurel looked down at it and nodded.

"She was our natural history student," John says. "She was interested in anything in nature. She was great at recognizing flowers by what family they were in. She'd say, 'What's the name of this flower? It looks like it's part of the pea family, right?' If you met Laurel in the grocery store, you'd have no clue what she did for a living, but you would know she was a wife and mother. She was passionate about her work, but it was second to being a good mom and wife."

"Laurel was unassuming and totally approachable," Andy explains. "She reminded me of the person next door—she was amiable and not at all pretentious. She was a mom who was focusing on raising her son, but then you'd talk to her and discover all these amazing things about her background [she was a naval submarine doctor, a flight surgeon, an avid outdoorswoman], but she was humble about all of it."

The next morning was Rick and Laurel's day to lead the team over Coon Pass, an arduous climb that would be like climbing a ninety-story building without any stairs; they wouldn't even have a trail. There would be fallen trees, slippery plants, uneven footing, a nine-hundred-foot elevation, and a boulder field.

"It's a challenge, to say the least," John says, "but Rick and Laurel did an excellent job leading us, even though Rick had been sick the night before. Rick was an outstanding leader, regardless of the environment he found himself in. He saw unfamiliar situations as learning opportunities and confronted them with excitement."

It was a long, rough day, but John and Andy said the crew laughed and joked their way up Coon Pass. "It was obvious that they enjoyed being with each other," John says.

Once camp was set up, Willie instigated another cribbage match that night. "It had become a quest for him to win," John says, "but he lost again. It was starting to get funny for the whole crew."

"Willie loved to interact with people," Andy says. "He didn't shy away from conversing with a person on the most intimate level, and that level means talking about what's going on right here, right now, with and between us. He was comfortable with who he was and what he was doing and always a great deal of fun. He knew how to *not* let moments get away and he grabbed hold of them. Not everyone can do that. Willie did more in one day than most people can accomplish in a week. I've met few people who could keep up with him."

They needed to turn in early that night because they had to get up at 4:45 the next morning to climb 2,500 feet to the summit. It wasn't going to be easy; John and Andy let them know that it was difficult terrain. The climb entailed getting around boulders the size of washing machines that could roll at the slightest movement. Mike and Willie were scheduled to navigate that day, but Mike said he might not go on the climb.

"The shuttle was his livelihood, and he didn't want to risk any sort of injury," John says. "The boulders are unstable, so they are a hazard. All of them had a lot to lose if something happened on that climb. Mike was looking at it and asking, 'Why take that risk? I have a wife and children to support.' It was an excellent point, and it gave them all something to think and talk about."

"If he had his druthers," Andy says, "I know Mike would have rather been with his wife and girls, but he jumped into this wilderness expedition for the team and NASA and for Rick. He was a great team player and wouldn't do anything that would jeopardize the team."

Others thought about the potential of injury on that day's climb, and some thought it might be wise to break into two teams: those who would climb and those who would stay behind.

"We pointed out that two days earlier they had said they were an all-or-nothing team," John says. "It was like a light turned on with them: 'We said we were like this, but now when the rubber hits the road, how are we really? What will we do?'"

After a lengthy discussion, it was determined that they would all climb as high as they could, and if someone got tired, they would all stop there and call it a day. Nothing stopped the STS-107 crew. They climbed the entire peak and made it to the top at 10:45 A.M.

Rick wrote,

The "plan" was to go as two groups but we ended up staying together all day. Everyone wanted to make it to the peak.

"They were so happy," John recalls. "Mike held the plastic emblem of the 107 and the team gathered around and we took a shot of them with nothing but the sky surrounding them. They milled around a little, and then Rick started singing 'The Doxology' as several joined in. It got very quiet and still, and the sky was cloudless. Andy and I commented several times during the trip how impressed we were that the crew could sustain such comfortable periods of silence with each other."

Rick wrote,

The views *were awesome!* I was thanking God the entire way for the beautiful, clear, cloudless day that He had blessed us with.

After the crew rested and ate, John pulled out a cell phone he hadn't told them about and dialed Monika Schultz, the astronaut expeditionary training manager at NASA. She didn't answer, but they left a message on her voice mail: "*Columbia* has landed," they said, whooping and hollering into the phone.

Each person signed the plastic emblem and left it in a peanut butter jar at the top of the peak. "We heard later that another group of climbers saw it there," John says.

Day six ended up being a layover day for the crew so they could rest from the peak climb. They broke into three groups: Rick, Willie, and Ilan went rainbow trout fishing while John, K. C., and Mike stayed at camp. Dave and Laurel went with Andy back to Lake 107 to retrieve the coffee filter.

"Coffee became an important social event for some members of this group—foremost, Ilan," Andy says. "We were ever in search of the perfect brew morning, afternoon, and evening so we had to have that coffee filter."

At the end of the day, when everyone reconvened, they ate a delicious fresh fish chowder, compliments of Rick, Ilan, and Willie. Dave documented many of the day's events again, but this time he was getting bolder in his approach, no longer satisfied to just lurk in the background holding the camera.

"He no longer just took video," Andy says. "He started filming, directing, and producing a movie!" We would all get an edited mini-version of what Dave filmed when they returned from the expedition. He even starred in a portion of it with Laurel that highlighted the importance of communication. They sat on rocks beside a river, facing each other.

"I've learned some new communication skills out here," Dave said. "And I think you're a jerk."

Laurel nodded. "I've decided you're a jerk too."

It was hysterical because neither of them could pull off the dialogue. It wasn't in either of their personalities to talk that way.

Willie pulled out the cribbage board again that night, but still with no luck. "It was driving him crazy!" John says.

Laurel and Dave were the leaders on the seventh day. Willie thought it would be fun to make the hike more interesting by challenging John and Andy to a competition. "It was classic Willie," John says. "He was always up for anything that would make a day more exciting and challenging."

The crew decided that they would get a head start over Andy and John, navigating the hike on their own that day—John and Andy would shadow behind them thirty minutes later. If Andy or John saw them, without anyone from the crew noticing, Andy and John would win, but if any member of the crew was able to sneak up on either Andy or John, the crew would win. Sort of "touch the enemy without them knowing it."

"Andy and I were confident we were going to win that game," John says. "We purposely went off trail because we knew they'd stick to it. They didn't know the region like we did."

John and Andy kept a watchful eye for movement on the trail; they were sure they'd see one of the crew at any moment. Both men knew they'd be funneled into a ridge that would force them back toward the trail. When they got to that area, they snuck back toward the trail, careful not to make any noise.

What John and Andy had forgotten was that, with the exception of K. C., the crew of the STS-107 had a background in the armed forces. They looked at the game as a military operation, realizing that John and Andy *would* go off trail and that they *would* get pinched between the ridge and be forced back to the trail. They took their spots, hiding behind boulders or downed trees, and waited with great patience for the "enemy's" approach.

"We stepped onto the trail and heard whooping and hollering," John says. "We looked up to see the crew running down from their hiding spots screaming, their arms raised above their heads. We were ambushed in a humiliating way. It was a crushing blow for us!"

"K. C.'s eyes were just shining with victory," Andy says. "She was so mischievous but so caring at the same time. When I first met her, she reminded me of someone who was an old soul. I've met few people who are as focused and calm as K. C. She had these laser eyes that would zero in on you when she talked, and you knew exactly what she was saying because she was always so honest. K. C. was to her core a person who emphasized action, being direct, and making things happen. At one point on the trip we were taking an afternoon to explore each other's leadership styles. During our conversation, K. C. stopped the group at one point and sternly said to all of us in her lilting Indian accent, 'I don't think I am such a driver as you all are saying I am.' But before she could get any further, we all burst out laughing. The laughter was a mirror shining back at her because K. C. was a 'type A' person if ever there was one. She stopped in her tracks and started laughing with us. She knew she'd been caught. The moment was stunning because we could see how much everyone cared for each other and how they held each other accountable. It wasn't about stereotyping. It was about exploring. She was one of the best explorers of what was one of the most stunning and accomplished teams that I've met. She was always ready to rumble, play, and listen to the quiet. Though I never quite figured out how she could do it, she could do all three at the same time."

That evening, Andy and John asked the crew about what would happen on the launch and mission. The crew huddled together for several minutes before coming back to the campsite where they proceeded to "put on" their space suits and walk in formation down the gangplank, waving at the media. They walked into the "orbiter" in the order they had already practiced for launch day and lay down on their backs, the position they would be in for launch. They began to toggle imaginary switches, and Rick went through the communication checks with "Houston."

"He was cracking us up," John says. "He was doing the dialogue for both him and Mission Control and was keeping a straight face, but the rest of us were howling."

The crew began to shake violently as the "g forces" hit their chests, keeping their heads firmly in place. Once they were in space, they took their suits off and were weightless moving about the campsite, bumping into each other as if floating in space. They performed some of the experiments they would be doing in space before getting back into their suits again for reentry.

"It was truly a laugh-filled impromptu show," Andy says. "It high-lighted why we were out there and why they were a team."

Rick and Mike led the crew on Day 8. In his journal Rick wrote,

> Read Psalm 8: O Lord, our Lord, how majestic is your name in all the earth!
>
> It was another gorgeous day and I continued to thank God for that.

The crew hiked to Twin Lakes without assistance from Andy or John. About that hike Rick wrote,

> I taught everybody the "Hot Dog" jingle by PDQ Bach that David Jones and I learned in high school.

The song is sung in rounds, and when it is put together, the two groups sing "hot dog" at the same time. They sang,

> Loving is as easy as falling off a log
> A cat'll love a cat and a dog'll love a dog
> When you're hot you know you're hot
> And when you're not you're not.

Now you know what astronauts do in their off time! With all their intelligence, each of them has a wire crossed in the brain that can remember ridiculous trivia.

They hit a few navigational snags but still made it to a lake in time for a swim before dinner. They had a class in conflict management, and when that was finished, they played "Survivor of the Weakest Link," a game John and Andy had made up to test them on what they'd learned on the wilderness course and about each other's personal life.

"They had to remember things like, Where did Willie do his under-graduate work?" John says. "Or what is Rick's middle name? Rick won, and we had a blast laughing throughout the game."

Rick noted in his journal that night:

> The 107 Players did the Hot Dog jingle and Willie and Laurel finally won a cribbage game!

"We let them win," John says, laughing. "It's not a pretty picture when astronauts cry, especially on issues of strategy and competence! We didn't want to demoralize them."

On their ninth day, Rick, Willie, and Ilan caught fish for the entire crew, and everyone enjoyed fish chowder—Israeli style. It ended up being another "Mm, mm! My favorite! I love it! Thank you!" meal.

On their last day, the crew hiked four miles to the road where they were being picked up and driven to their hotel. A huge barbecue would end their time in Wyoming but not their friendships.

"I had great one-on-one conversations with so many of them," Andy says. "Willie and I would get up and run together before breakfast and talk about faith and why we do what we do. I remember having several discussions with Rick about his family and faith and how that fit in with his being an astronaut. I knew I'd be able to call Rick and talk with him someday in the future with any questions I had about faith. He's one of those guys you look at and think, *How can he be so sure about what he believes?*"

"Rick didn't have the 'faith' language that can be alienating to people," John says. "Rick never used his faith to an end. He wasn't using it to impress anyone. He just lived it simply. It was as much a part of him as his sense of humor. I believe that the crew saw it that way as well. There was a comfortable space in his faith for everyone."

That trip was a highlight in Rick's life, and he felt that every crew should go through an NOLS course before flying in space because it really pulled the STS-107 crew together.

When he came back to Houston, Rick felt that now, more than ever, they were ready for their mission.

10

Launch Slips, Lice, and Blessings in Between

Rejoice always, pray without ceasing, give thanks in all circumstances;
for this is the will of God in Christ Jesus for you.

—1 Thessalonians 5:16–18 NRSV

THE HUBBLE MISSION THAT SUPERSEDED THE STS-107 FLIGHT was bumped to March of 2002, when it was finally flown with great success. (Unfortunately, the first launch of the Hubble in 1990 received more press. At that time, the mirror's shape was incorrectly ground, which basically made the telescope nearsighted and required additional money and time to fix. However, scientists and astronauts will argue that the Hubble is one of the greatest scientific platforms ever built. It is still pumping out volumes of information about the universe today.) With the Hubble mission out of the way, the STS-107 mission was on track for launch in the summer around a target date of July 19.

For the past few years it had become a family tradition to stay on different military bases in the San Antonio area for spring break. We loaded into the van and made the trek that spring, but our trip was cut short the second day when my maternal grandfather died. I called our neighbor Beth Cotten in Clear Lake and described what clothes we needed from our closets for the funeral so she could ship them to my parents' house. My grandfather had always been very fond of Rick, and my mom asked if he would sing at the funeral. Rick stood in the chapel on the grounds of the Llano Cemetery and sang "How Great Thou Art." I knew it was difficult because Rick was grieving for my grandfather as well, but he overcame his emotion and blessed us all with the song. When he sang the last note, there wasn't a dry eye in the chapel. After the funeral, I stood on the steps outside the chapel with Rick and my cousins, and we all shared memories of my grandfather. There is no way I could have known that I would have two more visits to that cemetery in less than a year.

In late June 2002, as the *Columbia* was ready to leave the hangar for the Vehicle Assembly Building, shuttle program managers stopped all prelaunch preparations and grounded the entire fleet. Tiny cracks had been discovered in the propellant flow liners of the *Discovery* so inspections were ordered on the other orbiters as well. No one knew how long this delay would be because the task required removal of the Rocketdyne main engines.

As repairs and inspections continued, NASA reorganized its shuttle missions and decided to send two flights to the International Space Station before the STS-107's science mission on the *Columbia*. As a result, Rick and the crew found themselves waiting several months more to fly, but everyone remained upbeat and patient. "Good things come to those who wait," Rick often said.

Because the mission kept getting slipped, the crew became phenomenally proficient with every system in the orbiter. They did one training session where they never spoke a word, and it drove the training team absolutely crazy—they couldn't hear anything over the communication system and couldn't figure out what was wrong. The crew had worked so well together for so long that Rick said, "Let's just do this and see if we can pull it off without speaking." They used hand signals and different forms of communication and never said a word to each other but did everything they were supposed to do. They were like a well-oiled machine. I know I'm probably prejudiced, but I think they were probably the best-trained crew that ever flew.

They made trips to labs in Holland, Alabama, Kennedy Space Center, and other places to learn from scientists how to operate, maintain, and repair the different equipment and tools used in the experiments. The experiments ranged from how to reverse osteoporosis and fight prostate cancer to how to design cancer drugs with fewer side effects and reduce pollution-causing emissions. The crew would become the eyes, ears, and hands on orbit for the scientists, so they needed to learn every detail of how an experiment would be carried out. It was important to Rick that they get every detail right, and the crew worked very hard toward that goal.

There were some initial reservations about a fighter pilot of Ilan's stature taking part in a scientific mission, but Ilan quashed those doubts at the outset. In a Discovery Channel special, *Sixteen Days: Columbia's Final Mission,* Dr. John Charles, NASA mission scientist for the *Columbia,* said Ilan came to him after one training session. "I'll do anything you want me to do," Ilan said. "I'll do it all. I'll do it the best I can. You'll be happy you've got me."

Lora Keiser, the lead crew trainer, said, "He did get the nickname of 'The Machine' because he could just pick up a procedure, read the procedure, and do it. There wasn't a lot of discussion. There wasn't a lot of questions. Ilan just did it."

I don't know how the crew could learn all the logistics of every experiment and how each tiny part fit into a machine or device, but they knew that information inside and out. As payload commander, Mike took that time of learning very seriously. He was the perfect payload commander because he was detail oriented and professional in every way. Mike wanted his work to honor the Lord as well.

Both Rick and Mike said that God had a special purpose for their flight; they had a sense that God was moving and doing something. "Rick and I both feel we were put on this mission for a reason, and we have tried to meet all those challenges with prayer," Mike said.

"I don't know what it is, Evey," Rick told me, "but I know God is up to something with this mission." Rick always had tremendous respect for the nation of Israel and its rich history and culture, and for the longest time he felt the mission was unique because Ilan was on the crew. Neither Rick nor Mike would ever know how special their mission was.

The STS-107 crew worked an incredible number of hours training for the mission, but the launch date was slipped time and again. Rick felt that everything would happen in God's timing and looked at the slips as a way to take advantage of their training and as time off for the families, even surprising me with a trip to San Francisco for our twentieth wedding anniversary. He planned it down to the last detail and did it all on his own, keeping much of it a secret.

At that time, Rick was very, very, busy and his time was precious, so the fact that he somehow managed to plan everything meant the world to me. He took me to a bed-and-breakfast English pub in the Sausalito countryside we had discovered a year earlier when we took the kids to California for vacation. It was nice to be together, and Rick made me feel so special. As was characteristic of Rick, he left work at work and concentrated on us.

Shortly after flying back to Houston, Rick began rehearsals for the Easter service at church. He was going to be one of the soloists in the choir and had to prepare himself for five services over Easter weekend. The song the choir director had chosen for Rick was called "Were It Not for Grace," which I thought could be titled "Rick's Theme Song." He was the first to tell you that everything that happened in his life was by the grace of God. He stood in front of the choir and sang,

Were it not for grace, I can tell you where I'd be
Wandering down some pointless road to nowhere with my
     salvation up to me
I know how that would go—the battles I would face
Forever running, but losing the race,
Were it not for grace

I thought, *Rick, this is a summation for your life.* It was a verbalization of Rick's personal faith journey.

Between July and August of 2002, the crew staggered their schedules, and all of them took two-week vacations with their families. Against our better judgment, we had promised Laura and Matthew that we would go to Disney World, so we drove from Houston to Orlando in July, along with the rest of mankind. Rick said that going to Disney World was the closest a civilian can come to combat: you have to have the right shoes or else you die; you have to have a fanny or backpack filled with rain gear, food, water, maps, camera, and film. All tickets and miscellaneous information must be shoved into a safe pocket, and then you fly out the door at an incredible rate of speed in order to get your money's worth for the day. We bought a four-day pass and stayed five nights. It was exhausting. Why did we think it would be a good idea to stand in lines for two hours at a time in the middle of the summer? Even Rick's NOLS training couldn't prepare him for that.

Rick tried to take pictures of the kids with the Disney characters, but each time we got to the front of the line we received the same distressing news: "Sorry, folks, it's time for Goofy to take a break." Because of the heat, the characters could stay out only a few minutes. Not to be discouraged after several failed attempts, Rick finally got the idea to have the kids run beside the characters as they made their exit.

He'd run backward so he could get the perfect shot and call out directions to the kids. "Just keep your eye on the camera, Matthew," he said from behind the lens. "Don't look at Winnie. Just run next to him and I'll get the picture." Matthew and Laura tried to pose while running next to the character, and inevitably, there was a scowling security guard ushering Mickey or Pluto away from the crazy man with the camera. "Pay no attention to the grouchy man, Laura," Rick said, determined to take the picture. "Just look right here at the camera." Just as Donald Duck or Minnie Mouse was about to dart inside a door, Rick would throw up his hand and say, "Thanks!" He put down the camera and looked at me. "You just can't trust those characters," he said. "They never make eye contact with you." When we got home and developed the pictures, we saw several of Matthew and Laura posing with the backsides of the characters as they were escaping inside the door; the scowling security guard was looking right into the camera.

It was a hot, tiring trip, but I'm so thankful we did it together. It was a wonderful time for our family.

After repeated slips, the launch was finally scheduled for January 2003. (Someone has said it was delayed up to seventeen times, although I'm not certain of that.)

On October 14, only five days after her ninety-eighth birthday, my father's mother died. Again, Rick was asked to sing "How Great Thou Art" at the funeral at First Presbyterian Church in Amarillo. We stood beside her graveside in Llano Cemetery, and Rick held on to my hand. My grandmother had been such an important part of my life. She had supplied my very first piano and had paid for my first lessons. She planted seeds that have lasted a lifetime of a love for literature, poetry, and using words creatively. I was getting tired of visiting that cemetery.

On November 20, 2002, the eighteen-story-tall *Columbia* was moved from its hangar to the Vehicle Assembly Building. Also in November, Rick gave the entire crew a week off for Thanksgiving. Rick felt that all work and no downtime was the making of an unhappy crew. He felt convicted to give that break at Thanksgiving and then a week and a half for Christmas. It's unusual for a crew to have downtime so close to launch, but this crew experienced it again and again. My parents came for the week of Thanksgiving, and we were able to actually relax and enjoy each other's company.

On December 9, the *Columbia* was attached to the external tank and solid rocket boosters and rolled out to Launch Pad 39A at Kennedy Space Center in Florida. On December 20, Rick and the crew performed a launch run-through at Johnson Space Center in Houston, going step-by-step through what the big day would be like. From December 17 through 20 the crew members were in Florida for terminal countdown, where they had a dress rehearsal for the launch and practiced emergency procedures in case anything went wrong. On the twenty-third, the crew took off for Christmas and wouldn't have to be back to work until January 2.

Rick was involved in all aspects of Christmas 2002. He loved Christmas every year, but 2002 was different; I could feel Rick's excitement. I usually did all the shopping, but that year I was running behind and Rick drove all over Clear Lake buying Matthew's presents. He'd call me and say, "Okay, I'm going into Toys 'R' Us now. I'll call you when I'm done." He'd drive to a little specialty shop and call me again: "I just found such and such." He had a great time.

We shopped in an electronics store together, which can be a test of your marriage, but Rick was ready for it. Although he didn't like to spend money, he went wild when it came to certain occasions, and that Christmas was one of those occasions. We bought a new TV for upstairs, a Game Cube for the kids, a digital camera, a 35mm camera, and a scanner. Making all of those purchases was unprecedented in the history of our marriage and uncharacteristic of Rick, but he loved doing it.

We played games for hours during that Christmas vacation. We actually played Twister, which is not designed for anyone over forty—it's alarming how you have to contort your body, and my body soon decided that it was not in the mood! I finally designated myself as the official "spinner." I spun the game piece, it spun around the colors till it landed on one, and Rick, Laura, and Matthew sprawled across the mat, reaching for yellow or red. It was more than amusing. Rick bought the game Jenga, which involves building a tower without making it fall and then carefully pulling it apart, piece by piece, without making it collapse. That game was designed for our family; it brought all of our personalities out in a way that Twister never could. Laura was very dramatic as she swooped in on a piece, and it unnerved Matthew because he was certain her dramatics were going to topple the tower. Then Matthew zeroed in on a piece and, with great focus and resolve, methodically pulled it away without breathing.

On New Year's Eve we let the kids stay up till midnight, something we had never done before. I made hot chocolate, and we went out to the backyard and looked through the telescope at the stars and saw Jupiter and the rings around Saturn. Rick painstakingly set up the telescope, focusing on a star of significance, but then an argument ensued.

"I get to look first this time," Matthew said.

"You looked first last time," Laura said. "I get to look first this time."

Rick tried to keep them from bumping the telescope by holding out his hand. "Careful," he said patiently. "Don't bump the telescope."

Inevitably, one of them did. Then, they looked through the lens and groaned. "There's nothing there!"

Rick looked through the lens and sighed before meticulously setting it back again.

It was freezing, but it didn't matter. That Christmas season was the first one we'd been alone together as a family, and Rick cherished every second. At midnight, people in the neighborhood were making noise, and Matthew got the biggest kick out of that and started hollering things too. Part of me questioned our judgment in letting a seven-year-old stay up till midnight, but since Rick had to be back at work on the second and would be going into quarantine on the ninth, I knew it was the right choice. Matthew and Laura loved spending that time with Dad.

I didn't know it at the time, but beginning on January 1, Rick started a journal for me, leading up to the day of the launch. He documented his days from beginning to end. Again, I don't know how he ever found the time to do it, but he wrote down every last detail of what he did at work and what we did together as a family.

That Friday, he woke up early with heartburn (I remember that because he wrote it in the journal). He finally decided to get out of bed and head into work so he could fit in some exercise. Astronauts don't exercise out of vanity, trying to obtain bigger muscles or a slimmer physique; they exercise because it's crucial for their health in space and their ability to tolerate entry after living in a 0g environment. When they get into space, astronauts' muscles atrophy (more so in a long-duration flight than a space shuttle flight, although it still happens) if they don't use them. Also, their skeletal structure starts weakening because their bodies have realized they don't need the heavy "1g" frame. Exercise is crucial to maintain muscle mass and skeletal structure.

Unfortunately, Rick's schedule was so full that he rarely found the time he wanted to devote to it. That morning he also worked in the simulator for four and a half hours practicing ascents before heading to his office to change into his blue denim crew shirt. A press conference was going to be held that afternoon. Rick stepped into a room across the hall and tried to call me at home.

He wrote in the journal,

I called home and left a message, then called Evey's cell phone and still got her phone mail and left another message. Then I walked back to my office to review some notes for the press conference when lo and behold, Evelyn and the kids were there waiting for me! It sure was great to see their smiling faces!

After a brief visit, we walked to the elevator and Evey and the kids headed for McDonald's for lunch. Matthew was especially looking forward to going to McDonald's. So they had their lunch and made it home in time to watch the press conference at 2:30.

Laura, Matthew, and I sat down in the living room and watched the crew file out and take their seats; they were all smiling. Most of the questions were for Ilan, since he was the first Israeli in space.

Rick wrote,

The press conference went very well, with most of the focus being on Ilan. He and K. C. always leave me in awe of their eloquence. Poor Dave Brown got to introduce himself and that was it! But for most of us, that's a great way to have it go.

At one point, a reporter asked Rick to compare this flight to his previous flight in 1999. He said, "There's less nervous anticipation about the unknown than there was on the first flight." He'd been up before; he knew what to expect.

That night, Rick and I had our last date night together. I felt very tired before we left home but knew somehow that it was too important to cancel. We went to the Outback for dinner and went to see *Antwone Fisher*, the latest Denzel Washington movie. The waitress took our picture in the restaurant, and Rick included the photo in the journal.

Under the picture he wrote,

> Dinner and a movie—a "couple" of our favorite things! Little did we know what the next day's events would be!

Saturday, January 4, began the last weekend Rick had at home before he went into quarantine, and he had a to-do list that just never ended. Rick was famous for his lists, and sometimes at the end of them he would write "Build Rome in a Day," because he knew it was impossible to get everything done. That day, he had an impossible list: he wanted to be sure the cars were in good shape, the finances were in order, and small repairs were done around the house so that everything was in working order for us during his absence. But first thing in the morning, we wanted to get together with Mike and Sandy Anderson to pray for the launch and mission. Laura was having trouble with a science project, and in the journal, Rick admitted he was in a "foot dragging mood," so we moved our prayer time to ten. When Mike and Sandy arrived, their children, Kaycee and Sydney, ran upstairs to play with Laura and Matthew, and we didn't hear a peep from any of them for the two hours we were together.

Rick wrote,

> We had a *great* prayer time with Mike and Sandy. It was so nice to pray through all the "stuff" that was on our minds and to lay everything at the feet of Jesus. I felt *much* better after we prayed!

Something poignant happened during our time with Mike and Sandy. We sat at our dining room table, and Mike brought up Ron McNair, an African-American who was on the space shuttle *Challenger* when it exploded. Mike related what Ron's family had gone through as a result of the *Challenger* accident and how he didn't want to put his own family through that.

"One of the hardest things you do is say good-bye to your family," Steve Lindsey says. "You think about your kids—*will I see them again?* I'm not worried about me when I go up. I know where I'm going if something happens, so I'm not afraid to die. I'm afraid that I won't be there for my kids. That's what worries me. That's what worries every astronaut."

Sandy held on to Mike's hand that morning and we prayed for the mission and for all of the crew members and their families, and we prayed that all of us would have peace about every aspect of the mission that was less than two weeks away.

We said good-bye to the Andersons at noon, and Matthew and I headed to Kroger to pick up some groceries while Rick started fixing things around the house. My cell phone rang, and I saw that it was Rick.

"Evelyn, Laura has head lice," he said.

For two weeks, Laura had told me her head was itching, but I kept dismissing it as something in the air because we'd been running the heater for two weeks straight or as an allergic reaction to shampoo. I kept blowing it off because I was busy and didn't have time to focus on an itchy head. My defenses went up immediately.

"No, she doesn't," I said.

"Yes, she does. I found something in her hair."

"She doesn't have lice."

"I looked it up on the Internet and it's identical. It's the same thing. She has head lice."

I was defensive because I felt my mothering skills were being challenged to the limit. If she had lice, that meant I had failed my family, and the ramifications were huge. Rick was only a few days from quarantine, and if we couldn't eradicate the problem and the crew members got head lice, the mission could be delayed again, and it would be Evelyn Husband's fault! In my mind, I could already see the newspaper headlines.

Laura has long, beautiful hair that she washes more often than even I think is necessary; she takes excellent care of it. We discovered that cleanliness has nothing to do with head lice. We called the NASA flight clinic, and they told us all the disgusting things you have to do to get rid of the lice—none of which were going to be simple or quick.

Rick and I had opposite personalities: he was very slow and deliberate, extremely meticulous and calm, while I bounced off the walls.

We decided that he would take care of Laura that afternoon while I tried to get the bugs out of our house. I ran upstairs and ripped the sheets, blankets, pillows, and comforters off our beds. I threw the sheets and blankets in the washer and took the comforters to the dry cleaner.

In the journal Rick wrote,

> Laura and I settled down in the big bathroom for "treatments" while Evelyn started washing or bagging everything in sight! Evey's outlook on life wasn't too high at this point either!

My outlook actually stunk at that point! The washing machine overflowed into the dining room, and I quickly cleaned up that mess and started the washer again. Several minutes later it overflowed again. At that time, I thought it was necessary to have a little conversation with God. "Didn't You hear us ask for peace three hours ago when the Andersons were here? Have You seen the to-do list Rick has today? Don't You know he's going into quarantine in a few days? What's the deal?"

As I mopped up buckets of water from the floor, Rick gently washed Laura's hair in Rit, the shampoo NASA had prescribed, and repeatedly told her how beautiful her hair was and that everything was going to be okay. When Matthew knew what was happening, he made himself scarce, careful not to invade our space during that tense time. While I continued to run through the house and bag up the stuffed animals for a two-week quarantine of their own, Rick proceeded to painstakingly take little sections of Laura's hair and comb it with a tiny comb that gets out the eggs. Then he had to twirl each section up and pin it before he could move on to another section. It took hours, but Rick never made Laura feel as if he had anything else to do. He kept telling her how proud he was to have her as a daughter and how much he loved her and how thankful he was that she loved Jesus. Rick's "Build Rome in a Day" list was long forgotten; Laura needed him.

As I ran through the house tearing things apart, I could hear them talking and laughing together, and I could hear Rick's deep voice speaking tenderly to her. He knew that she was embarrassed and that her self-esteem had taken a hit, but he kept loving her and telling her again and again that everything would work out just fine. He was so gentle and good to her that day.

Laura was supposed to go to her best friend's birthday party, and I was going to drop her off at a meeting point at five o'clock in Clear Lake. She didn't want anyone to know that she had lice; I had to call and say we were running late. Several minutes later, my friend thought she'd do us a favor and drove to our house to pick up Laura. When I answered the door, my crazy eyes must have told her it had not been the best of days. Rick and I were also supposed to be at a crew dinner with all the spouses that night at seven o'clock. I knew there was no way we could get everything done.

Rick finished with Laura around 6:30, and I sped across Houston to get her to a birthday party that was forty-five minutes away. But she breezed in with beautiful, lice-free hair. Rick gave Matthew a preventive treatment and then did one on himself before showing up at the crew dinner thirty minutes late. It was 9:30 when I finally arrived from the other side of town where I had dropped Laura. I didn't say what had happened because Laura was embarrassed by it, so I just said we had a bad day. Someone later said I should have told them we had a bad hair day, which would have been the understatement of the century!

At the end of that day's journal entry, Rick wrote,

God, as always, took care of us through a very challenging day in which we prayed a lot!

During my quiet times, I had been working on giving thanks for everything but found it difficult to thank God for Laura's head lice. How could anyone be thankful for *that*? Almost immediately, a scene from the book *The Hiding Place* came to mind about Corrie Ten Boom and her sister, Betsie, who were prisoners in a Nazi concentration camp. Their quarters were infested with fleas, and they itched day and night. Corrie was complaining, and Betsie said they needed to give thanks to God for the fleas because they needed to be thankful for everything. Corrie couldn't see it that way. As it turned out, the fleas kept the guards from entering their barracks, and they were able to have Bible studies with the other women and minister to them without anyone bothering them. Their fleas had been a blessing from God.

I felt as if the Lord was saying, *I gave Laura five uninterrupted hours with her dad.* I was laid low by that because I thought about how lovingly Rick had attended to Laura and how differently I would have handled it. He was patient; he loved on her; he edified her; he told her how beautiful she was. They wouldn't have had that time together were it not for the lice—our list of things to do that day would never have allowed it. We never got to any of the items on that list, but who cares! God gave us a blessing instead.

11
Ready to Fly

God is the most important thing in my life.
Only through God can I really do anything worthwhile.

—Rick Husband

WE WENT TO CHURCH ON SUNDAY, JANUARY 5, AND DURING THE
service, Pastor Riggle asked our family and the Andersons to come up
front so he could pray for the mission, the families, and God's guid-
ance and protection over all of us. Rick told the congregation about
the mission and how the crew had bonded during the nearly two and
a half years of training. "It's been a really interesting journey up to
this point," he said. "Certainly, we've been praying a lot for the mission and for the crew and all the people who work on the mission and
make it possible for us to go and fly a mission like this." He handed
the microphone to Mike.

"Rick and I have prayed for a successful mission," Mike said, "but
also that somehow God would allow everyone to see our faith in
Him. We'd really like to ask for your prayers as we get ready to go
on this sixteen-day mission. And not only prayers for a safe flight but
also that in some small way we can use this platform to really let
people know what we believe and let God's message get out there." It
was how all of us felt, and Mike said it beautifully.

Pastor Riggle prayed for all the crew families, and we took our
seats. Rick was very moved that the church took time to do that for
us. Rick was so easygoing that day that you would never have known
he was just eleven days away from going to space. However, the next
two days were whirlwinds.

Rick and the crew were at Johnson Space Center early each day to
go over last-minute details and prepare for quarantine. On Wednesday,

January 8, the day before he actually went into quarantine, Rick came home for lunch with camera equipment he'd borrowed from NASA and began filming the video devotionals for the kids. Laura and Matthew were back in school, so they knew nothing about this very special project.

He set up the camera and recorded the first devotional for Matthew. His demeanor was calm throughout the taping; the kids would never know it by watching the tape, but I knew Rick was terribly short on time. I knew his schedule was weighing on him, but it didn't take precedence over what was taking place while that camera was on—this, not space, was Rick's highest calling in life.

He sat relaxed on our living room sofa and looked into the camera to begin filming the second devotional.

"Okay," he said, his eyes brightening. "Now it's time for our second day of our devotionals. Howdy, Matthew! I love you! This is the second day that I am in space."

Rick opened Matthew's Bible and turned to Philippians 4:6–7: "Do not be anxious about anything, but in everything, by prayer and petition, with thanksgiving, present your requests to God."

He held his finger on the Bible to mark his spot and looked up into the camera, speaking to Matthew: "So that means don't worry about anything, but in everything, just ask God to help you."

He looked back down to finish the verse: "And the peace of God, which transcends all understanding, will guard your hearts and your minds in Christ Jesus." He looked back into the camera again: "So that means Christ Jesus will give you peace."

Rick had learned over the years to hand his worries to God; he had learned to pray about things that bothered him instead of agonizing over them, and he had experienced the peace that comes only through Jesus. Those weren't just words on a page to Rick; they were the truth that had set him free. It was the perfect devotional for him to relate to Matthew.

He read the story from Matthew's devotional book and then prayed for him: "Lord, I pray that You will help Matthew not to carry any worries or burdens around but to cast them on You, Jesus, because You care for Matthew. Help him to know that because You love him so much that You want to help him out and carry the weights that bother him."

He glanced up: "I know up in space right now I'm sure missing you and Mama and Laura, but I know that the time will go by fast and I'm sure looking forward to seeing you. I love you! Bye-bye!"

He looked into the camera and smiled. Day two was finished. He filmed as many as he could on his lunch break and then headed back to work. I knew that Rick's "Build Rome in a Day" list at work was longer than anything we could put together at home, but he always managed to get home in time to have dinner with us and to play with the kids. Rick never had a sense of panic or made us feel as if he was leaving things unfinished at work.

We watched a movie with the kids that night after dinner, and then Rick helped Matthew with his bath.

In the journal for me he wrote,

Had to get after Matthew at bath time—I think he was feeling cranky about me going into quarantine tomorrow. We had a great wrestle time on the floor of his bedroom afterwards with *lots* of giggling.

Rick would go into quarantine on the evening of Thursday, the ninth, but he was able to have dinner with the kids and me and visit for a while before he headed to crew quarters (the purpose of quarantine is to keep infections, illness, and germs away from the crew for seven days so they can be as healthy as possible in space). During his last hour with us, Laura looked up as if she heard something.

"Mom, I just heard the gate shut," she said.

"No, I don't think so," I said.

She looked up. "There's somebody with a flashlight in our backyard."

"No, there's not," I said, getting up to look just in case. Sure enough, there was somebody with a flashlight in our backyard! It was a policeman. With an Israeli scheduled to be on board the shuttle, security was especially tight in case of terrorist threat so every crew member's home had police protection. We had had it for Rick's first flight into space in 1999, but this time, security was ramped up even more. Weeks earlier, someone came and sketched our home, marking where the shrubs were so they'd be able to search for anyone who might try to hide in them. For the last hour Rick was home, searchlights flicked past our windows as policemen scoped the area around our house.

He didn't have to arrive at crew quarters until 9:00 or 9:30, so Rick stayed with us as long as he possibly could. He prayed with both Laura and Matthew, we prayed together as a family, and then Rick said his good-byes. Laura cried when she hugged him, knowing that with the time in quarantine and space, it would be well over three weeks before she saw her dad again.

Rick would spend the next three nights in Houston before flying to Florida, where the crew would finish the quarantine. The next morning while in quarantine, Rick got up and set up the video camera again. He still had Laura's seventeen video devotionals to complete. He sat in a stark, white room in crew quarters, and again, he took his time talking into the camera: "Hi, Laura, I hope everything's going well for you. I wanted to make this tape for you to let you know how much I love you and to let you know that I'm thinking of you. And this is my gift to you for having to wait such a long time while I'm up in space."

He was animated reading through Laura's devotional, adding inflections and voices for the characters in the story. He prayed for her and then looked into the camera, smiling. "All right, I love you very, very much, and I'll see you tomorrow for our next devotional. Bye-bye!"

On the second day of Laura's devotions, Rick read through the Scripture and story and then looked into the camera. "How about *you?*" he said, pointing and smiling into the camera. Rick loved the "How About You" section of the devotional for no other reason than he loved to point and emphasize the word *you*: "Do *you* find it hard to resist temptation?"

He stopped reading and looked up. "That's one thing that I pray for both you and Matthew: that you guys will both be strong in resisting temptation because that's a really important thing in life and because I love you so much, I pray for you."

He looked down at the book. "The key down at the bottom here says, 'Maintain your spiritual life.'"

He looked back up. "And this is *me* talking: it's as important to keep your spiritual fitness up as it is to keep your physical fitness."

Rick wanted both Laura and Matthew to know that it was a daily relationship with God that would help maintain their spiritual lives. It wasn't simply going to church on Sunday for an hour and being a good, decent person; it was something that would have to be maintained on a daily basis. It's what had changed Rick's life at the end of our time in California and during our stay in England, and he knew it would sustain Laura and Matthew for the rest of their lives.

After breakfast on the tenth in crew quarters, Rick went home to finish Matthew's devotionals (he could be in our home as long as the house was empty). He hurried back to NASA for lunch with the rest of the crew, then went through more training. That afternoon, I took the kids to crew quarters and sat in a huge office. Rick entered through a door from crew quarters and sat on the opposite side of the room while we visited with him. (Rick determined that a brief visit with a distance of twenty feet between us would be okay. A NASA flight doctor stuck his head in the door to check on us and say hello and all was well.)

A few hours later, the spouses were allowed to have dinner with the crew. The crew would be working in shifts in space, so they had already started sleep shifting; the Red Team was awake while the Blue Team slept or vice versa. The Red Team was made up of Rick, Laurel, K. C., and Ilan; the Blue Team consisted of Mike, Willie, and Dave. I showed up at six o'clock for dinner and said, "Good morning," to those who were just getting up and eating breakfast. It was a strange experience, but their bodies had to get used to sleep shifting for the sixteen-day mission.

On Sunday morning, January 12, Rick got up at 5:25 and had his quiet time before finishing Matthew's devotional tape. He packed his bags for Florida and briefed the crew on the upcoming flight to Kennedy Space Center. Usually, they flew in four T-38s, but the weather was horrible that day, too stormy for the T-38s. Instead, they would fly to the Cape in a NASA Gulfstream-2 business jet.

Rick wanted to drop off the Camaro at our house so it wouldn't be left at Ellington Field and also leave Laura and Matthew a gift during his time away. He had decided to buy two inexpensive cameras and film for the kids' trip to Florida the next day as their gifts.

Our neighbor Beth Cotten was going to stay with the kids while I drove Rick to Ellington Field where the crew would get on the G-2 for the flight. Beth had told both Laura and Matthew that Rick was going to bring the Camaro back, but that they couldn't hug him or get close to him and they both understood that. Rick pulled the

Camaro into the garage and walked through the door that leads into the kitchen to leave the cameras and film on the counter. Matthew saw him and forgot the conversation Beth had had with him only minutes earlier. He yelled, "Daddy," and took off toward Rick in a dead run. Beth and I both started yelling, "Matthew, no!" Matthew froze about fifteen feet away from Rick, and Rick blew him and Laura big kisses and hugs. It was the last time they would ever see their dad.

Laura, Matthew, and I flew to Florida with the other crew families on Monday, January 13. From the journal that Rick kept for me, I know that he got up early that morning and opened the pocket Bible he was going to take into space with him and saw that 2 Timothy 1:7 was underlined in red. He read it and realized that our pastor had mentioned that same passage in church and that the Billy Graham devotional calendar we had at home listed that as the verse of the day for January 16, launch day. It says, "For God did not give us a spirit of timidity, but a spirit of power, of love and of self-discipline." It was as if God was reassuring Rick that there was no reason to fear the upcoming mission.

NASA made arrangements for the crew families to stay at Patrick Air Force Base. It was typical for the families to be placed in a hotel, but given the pending war with Iraq and the fact that Ilan was traveling with the crew, NASA felt it was necessary to take all precautions and protect us at the air base. If we left the base, there was always a huge motorcade in front and in back of us. I was able to see Rick that evening for a dinner at crew quarters with all of the spouses. I walked in and Rick gave me a big hug.

"In all the years I've known you, Rick," I said, "it's never been such a production to get us together. I've got my own special agent and police protection! I think this is a good week for Laura and Matthew to mind their p's and q's."

He laughed. "Not only can you give them 'the look,' but now you have thirty other people who can mimic it as well."

"My special agent scolded me because I rode with Clay Anderson to the security briefing. How was I supposed to know?"

Rick laughed again.

When we arrived at the security briefing, my agent met me at the car door and said, "I'm supposed to be with you at *all* times." I thought, *I'm willing to be a sheep; I just don't know who my shepherd is!*

I buried my head into Rick's chest, hugging him. "I'm so glad to be with you again." I looked over my shoulder. "There isn't an agent or policeman behind me, is there?"

He laughed and kissed me. "How 'bout I take you out to dinner?" Rick opened a door that led into a room at crew quarters where the ladies who work at crew quarters had put together a beautiful candlelit meal for all the crew and spouses. Smith Johnston, the crew's flight physician, played the guitar for us in the background, and Dave Brown put a plate next to him. We all scrounged up $1.07 to tip Smith for his efforts. It was a relaxing evening for all of us.

That night, on the way back to Patrick Air Force Base I needed to grocery shop but had no idea what I was getting myself into. There were six to eight police cars in front, back, and around the car Steve Lindsey and I were in, and they all pulled into the grocery store parking lot. I thought, *Surely, they're not going to go into the grocery store with me!* But they did. I was flanked by ten officers as I shopped for milk, orange juice, and other items I could no longer think of because I was so tense and nervous. The other shoppers in the store just stopped dead in their tracks and stared at me, wondering who I could possibly be and what in the world I had done to warrant a police escort at the grocery store!

Out of nervousness, I finally sent some officers throughout the store: "I need milk." "Could you find a cereal that crunches?" "Any sort of bread will do." We moved along as a huge unit throughout the store, and when it was time to check out, the police put me through an empty line and then blocked it off, making sure no one else got in the same line.

The cashier quietly rang up my items and glanced up from time to time, trying to figure out who I was. "Is this all for you?" she finally whispered.

"I'm afraid it is," I said.

From then on, I thought I'd rather starve than go back to the grocery store.

On Tuesday morning I met Rick at the beach house on the property of Kennedy Space Center.

He wrote in my journal,

> Went to the beach house and saw sweet Evey. My stress level immediately decreases when we are together!

I was so happy to see and hug him again. We were both at our best when we were together. We took a launchpad tour along with the spouses of the rest of the Red Team: K. C., Ilan, and Laurel. We stood beside the massive shuttle *Columbia,* and it was breathtaking, so enormous. I stood within an inch of it, and it was all I could do not to reach out my hand and touch it. It was amazing to be right there beside it. Rick and I stood by the external tank, and he put his arm around me while someone took pictures of us. They are our last photos together.

On the fifteenth, Rick was up at 5:30 and at 6:00 went through a last review of suit-up, strap-in, and communication checks prior to the next day's launch. At 6:45, he and Willie headed to the Shuttle Landing Facility to fly the STA. They flew for an hour and a half, and Rick wrote in the journal that it was "a *gorgeous* day!" He came to see me at the beach house later that morning, and we took a walk along the beach.

He wrote,

> We took a wonderful long walk on the beach and talked about how we could see God's hand in everything and how "at peace" we were—having fun running around inside His hedge of protection. It was a *glorious* day!

It was so relaxing—just like a minidate out on the beach. We felt certain the launch would happen and wouldn't be delayed again. Rick was ready for the mission, and we just enjoyed each other's company without any stress or pressure. I said, "Rick, I have such a sense of peace this time, so different from your first launch. I'm not stressed at all about anything."

"Isn't it fun to be inside the hedge of God's protection?" he said. "To be running around in this Holy Spirit bubble?" Both of us felt completely covered and at ease and knew that sense of peace came from God.

"Keep these to remember our walk by," he said, handing me two seashells. We picked up seashells for the kids, and Rick sang "Be My Love" to me, a song he had been singing to me since college. I teased him that security agents were going to rise up out of the weeds, applaud, and then duck back down into the weeds again. We prayed together for the launch and the mission, and Rick prayed again for the landing on February 1. He had often discussed the landing with me, stressing how important it was to have a safe landing. He wanted nothing more than to do his job well and bring his crew safely home. We held hands along the beach, and I still marvel at how relaxed we were.

That afternoon, with the help of Dan Dillard, a dear friend from Orlando, I hosted a reception for all our invited guests and any of the crew's families who wanted to come. It was held at nearby Calvary Chapel, where I'd held the first reception in 1999. Dan and his wife, Malia, helped with both receptions and organized everything from choosing the cakes to lining up the speakers. I had met Dan years before at the church we attended in Apple Valley, California. He and Malia are on staff with Campus Crusade for Christ, and we have supported their ministry for years. Doug Stringer, a pastor from the Houston area, spoke; Zola Levitt, a Jewish author who was educated in the synagogues but was brought to belief in Christ in 1971, said a prayer for us in Hebrew; and Sally and Clay Clarkson, who had written many books on homeschooling, also prayed. Although I was no longer homeschooling Laura, I had always enjoyed their books on homeschooling and was so pleased that they could be with me at the reception. Sally prayed for Laura and Clay prayed for Matthew, and they were two of the most beautiful prayers I had ever heard. Steve Green sang a few songs to celebrate the occasion. It was an awesome afternoon.

Rick and I had an hour at the beach house that evening with the crew and the spouses, and near the end of our time together, we made toasts to the upcoming mission. Rick quoted Joshua 1:6–7:

Be strong and courageous, because you will lead these people to inherit the land I swore to their forefathers to give them. Be strong and very courageous. Be careful to obey all the law my servant Moses gave you; do not turn from it to the right or to the left, that you may be successful wherever you go.

When Rick said, "Be strong and very courageous," his lip started quivering. It was an emotional verse for Rick and an emotional time with me and the crew he loved. Rick was not demonstrative with his faith; he never pushed it on anybody, but he also never denied it. The crew members were quiet; the emotion was real, and as we stood together that night, we were all one unit. We were minutes away from saying good-bye to each other.

"The hardest part of space flight for me is saying good-bye to Diane and our three children," Steve Lindsey says. "Even though I'm always fully confident in the mission, the vehicle, my crew, and the team of ground and flight operations people, when I say good-bye, it feels somewhat permanent, and there's a part of me that wonders whether or not I'll ever see them again. When I walk away the night before launch from Diane, I have a sick feeling in my stomach. Each time I fly it gets harder and harder to do."

We all went off with our spouses for what little time there was left, and Rick and I hugged and kissed and said how much we loved each other. I wasn't teary-eyed. I had been through this before; I was at peace.

"Evey, I just want to tell you one more time how much I appreciate your support," Rick said. "I couldn't do anything without your help. I still have such a sense that God is up to something special with this mission. I'm really going to miss you and the kids, but I am so excited to finally get to fly this mission!"

"Rick," I said, holding on to him, "I hope that you have a great time and that everything goes smoothly and that you'll get some downtime so you can really enjoy it. I know you and the crew are going to do an incredible job." I squeezed him hard. "I just hope the sixteen days will go by quickly for all of us."

"It'll go by quickly," he said. "It'll be over with before we know it."

We prayed together. Rick prayed that Laura and Matthew would be obedient and that time would pass quickly for us without him. I prayed that Rick would feel well in space and that the landing would be perfect. I hugged him close.

"I love you with all my heart," I said, kissing him. "I am so proud of you."

"I love you, Evey." He pulled me back and looked at me. "You are a beautiful woman, Evelyn Husband."

Rick walked me to the car and kissed me good-bye. Lani McCool said good-bye to Willie and got in the backseat with her special agent. I turned to look at her and saw tears in her eyes. "Lani, this is the hardest part, but it's going to be okay," I said. That first flight is nerve-racking.

That was the last time we would be together. The next day, Rick and the STS-107 crew were boarding the *Columbia* for their sixteen-day mission.

12

The Final Flight

They made the ultimate sacrifice, giving their lives in service
to their country and for all mankind.

—Rick's comments aboard the *Columbia*
on the seventeenth anniversary of the space shuttle
Challenger tragedy

AT 3:06 A.M. EST, SHUTTLE MANAGERS GAVE A "GO" FOR TANKING, and the *Columbia*'s external tanks were filled with millions of gallons of liquid oxygen and liquid hydrogen, an operation that took three hours to complete. Once the directive for tanking was given, it indicated that launch countdown was progressing normally with no major problems. Confidence was high that everything would be ready for a 10:39 A.M. liftoff.

At 6:10 A.M. EST, the final inspection team checked every inch of the external tank, solid rocket boosters, and orbiter for any signs of trouble and gave an all clear.

At 7:30 A.M. EST, Rick and the crew were ready to board the van at the Operations and Checkout Building that would take them out to the launchpad. In a rare moment, before the crew left their quarters, Rick paused and stood with them in a circle and prayed for the mission ahead. They rode to the Operations and Checkout Building and took an elevator up to the 195-foot level where the closeout crew waited to help them into the orbiter.

At 7:52 A.M. EST, the crew began entering the *Columbia*. Rick went in first and took his seat on the flight deck, Ilan took his seat on the mid-deck, then Willie went in and took his place in the pilot's seat on the flight deck next to Rick. Mike entered and took the left seat on the mid-deck, Dave Brown sat behind Willie on the flight deck, then Laurel sat down in the middle seat of the mid-deck. K. C. was the last to board that morning. She sat in the center seat on the flight deck, behind Rick and Willie.

At that time, the crew's families were driven forty minutes from Patrick Air Force Base to Kennedy Space Center. The motorcade was much larger than anything we'd experienced up to that point: a large convoy with a huge security escort that stopped all the traffic for us along the way. We were taken to the top floor of the Launch Control Center and into a suite of offices that overlooked the launchpad. Tables of food were set out for everyone, and the kids were able to color on the dry marker board just as they had done for Rick's first mission. NASA personnel supervised the children as the crew spouses stayed in the office suites, waiting for launch. Just as the procedure had been for the flight in 1999, we would not go up to the roof to watch the launch until the nine-minute hold was over. When the all clear was given, our astronaut escorts led the crew families to the roof, overlooking the launchpad. It was a clear, beautiful day.

At 10:36 A.M. EST, Launch Director Mike Leinbach instructed the crew to close and lock their helmet visors. "If there ever was a time to use the phrase 'good things come to people who wait,'" Mike said, "this is the one time. From the many, many people who put this mission together, good luck and Godspeed."

"We appreciate it, Mike," Rick said from the flight deck. "The Lord has blessed us with a beautiful day here, and we're going to have a great mission. We're ready to go."

Many people have commented on the words Rick said that morning. Newspapers and magazines printed them in a positive way, reflecting the crew's excitement for the mission, but there was more than just excitement in Rick's words.

Steve Green was at Kennedy Space Center and heard the communication between Mission Control and the shuttle. "I thought . . . given the stress, the danger, the responsibility . . . would I have said that? I don't know if I would have," Steve says. "I don't know if I would have had the presence of mind to very purposely say, 'The Lord has blessed us with a beautiful day here,' but Rick did. In saying that, he was acknowledging that what was about to happen wasn't occurring by happenstance. It was a gift from God."

I stood with Matthew and Laura by my side along with Steve

Lindsey. A group of astronauts stood behind us, careful not to disturb the families as we waited for launch. I prayed briefly with the kids that the launch would go well and that God would give us peace. I started to play with Laura's hair; for whatever reason, it's always calming for me and probably for her as well.

At about ten seconds out, we could hear the engines roaring to life. They can abort a mission to the last second, but when you hear everything firing, you know you're closer than ever to launch. The countdown began, and when it got to zero, I held tightly to Laura and Matthew as tears streamed down my face. It's impossible to watch something like that and not feel emotion. All the families were quiet as we watched the shuttle lift off and then climb. The ground was shaking for miles around us as the *Columbia* gained speed, and then at about 2,000 feet, the *Columbia* broke through a thin layer of clouds and a shadow stretched across the sky, forming a cross. It was identical to what had happened during Rick's first launch on the shuttle *Discovery* in 1999. I thought, *Lord, I know Your hand is in this.*

We watched the shuttle climb higher and higher to 50,000 feet and waited for Mission Control to give Rick the command, "Go at throttle up." It was the last communication that Mission Control had with Dick Scobee on the *Challenger*. Mission Control gave him the command, and Dick repeated, "Go at throttle up." At that moment, the *Challenger* exploded. It's a tense time for families on the ground to get past that command, but I just knew they were going to be okay because I felt unbelievable peace. Rick repeated, "Go at throttle up," and the STS-107 crew was on the way to space.

Two minutes in, at 150,000 feet, we watched as the solid rocket boosters disengaged from the shuttle. After the eight-and-a-half-minute ride to orbit, the families celebrated because the biggest stress was over. Steve Lindsey handed Laura and Matthew the devotional tapes that Rick had recorded for them. On the side of each tape Rick had written, "With love from Daddy. I love you." He gave Matthew chocolate bars, Laura and I received roses, and I got the journal that Rick had been putting together for me. The crew patch was stuck on the outside, and the first page had a five-by-seven-inch photo of Rick and me taken in college at an ROTC banquet. Beneath it he wrote,

Well, Evey, this isn't quite where it all started for us, but it's pretty darn close! Judging from this picture, I've aged a little, but you haven't changed a bit! Wa Wa Wa!

I love you so much and I surely do appreciate all your love and support for these many years. There is no doubt in my mind that I never would have made it this far without you! You are a wonderful woman, wife, and mother, and I am so glad that God blessed me with you and our two wonderful children.

We were each given cards, and he'd taken time to write cards for Jane and Keith as well. My card had a picture of a field of bluebonnet flowers in south Texas, and they were so beautiful.

Rick wrote,

Evey—

Well, we're in space! I can't tell you enough how much I love you. If I filled this card with "I love you's," it wouldn't do it.

Thank you so much for your love and support and prayers, and everything! Thank you for being my friend, my wife and [a] wonderful mother.

I hope you enjoy the album [referring to the journal he had made for me]. I'll see you in 16 days!

Love, Rick

To Laura, he wrote,

You are a dear, sweet, beautiful girl and I love you so very much! Well, we made it to orbit!

Thank you so much for loving me like you do and for being such a great daughter. God has made you *very* special and I feel very blessed that I get to be your dad.

Have a great trip home and I'll see you in 16 days! I hope you enjoy your video.

Love, Daddy

In Matthew's card, he wrote,

Well, I'm in space! I hope you liked the launch! Pretty loud, huh?

Matthew, I am so very proud of you. You are a fine, sweet boy and I love you so very much! Thank you so much for loving me so much and for being such a *great* son. God has made you very special and I feel very blessed that I get to be your dad.

Have a great trip home, be a good boy (I know you will) and I'll see you in 16 days!

I hope you enjoy your video!

Love, Daddy

When I look at the cards now, I can't keep a dry eye. When he says, "I'll see you in 16 days," I think, *No, we won't see you in sixteen days, Rick. It'll be a whole lifetime before we see you again,* and the thought absolutely kills me. There's such an emptiness when I read those cards. We have the knowledge that we'll see Rick again in heaven, but the wait is going to be excruciatingly long.

After the launch, we made our way off the roof and gathered in a room where Sean O'Keefe, NASA administrator, and other NASA executives greeted us. We went through the bean-eating tradition again, but this time I couldn't swallow even one bean. Then we watched as the STS-107 patch was stuck to the door along with all the other missions that had been flown since the *Challenger*. (I have often wondered what NASA will do with that door now that we have faced another tragedy.) Thirty minutes later we were taken to the NASA airplane that was waiting for us, and we flew back to Houston, landing approximately four hours after the launch of the *Columbia*.

I needed to make a trip to the grocery store and laughed, thinking of my last trip to the supermarket in Florida. This time it was just me, Laura, Matthew, and the grocery cart—not a policeman in sight. We went out to eat at a Mexican restaurant, and I thought, *Does anyone have any idea what we've done today?*

Each morning, a crew member got a wake-up call in space, and since the Red Team was up first, that team got the first call, but someone from the Blue Team would also get one once that team woke up later in the day. I had chosen a song called "An American Anthem" for

Rick, a song written by Allan Naplan. We invited him to watch the launch, and he was thrilled to be there for it. The song featured the Elementary Honors Choir at the Annual Texas Choir Directors Association Convention. Laura had been selected as a member of the choir, and the convention took place in July. Rick was thrilled that Laura shared his love for singing.

NASA played the song, and then the person working CAPCOM that day recorded communication between the *Columbia* and Mission Control.

NASA: And that wake-up music for the Red Shift is brought to you by the Texas Elementary Honors Choir with the beautiful Laura Husband as a featured member.

RICK: Thank you very much. It's really great to hear that music and also know that Laura was singing with the choir. And it's really nice to have a nice reminder of our families. I'd like to say hello to Laura and also to my son, Matthew, and my wife, Evelyn. We're having a great time up here and just appreciate all your support. Thank you so much!

NASA: Thanks, Rick. We'll make sure they get the word.

Once in space, the crew immediately set up the shuttle as an orbiting platform for science research. They would be working with a menagerie of rats, fish, silkworms, spiders, ants, and even bees.

One of the first experiments was called ARMS (Advanced Respiratory Monitoring System), which was developed by the European Space Agency. The crew members had to ride a bike in the SPACEHAB module, and ARMS measured each person's breath composition and heart rate. The data they gathered would help in developing treatments for patients who experience muscle loss similar to what happens to astronauts in space.

An experiment that received a lot of attention was the Mediterranean Israeli Dust Experiment (MEIDEX), which was one of the reasons Ilan was flying on the mission. The experiment would track the movement of dust clouds and help predict weather patterns and the spread of communicable diseases.

Though he was busy, Rick sent Laura and Matthew and me our first e-mails that day. To Matthew, he wrote,

Hi, Matthew!

We had a great ride to space!! Was it loud from where you were? From where we were, it wasn't too loud, just really fast!!!! I hope you had a great trip home and I hope you enjoy your devotional tape! I love you very much!!

Love, Daddy:)

The kids were thrilled to get their first messages from their dad. They quickly got on the computer and sent letters to him. Laura typed hers first:

Dear Daddy—

Is it fun floating in space? It is fun walking around on earth. I saw you on TV today. I love you. Talk to you soon. I can't wait to see you again.

Love, Laura

I typed Matthew's letter for him but typed exactly what he wanted to say:

Dear Daddy—

I hope you have a safe flight home. I hope you have a great time in space and that you will have a great time with your crew and that you'll have fun and that you do great on the experiments. Have a great time with Dave and Willie and Mike and Laurel and K. C. and Ilan. I like your devotional tape and thank you for the big, big chocolate bars and the almond chocolate bars. Have a nice time in space and I saw you on TV and Mom saw you say you love her back.

P.S. Love, Matthew

Rick e-mailed Matthew and said,

I'm glad you like the devotional tape and that you saw me on TV. Is it weird seeing me on TV floating around? It's really fun! Floating and looking out the window are probably my two favorite things to do in space! I love you very much and miss you, Mama, and Laura. As each day passes, we're closer to the time we get to see each other again!

That's now become the motto for the rest of our lives: as each day passes, we're closer to the time that we get to see Rick again.

I e-mailed Rick and let him know how proud I was of him:

Congratulations for doing such a superb job. I already know the entire mission will be tremendous. Hugs and kisses to all the crew. We all love you soooooo much.

Rick had suffered from nausea during his first mission to space, but neither he nor any of the STS-107 crew experienced any discomfort. He e-mailed me and said,

We had a great ride to space and I feel great! So much better than last time—it is a real blessing . . .

He was amazed at how well all the rookies took to space. He went on to say,

Everybody kicked in like they had been here before and we're having a great time. Red Shift is on their way to bed now. I love you so much! God really is faithful!!

Love, Rick

In an interview from the orbiter, he said, "I think from my perspective as the commander, my 'Oh, wow!' has been watching everyone perform as a team. The crew has performed just marvelously and I really love seeing a team come together. It's such a great feeling for me to see everybody working together as a team like that."

He e-mailed John Kanengieter and Andy Cline, his NOLS instructors, and bragged to them:

John and Andy—

We're having a great time up here. It's been a long but very enjoyable road and we're all very glad for the role you two have played in our lives in preparing for this mission. We have talked several times already since we got up here about our experience with you guys . . . The parallels are absolutely uncanny . . . Suffice it to say, we'd love to have you guys up here with us—certainly you are with us in our thoughts as we go through the daily routine working together as a crew . . . I am so proud of my crew I could pop.

"It sounded just like Rick," John says. "He was so proud of that crew."

On Tuesday, January 21, the Red Team (Rick, K. C., Laurel, and Ilan) got a call from Israeli Prime Minister Ariel Sharon. Ilan told the prime minister about a small scroll filled with scripture from the Torah that a professor who had survived a concentration camp gave him to carry into space. "This represents, more than anything, the ability of the Jewish people to survive," Ilan said. The prime minister invited the entire crew to visit him in Jerusalem.

"We really appreciate the invitation," Rick said, "and if the people of Israel are as nice as Ilan and his family, we know that we will be expecting a very warm welcome when we come to visit Israel." Rick e-mailed me later and said he was so excited about that invitation. He had always wanted to visit Israel so that he could walk the land that Moses and Abraham and Jesus had walked. He couldn't wait to do it with Ilan and the rest of the crew.

I e-mailed Rick later that day after the interview aired:

I watched your interview with Sharon this morning and then they showed it again this afternoon with a translation. You looked great and maintained a very pleasant look throughout the Hebrew interview!!

Rick was humbled and honored to speak with the prime minister that day. I could see the excitement on his face throughout the interview.

Laura and Matthew anticipated each day's devotional that Rick taped for them. I wanted Rick to know that the kids loved them, so I e-mailed him:

We watched the devotional videos last night and this morning. They both are really loving their time with you. What an incredibly personal gift you gave them . . . It was worth every precious minute you spent making them. They both have lots of smiles watching them. Thank you so much.

Of course, none of us could have anticipated what those tapes would really mean to the kids—they are a priceless gift, a legacy of love from the father who deeply loved them.

On Tuesday, January 21, the Red Team was greeted with a song called "God of Wonders," sung by Steve Green.

NASA: That music was for Rick—"God of Wonders" by Steve Green.

RICK: Good morning, Linda. Boy, looking out the window you really can tell He's a God of wonders and we sure appreciate being able to take a look out and enjoy the view. We're looking forward to another great day. Also like to say hello to Steve Green. He's a good friend of mine. Good to hear your voice. We're ready for another great day in space.

Steve was in concert on January 24 in Houston, and I was able to play the wake-up recording for him. He smiled listening to the tape. "Rick was unashamed with being identified with God," Steve says. "When he said, 'Boy, looking out the window you really can tell He's a God of wonders,' I thought, *He can say that because he has lived so well with this crew, with an unblemished testimony, that he's been given the right to have a verbal witness because he's first had a living witness.* A lot of people blurt out religious sayings, but their lives don't bear evidence to what they say. Rick's did."

Sandy Anderson went to the concert with me, and Steve asked us to stand up. He introduced us and prayed for Rick and Mike and the rest of the crew and all the families. It was such a blessing to be there.

Several news outlets interviewed the crew from space. CBS News interviewed Rick, Ilan, K. C., and Laurel and addressed a question to Rick.

CBS: From your perspective, how has it been going? Batting a thousand?

RICK: Well, actually, things are going really well. Things have been working well. Columbia is in great shape and working absolutely

perfectly. The experiments are working very well also so no place
to go but up!

*The crew was unaware that something was indeed wrong with the
Columbia. Rick's last words were prophetic, but he had no idea what
he was saying . . . there would be no landing, for there was no place
to go but up.*

The training team at NASA selected the wake-up music for the Red
Team on January 24. Throughout their training, Rick and the crew
used a little stuffed hamster that was dressed like a kung fu fighter as
a sort of mascot. They brought it into the simulator with them and
pressed a button that played "Kung Fu Fighting," and it provided lots
of humorous mileage for the crew.

NASA: *Columbia,* Houston, good morning to Rick, Laurel, K. C.,
and Ilan. That music was "Kung Fu Fighting" selected especially
for you by your dedicated training team.

RICK: We really appreciate it, Houston. I'll tell you what—our
training team has been such a fantastic group. We owe such a
certain debt of gratitude to each and every one of them. I really
appreciate everything they've taught us and we know that all that
training has paid off and is paying off as we go through this
mission. We just want to thank them very much for that great
music as well. It's kind of been one of the enjoyable jokes we've
had as we go through our training. So we really appreciate it.

Since landing day was in sight, it seemed the days were crawling by
without Rick. The kids and I couldn't wait for him to come home so
we could get back into the normal swing of things. Everything seemed
empty without him at the center of our lives.

On Saturday, January 25, Rick's wake-up call was "The Prayer,"
sung by Celine Dion and Andrea Bocelli. Rick had only one more personal wake-up call before coming home. Later that day, I received an
e-mail from Rick with a subject line that read, "Sorry for few e-mails!"
He said,

Evey—

I love you very much! Things are going great but very busy—that's why I'm not able to send many messages. I'll try to do better but please know I love you, Laura, and Matthew so very much! Tell your mom happy birthday!

Love, Rick

I knew Rick was extremely busy with the experiments on board the shuttle, but even in space he was thinking of us, concerned he wasn't spending enough "time" with us. His e-mails were short, but in every one I could sense his love.

We were scheduled to have two family video conferences during the sixteen days Rick was in space. For STS-96 in 1999, we had only one conference, but because this mission was longer, each family got two. Our first one took place approximately seven days into the mission. Laura and Matthew and I went into a special room at Mission Control that was set up with a camera and a huge TV screen that was divided in half. We could see Rick floating up and down, and he could see us. We communicated through a speaker phone, but because Rick was in space, we had a one-second delay, which made the conversation more than interesting. I would laugh and then hear that same laugh a second later on the space shuttle. Our conference lasted thirty minutes, and when it was over, we told Rick we loved him and then headed home.

Our second conference was scheduled for January 28, the seventeenth anniversary of the *Challenger* explosion and the anniversary of our first date in college. (Rick sent me an e-mail the night before so I would get it on the twenty-eighth. It said, "Happy dating anniversary! I love you!" I didn't see it until we got home from the video conference.) That conference was scheduled at 6:08 in the morning, which meant we'd have to be there at 5:30. I had no idea how I'd get all three of us up and out of the house and into NASA at that awful hour!

Laura, Matthew, and I decided that they would hide out of sight of the camera so that Rick would think they stayed home in bed. I sat down in front of the camera, and a few minutes later, after a couple of failed attempts to connect us to the shuttle, I could finally see Rick floating in front of me. I told him it was just too early for the kids, and I could see the look of disappointment on his face. Then Laura and Matthew burst onto the screen, and he smiled. Rick adored our children, and his face lit up when he saw them; he was so happy they were there. He threw a pen into the air, and the kids laughed watching it float, then he threw a small timer and we watched it spin in front of him. A couple of times he dipped down out of sight of the camera and then floated back up, smiling. He was having a great time.

Laura got the idea to hold Matthew sideways and move him into the field of view so that it looked as if he was floating as well. "Look at me, Dad," Matthew said, with Laura's hands squeezing into his sides. "I'm floating!"

At seven years old, Matthew can be still and calm for about fifteen minutes, but for a thirty-minute phone conference? Forget it. Fifteen minutes in, Matthew felt Laura was getting too much camera time and stormed off to where Rick couldn't see him. Laura picked up the camera and pointed it in his direction, tracking him around the room, even as he ducked under the table. Rick looked into the camera and said in a booming voice, "Matthew, get back over here." It was a direct order from the space cowboy himself. Matthew came back, and we finished our conversation. We were told we had five minutes left and we all said that we loved each other, but then the screen froze. We kept calling Rick, but he couldn't hear us and we couldn't hear him. We called again and again.

"Dad," Laura said.

"Dad!" Matthew shouted.

Nothing but his frozen image in front of us.

"I guess that's it," I said, disappointed that our time ended so abruptly.

After several seconds, still looking at his frozen picture on the screen, we could hear him.

"Hello," he said.

"We lost you," I said. "All we have is a frozen image of you."

"That's what I have up here. A frozen image of you."

"The last thing we heard you say was that you loved us."

"Well, at least we took care of all of that," he said.

We were given the two-minute call.

"We have two minutes now," I said, looking at his frozen image.

We chatted briefly and said again and again that we loved each other; then the screen went blank. I was so thankful we were able to finish the video conference that day. It was the last conversation we ever had, exactly twenty-six years to the day after our first date.

Later that day, Rick and the crew took a few moments to remember the *Challenger* disaster. He said, "It is today that we remember and honor the crews of *Apollo 1* and *Challenger*. They made the ultimate sacrifice, giving their lives in service to their country and for all mankind. Their dedication and devotion to the exploration of space was an inspiration to each of us and still motivates people around the world to achieve great things in service to others. As we orbit the earth, we will join the entire NASA family for a moment of silence in their memory. Our thoughts and prayers go to their families as well." Of course, no one knew that just four days later the world would be applying those words to Rick and the STS-107 crew.

Rick's last wake-up call was scheduled for January 29, and I chose "Up on the Roof" by James Taylor. Rick had always loved his music, and I knew he would appreciate hearing one of his favorite songs.

NASA: *Columbia,* Houston, good morning to the Red Team. That was "Up on the Roof" for Rick.

RICK: Good morning, Stephanie. It's really great to hear your voice. It's really great to hear James Taylor. He's one of my favorites. We are way up on a roof up here and you can look at the city lights below from here. It happens to be dark outside right now. It's just a gorgeous view from up here and we're really enjoying our mission. We've got just a couple more days to go before we'll be coming back and seeing everybody who's supported us so well on this mission, including our families. I'd like to take this opportunity to say hi to them as well and thanks for all their support.

With quarantine, Rick had been gone two weeks. The daytime hours went by quickly because Laura and Matthew were busy with school, but I desperately missed having long conversations with him in the evening. Every day when Rick was at work, he would call me at least once a day to catch up, and I missed hearing his voice and knowing he was just a phone call away. The weekends dragged by because that's when Rick was always with us. After two weeks of being without him, I was counting the days till he came home.

Later that day, I e-mailed him:

> Mother went home today. We had such a wonderful visit. What a blessing to have such a nice mom . . . I feel like a horse that has just sighted the barn. I am starting to trot toward Saturday and your landing! Laura and Matthew are all aglow with a four-day weekend spread before them, not to mention the homecoming of their dad!! . . . Laura has been praying for you to have the most perfect landing ever in the history of the shuttle program . . . that'll work!! We are very excited to see you. Won't be long now!!!
>
> I love you!!
> Evelyn

Mike Anderson received the wake-up call on Friday, January 31, the crew's last full day in orbit.

NASA: *Columbia,* Houston. Good morning to the Blue Team. That music was for Mike. It was "If You've Been Delivered" by Kirk Franklin. We're looking forward to our last day on orbit with you.

MIKE: Thank you, Houston. That should certainly wake you up. And thank you for waking us up on what is Blue Shift's last day. It's kind of with mixed emotions that we get ready to come home, but we have enough fond memories to last us for a lifetime. We'd like to thank our families, our wives and our kids, for providing us with all the wonderful wake-up music each day and getting us off to a great start. As you know this is a very busy day today. We have a lot to do to prepare the orbiter to come home so we want to get to work and get all those things done, and hopefully, we'll see everyone by the end of the day!

NASA: Thanks, Mike. We've all enjoyed the mission down here, and I think that music woke up the Control Center too!

I sent my last e-mail to Rick that day:

Dear Rick—

This is probably the last e-mail I'll send. I know you have been extremely busy. We are really looking forward to seeing you. We all love you very, very much. We are praying for the landing to go perfectly. Hope to see you Saturday!

Love, Evelyn

Rick sent an e-mail to me later that day:

Hi, Evey!

Hopefully our e-mails crossed paths because I did send a note last night before I went to bed. Thank you so much for all the wonderful notes! Sorry mine were so few and short. You lift my spirits in so many ways and I really appreciate it. I can't wait to see you, Laura, and Matthew in Florida! Thank you so much for your prayers, love, and support!

Love, Rick

That was the last correspondence I would receive from Rick. I turned off the computer. The next time I thought I would see him would be in Florida.

Laura, Matthew, and I flew with the rest of the crew's families to Florida that afternoon in a NASA plane. We got into our condominium located on the beach, and I went out to dinner with all the spouses. Everyone was in a celebratory mood because our husbands and wives were coming home the next day. After I put Matthew and Laura in bed, I went out to the balcony and looked up at the stars; there must have been a million of them. I stood there and thanked God that Rick's mission had gone well and that he was finally coming home.

I was so excited that night, I didn't know how I'd ever get to sleep. I just couldn't wait to see Rick. I turned on the NASA channel and heard his voice: he was talking and going through final checks with the crew. It would take them several hours to prepare the inside of the shuttle for landing so they were busy getting the seats back into place and stowing equipment. I found myself talking back to the TV, saying things like, "I can't wait to see you. It's been a long haul since we've been together, but now we're down to just a few hours. I love you so much."

At 2:00 A.M., I went to the bathroom and heard Rick's voice again on the NASA channel going through the multiple checklists for the deorbit burn and landing. He sounded so relaxed and calm, and it was a tremendous comfort to hear him. I crawled back into bed and pulled the covers around my neck. I felt like a little girl on the night before Christmas.

On Saturday, February 1, Laurel received the last wake-up call from NASA.

NASA: Good morning to the Red Team. That was "Scotland the Brave" for Laurel.

LAUREL: Good morning, Houston. We're getting ready for a big day up here. Had a great time on orbit. Really excited to come back home. Hearing that song reminds me of all the different places down on earth and all the friends and family that I have all over the world. Thanks, and it's been great working with you and all the other folks.

That was it. The mission was complete. The crew was coming home.

13

The Longest Day

If this thing doesn't come out right, don't worry about me; I'm just going on higher.

—Michael Anderson

I LOOKED INTO THE SKY. *WHERE IS THE SHUTTLE? WHERE IS Rick? What is happening? Lord, please bring them home. Where are you, Rick? Oh, Lord, please help us. Please help us.* Keith was quiet as he looked at me. I had desperately wanted him to provide a logical explanation. Keith is a pilot with America West Airlines and has flown with the company more than a decade; he is no novice regarding flying. I was unaware he had been listening to communication with the *Columbia* and the subsequent loss of communication. Keith had heard his brother's last words.

We watched the landing clock count down to zero; then it started counting up again. My legs were shaky, and my ability to comprehend what was happening was impossible. *Father God, what's happening? Please don't let this be real. Please help me, Lord.* I could hear my heart pounding in my ears and feel the blood in my veins, a cold, icy rush that told me something horrible had happened. A huge wave of nausea hit me. People began to comment in the stands about what was happening.

"I heard someone say, 'Oh, they're always late,' or something to that effect," Steve Lindsey says. "And I thought to myself, *No, we're never late; we're always* exactly *on time.*"

When the bleachers started to empty and security personnel and astronauts scrambled away from the landing site, people began to wonder what was happening but kept the unthinkable out of their minds. "We were thinking they landed at Edwards Air Force Base or in New Mexico," Steve Schavrien says. Steve and his wife, Connie, and their daughter, Lisa, had been invited to the landing and were enjoying their time with Larry Moore and his wife, Sonya.

"Subconsciously, I kept thinking there was just a communications problem," Larry recalls, "but as the minutes rolled on, it became apparent that something was terribly wrong. Then when the clock ran down and started counting back up, the sinking feeling got very intense. I think I tried to ignore what we were all thinking in the back of our heads, but it was obvious something was wrong. Some people were using cell phones to call relatives who were watching television, and that's when the first of the real news began to spread."

David Jones couldn't be at the landing that day, but stood outside his home and watched for the shuttle. "They flew over west Texas about five minutes of eight [central standard time]," he says. "We stood outside and watched it come across the sky. We lost it about two-thirds of the way, but I just assumed I had lost its reflection in the sun or something. I had no idea of what was really happening. I didn't know it was breaking apart."

David and his family went inside to watch the landing on MSNBC, but first he called our home phone. "I called Rick and said, 'Hey, I just saw you fly over,'" David says. "'I'm sorry I couldn't make it to the landing. Congratulations on a great flight! I'll talk to you later about it. I love you, bye.' We started to watch the news, but when the landing time came and went, we knew something was wrong. Then we heard the first report of explosions over central Texas. I knew it wasn't good. I was shell-shocked. I'm still shell-shocked. I couldn't move. My wife got on the phone and booked us plane reservations immediately, and we flew out that day for Houston. I just stood in a daze while Risa packed our things. I couldn't wrap my mind around what was happening."

The news was reaching people across the United States, and at that moment, they knew more about what was happening than I did.

"I couldn't get the channel that showed the landing so I started checking e-mail," John Kanengieter says. "A few minutes later, someone called and asked if I was okay. I turned the TV on and saw the light streaking across the sky, breaking up. That was one of the worst moments of my life. I broke down and started sobbing. It was pretty clear what was going on at that moment. My wife and daughter came downstairs, and we all watched the news in shock, holding each other. Almost immediately, the media connected my name with the crew and started calling me. It was unbelievable! I had just lost seven friends; I couldn't talk."

Andy Cline was supposed to be at the landing, but he and his wife had just moved to Washington State and were going to move their belongings that day. "I knew I'd regret not going," Andy says. "We were staying at this little cabin in the woods that didn't have a TV so I knew I wouldn't be able to watch the landing. My wife needed to be somewhere around six o'clock that morning, which was nine o'clock eastern time, and I decided to get up and watch the sunrise so I could honor the crew's coming home. I had barely gotten out of bed when Molly pulled back into our driveway. I ran out to meet her, wondering what was wrong. She had heard on NPR that the *Columbia* was gone. I couldn't understand what she was saying at first—I didn't connect anything she was saying with the *Columbia,* but then it sank in and we both stood there crying in the middle of the woods. It was devastating."

Pat Daily and his wife were volunteering with a special project at a local elementary school in Houston that morning. "My wife was in another room when she got a call from a mutual friend telling her what happened," Pat says. "I couldn't believe it. There was no way this could happen, especially with Rick flying the shuttle. There had to be a mistake. I kept watching the TV and was in shock. There was this incredible grief. It was like losing a brother."

Steve Green couldn't be at the landing because he had two days of concerts scheduled in North Carolina. "All of our team was staying at the headquarters of Trans World Radio," Steve says. "I'd just woken up Saturday morning and was going into the kitchen to make breakfast when my cell phone rang, but I didn't answer it because the battery was low. I knew it was my wife, so I walked to the office area where I could call her back. The office phone rang, so I answered it. It was my wife, but she didn't recognize my voice. 'Why do you want to talk to Steve?' I said, playing with her. She said there was an emergency. I told her it was me, and she said, 'Honey, something's wrong with the shuttle. Something terrible.' I turned on the TV and was stunned. I sat there hoping, praying. One by one the team came out, and we sat around that TV for four hours or more praying, crying, and grieving."

Our friend Becky Gault from church was driving back to Clear Lake from a trip to Oklahoma; she was bringing her mother-in-law to Texas for a visit. They wanted to get back early enough to celebrate her daughter Kara's eleventh birthday. "Kara and Lauren were home alone that morning because Glenn was working," Becky says. "Lauren called me and she was upset. She said the shuttle was breaking up. I told her it was common for communication to break up. She said, 'No, it's breaking up over Dallas.' I kept telling her that she didn't understand. The other cell phone rang, and my mother-in-law answered it. It was Glenn telling her the same thing. I couldn't believe it was true. We were driving through Dallas, but the traffic was heavy. Off to the side we saw police cars and yellow police tape blocking something off. I looked and saw a huge piece of bowed metal that was from the shuttle. I had to pull off to the side of the road. I couldn't drive anymore because I was shaking so bad."

Our pastor, Steve Riggle, was in Guatemala with his wife on a missions trip when he heard the news. "We were about two hours outside Guatemala City," Steve says. "We were way up on a mountainside in the boonies where my cell phone would work for about a minute and then would be off for an hour. It rang, and my daughter said contact had been lost with the shuttle. I told her that often happens, but I didn't hear anything else because I lost service again. Several minutes went by, and my phone rang again. It was one of our pastors in Dallas who is also a police officer. He told me they'd lost contact with the shuttle, and I told him I knew that. He said, 'No. You need to know that they didn't make it.' There was total disbelief. It was hard to imagine. I knew we had to get to the airport but had no idea how we'd do that out in the middle of nowhere, but when we looked around, we saw a taxicab just sitting on the side of the road up on this mountainside. I couldn't believe it. It was the ride we needed in the middle of nowhere."

Angus Hogg was piloting a flight to Morocco when the tragedy happened. "I got out at Marrakech," he says, "and our engineer came in and said that the *Columbia* had come apart. I was almost physically sick, and I could hardly contain my emotions and was trying not to shake. We have known many people die in flying accidents whilst in the RAF, but I have never personally felt such a sense of loss as I felt at that moment. I phoned Carole and she was crying—I don't remember ever hearing her so upset. It just seemed almost surreal or some sort of bad dream, which would not disappear. Our engineer, himself a Muslim, was visibly upset by the accident and thought it was a terrible tragedy. It just showed that such an accident transcended national and religious boundaries, because it was not seen just as America's loss but also humanity's loss in the great endeavor of exploring the world beyond our own."

In Amarillo, my parents' house was already full of friends who were packing Mother's and Daddy's bags for them. "I'm normally in charge," my dad says. "I pack my own bags, make my own flight reservations, and take care of things at the house, but I couldn't do anything that day. Not one thing. The phone was ringing constantly, but I couldn't even answer it."

It's amazing how God puts special people in your life who are able to step in and take charge when you can't put one foot in front of the other. Someone called Southwest Airlines for my parents but was told the flight was full to Houston. Daddy got on the phone and said, "We have to be on that plane." He didn't want to go into what was happening, but he was able to tell the reservation clerk enough for her to get a supervisor on the line. "He got on the phone with me and said, 'Don't you worry, Mr. Neely. We'll make sure you're on that flight,'" Daddy says.

NASA has a contingency plan in the event of an accident, and within seconds it was being carried out. The next few minutes were surreal; I felt as if I was floating because I wasn't aware that my legs were working. I heard someone yell, "Get the crew families out of here," and Steve Lindsey took hold of my arm, leading me to our car. I pulled Laura and Matthew alongside me. I could hear myself breathing. It was the first time that I actually realized something horrible had happened but knew I immediately had to take care of Laura and Matthew.

"What's happening, Mama?" Laura asked, holding my arm. "Is Daddy okay?"

"I don't know," I said. "I don't think so, but we need to wait."

Matthew took hold of my hand but didn't say a word.

We passed my special agent who had been with us the entire week, and he said, "Evelyn, I'm so sorry." I couldn't figure out why he said that. I thought, *This is* not *happening*. We climbed into the car, and I turned around and looked at Matthew in the backseat. He looked so tiny and sad.

"Matthew, I don't think Daddy's okay. I don't think landing went well." He nodded, and that's all I could say.

Laura sat in the backseat and I sat in front, reaching my hand around so I could hold on to her. She was quiet. "Laura," I said, "they're going to take us to crew quarters, and it may be a while before we know what's happened to Daddy." She nodded.

It seemed we sat for several minutes in the car without moving, and Steve was getting frustrated.

"We couldn't move because everybody was in the way," Steve says. "Not everyone was in their cars, and there was press everywhere. I was afraid they were going to crush in on the families and start asking them questions. It was really tense."

Steve rolled down his window and yelled, "Get in the cars now! Let's go! Move! Move! Move!" We drove to crew quarters.

We walked in, and everyone gravitated to the bedrooms our spouses had been in sixteen days earlier, with their names still on the doors. We all looked so lost. In the hours and days previous to this one, crew quarters had been bustling with activity preparing for the crew's arrival, but now there was no crew to welcome. Laura, Matthew, and I walked into Rick's bedroom and saw his packed clothes for his return to Houston. We sat on his bed and held hands, waiting for word. Laura and I were crying, but Matthew just hung on to me. "We have to ask God to help us through this," I said, weeping. "We have to pray for help."

There were television sets throughout crew quarters, but they were off; we couldn't bear to see what the media were broadcasting. I called Daddy on my cell phone because I had to know something.

"I hadn't been able to answer the phone that morning," he says, "but for some reason I was right next to it when it rang and picked it up."

"Daddy," I said.

"Evelyn," he said. "Where are you, Precious?" His voice sounded shaky, and I knew he'd been crying.

"We're back at crew quarters. Do you know anything? Is it bad?"

He began to cry and my heart sank.

"Yes, Sweetheart. It's bad."

My hands were shaking. I asked Daddy if he wanted to say anything to Laura or Matthew, but he couldn't. He just couldn't talk. I hung up the phone and realized for the first time that Rick was dead. He wasn't coming home. I was thankful that my father, whom I love and respect so much, was the one who told me and not someone else. I broke down, sobbing. I scooped Laura and Matthew in my arms and fell onto Rick's bed, holding them. *This can't be true. It just can't be real.*

"I think Daddy has died today, but we have to be brave and hold on to each other and trust God a step at a time," I said, holding them tighter. My brain went into shock. Time stopped. Everything moved in slow motion. The other spouses and family members were in the same physical state. I knew that this was the *Challenger* all over again and that we were being ushered into a world that none of us ever wanted or believed we would live in.

It seemed like hours, but eventually, Steve Lindsey and Bob Cabana, the chief of Flight Crew Operations, came into crew quarters. The families were seated around a huge conference table that was covered with STS-107 T-shirts and pictures. The crew had been signing them before the mission but needed to finish them when they got back. Everything was still in place, waiting for their return. The families were holding hands. Our grief-stricken faces spoke volumes before a word was said.

"Before we went in to talk to the families," Steve says, "Bob said to me and Kent Rominger, chief of the Astronaut Office, 'This is what we know: the vehicle came apart over Texas at about 200,000 feet.' And I'll never forget this . . . he said, 'We have to go tell the families. And we can't give them any false hope that the crew survived.' I will never forget that. So, we went into the room and closed the door, and Bob said words to the effect of, 'This is the hardest thing I've ever had to do,' and basically told it straight. There was no other way to say it. Then the nightmare, well, the nightmare had already started, but it got worse."

Before Bob Cabana and Steve came into the room, I knew that Rick was dead. Sandy, Lani, and Rona knew that Mike, Willie, and Ilan were dead. Dave's brother, Doug, knew that he was dead. J. P. and Jon knew that K. C. and Laurel were dead. Yet when you hear those official words, you know that all hope is lost. You know that your spouse is never going to hold you again. You know that your children's father or mother is never going to see them graduate or marry or hold their children. You know that aging parents have outlived their own children. Then the weeping begins. We cried silently; we moaned; we wailed; we screamed. We sat together at that table and held hands and felt as if our hearts had been cut out. It couldn't be possible. It just couldn't be possible.

I learned much later that Jane, Keith, Kathy, and other family and friends were taken to an auditorium not far from crew quarters. On the bus ride to the auditorium, Willie's sister called her dad on her cell phone to see if he knew anything. She got off the phone, and she turned to Keith. "I think the shuttle blew up," she said. Keith didn't tell Jane; he knew it would be better to wait until they had official confirmation. What agonizing moments Keith must have suffered while they waited for word. After they had waited twenty minutes or more, Kent Rominger and Steve Lindsey walked in to speak with the group.

"Kent Rominger came in and said contact with the shuttle was lost somewhere over the west part of Texas," Steve Schavrien says. "There were about fifty people in the auditorium, but you could have heard a pin drop. He said that none of the astronauts' beacons [their location devices] had been activated and that they believed no one had survived. We were hoping they landed somewhere else because you just can't bring yourself to believe that," Steve says. "We kept hoping there would be better word that would come through, but of course, it never did."

Steve Lindsey escorted Jane, Keith, and Kathy to crew quarters to be with Laura, Matthew, and me. Keith wheeled Jane in (she has severe arthritis and can't walk long distances), and my heart broke all over again. She had lost her oldest son.

The White House learned that the *Columbia* was lost when Andrew Card, the chief of staff, saw preliminary reports while he was channel surfing at Camp David. His first concern was that the shuttle had been a target for terrorists since it was carrying Ilan, an Israeli war hero. President Bush was notified as he prepared for his morning workout at Camp David. When he heard, the president returned to Washington immediately.

NASA Administrator Sean O'Keefe spoke to President Bush on the phone and told him everything he knew at that point.

"This has got to be incredibly tragic for the families," President Bush said. "Where are they?"

"They are right here at Kennedy," O'Keefe said. "We have them."

President Bush asked to speak with us, and someone hooked up a phone. Sean O'Keefe talked to us beforehand and told us that in a few moments we would be talking to the president. O'Keefe was obviously shaken by the events.

In just minutes we were given word that the president was on the phone. In a matter of seconds I heard the president telling us how sorry he was. He was full of compassion and gave us his deepest sympathy, but it wasn't registering. I heard him speaking, but I couldn't process any of it. I was totally numb. I thought, *The president of the United States is on the phone, but I have no idea what he's saying because my husband is dead.*

It was impossible to fully take in what was happening. I think it's God's provision that you can't experience every emotion during a time of tragedy.

President Bush hung up the phone and prepared to tell the nation what had happened to the *Columbia*. "Tough day," he said, leaving the Oval Office with tears in his eyes. "Tough day."

People across the world sat in front of their television sets and watched as President Bush delivered the devastating news:

My fellow Americans: This day has brought terrible news and great sadness to our country. At 9:00 A.M. this morning, Mission Control in Houston lost contact with our Space Shuttle *Columbia*. A short time later, debris was seen falling from the skies above Texas. The *Columbia* is lost; there are no survivors.

On board was a crew of seven: Col. Rick Husband; Lt. Col. Michael Anderson; Comdr. Laurel Clark; Capt. David Brown; Comdr. William McCool; Dr. Kalpana Chawla; and Ilan Ramon, a colonel in the Israeli Air Force. These men and women assumed great risk in the service to all humanity.

In an age when space flight has come to seem almost routine, it is easy to overlook the dangers of travel by rocket, and the difficulties of navigating the fierce outer atmosphere of the Earth. These astronauts knew the dangers, and they faced them willingly, knowing they had a high and noble purpose in life. Because of their courage and daring and idealism, we will miss them all the more.

All Americans today are thinking, as well, of the families of these men and women who have been given this sudden shock and grief. You are not alone. Our entire nation grieves with you. And those you loved will always have the respect and gratitude of this country.

The cause in which they died will continue. Mankind is led into the darkness beyond our world by the inspiration of discovery and the longing to understand. Our journey into space will go on.

In the skies today we saw destruction and tragedy. Yet farther than we can see there is comfort and hope. In the words of the prophet Isaiah, "Lift your eyes and look to the heavens. Who created all these? He who brings out the starry hosts one by one and calls them each by name. Because of His great power and mighty strength, not one of them is missing."

The same Creator who names the stars also knows the names of the seven souls we mourn today. The crew of the Shuttle Columbia did not return safely to Earth; yet we can pray that all are safely home.

May God bless the grieving families, and may God continue to bless America.

We did not see the president's address to the nation, but friends and family throughout the U.S. and the world watched and cried throughout it. I was so thankful for a president who thinks so highly of the armed forces, respects the space program, and has a deep faith in God. This was not routine for the president—we knew he was mourning the loss of the crew.

As we sat in crew quarters, Laura looked at me and asked, "Who's going to help me with math? Who's going to walk me down the aisle? Will we move? Will you have to get a job?" She was processing it all much more quickly than I was, and she knew that what she had always known as normal was now gone; nothing would ever be normal again.

"Laura," I said. "I can't think about any of that right now. I'm just trying to get through today." I cried and held on to her. "We're just going to have to take this one step at a time." Laura and I went and sat down next to Kathy, Keith's fiancée.

Kathy had lost her husband of fifteen years a year earlier after a long battle with emphysema. John and Keith had been best friends since they were two years old. For years Rick and I prayed that Keith would find a godly woman. Kathy and John had also prayed that Keith would find a godly woman. Kathy had no idea that *she* would be the woman she was praying for. She was a great comfort to me that day. She ministered into my life in a way that no one else could because she was also a young widow; she knew what it was like and what I would be going through. She said God would walk me through my grief one step at a time.

Kathy and Keith were going to get married in April, and Rick was supposed to be the best man. I said, "Please don't change the wedding date. Rick would never want you to do that." I knew Rick would feel awful if he thought they were rearranging their lives. In April, Matthew would step into the role as best man at the wedding.

Kathy sat for the longest time and just stroked Laura's hair. Laura looked up at her and said, "I know God will get us through this."

I thank God every day that Rick had taught his children that God is always our help. He is always near. Matthew and Laura saw Rick and me lean into God through every situation, and now, in our darkest moment, Laura was living it.

NASA sent officials to pack up our things in the hotel. I had the presence of mind to remember to tell them about Rick's video devotionals that I had set inside the TV cabinet; otherwise they wouldn't have thought to look there. It was not an option for those precious, personal tapes to be lost or misplaced. I already recognized the incredible legacy they would be to our children for the rest of their lives.

We waited for a NASA plane to be readied in order to fly all of us back to Houston simultaneously. Many of the kids played video games to distract themselves. The rest of us sat around waiting. I looked at my watch, and it seemed as if it wasn't moving. I had no idea what time they had brought us into crew quarters nor did I have any idea how long we'd been there. All I knew was that I just wanted to get away from there.

When we boarded the airplane, we saw that it was filled with food. We had eaten hours ago, but I just couldn't think of food at that point. I didn't know when I would ever want to eat again. That two-hour flight felt like an eternity. It was very quiet on the plane. No one was talking. There was nothing any of us could say.

Matthew looked so confused and lost. I knew he was trying to wrap his mind around his life and what all this meant. "Matthew," I said, "when we get back to Houston, you can do whatever you want. You can play with your friends or with your Game Cube, or you can scooter. You can even play with Danny [his best friend from across the street]. You can do whatever you like."

"Really?" he asked. It was the first hint of anything close to normal for him, and I saw a look of relief cross his face. A seven-year-old should never have to process the death of his father, but Matthew was trying.

When we flew over Houston, Laura and I looked out the window of the plane and saw flags at half-mast throughout the city. "Mom, look," Laura said. "All the flags are at half-mast." I began to cry all over again. It was physical confirmation that what was happening wasn't just a dream. Since we didn't see the president's address, this was our first acknowledgment that the nation knew what happened and our grief was no longer private.

As we circled to land at Ellington Field, we saw the flags were also at half-mast there. We stood to get off the plane, and as I looked out the window, I saw rows and rows of astronauts and NASA personnel lined up in front of the buildings. General Howell, the center director for Johnson Space Center, was standing at the foot of the stairs. He took my hand in his and said how incredibly sorry he was and how much he thought of Rick. There were tears in his eyes, and I knew it hadn't been a good day for anybody.

We were escorted to Steve Lindsey's car while they found our luggage, and a few astronauts came over and spoke with me; I could see the pain in their eyes. Everyone was heartbroken. They'd lost close, dear friends when that shuttle exploded.

The police escorted us off the field, and as soon as we cleared the gate, there was a bank of media pointing cameras at us. I thought, *Welcome to our new life. A life I never wanted or expected.* I put my head down because I didn't want my picture taken. We pulled onto the road, and cars immediately pulled over to the side of the road, letting us pass. Men who were standing at the gate took off their ball caps in respect. Steve was driving, and we were all quiet on the drive.

We drove through our neighborhood, and nothing looked the same. It was terrible. This was the city I would now be living in without Rick. On our street, every tree had a blue ribbon tied around it in honor of the crew. I could see in the distance that police were already protecting our home. My heart started to beat faster because I didn't want to go in, not without Rick, not without the possibility of Rick ever being there again. Many people had left teddy bears and flowers on our front porch as a memorial to Rick, and when I saw them, the pain was too much. This wasn't the homecoming that anybody anticipated. The street was quiet; the neighbors were in their homes.

Before we had arrived at the house, all the neighbors on our street had a meeting. "The media contacted all the neighbors immediately," my neighbor Beth Cotten says. "They were trying to get any information they could, so we met in the street and decided not to say anything. We wanted the house to be a safe place, so the neighbors worked as a unit to maintain privacy and respect."

Steve helped with our luggage, and before we entered the house, a reporter tried to get to me, but Steve waved her off. I walked through the front door and saw all the paper chains decorating our wall that Matthew and Laura had made for Rick's return but he would never see any of it. There would be no sweet homecoming with tiny arms wrapping around Rick's waist to welcome Daddy home. Stepping into that house was the most painful thing I've ever done. On the mantel I had left a huge picture of the crew, but I couldn't look at it. It took me weeks to grieve for the others. My brain could handle only so much at a time, and it was consumed with the loss of Rick. I couldn't grieve for all seven of them at once. I looked at my watch: it was 3:30 CST. I thought, *Rick's been dead only seven hours, but it feels like seven years.*

I took my things to the bedroom I had shared with Rick for the last seven years, and I doubled over, sobbing and wailing. Sounds were coming out of me that I didn't recognize. It was the first time I had been alone, and I felt I could grieve freely.

"I can't believe this is happening," I said again and again. "Rick, I can't believe that you're gone." Before Rick had gone into quarantine, he took a bar of soap and wrote, "I love you, Evey! Love, Rick," on my makeup mirror. Every time I looked at that mirror, I wailed. Everything in that bedroom reminded me of Rick, and I sobbed at every turn, cries that were deep into my gut, cries I couldn't even distinguish as human; they sounded like something an animal would make. "You're not gone," I moaned. "Rick, you can't be gone."

David and Risa Jones arrived within an hour. They walked through the door, and we just held each other. There is no way to describe the grief. Friends from all over were arriving, including Dan Dillard, our friend with Campus Crusade for Christ. Dan, along with all of our friends, wanted to help however he could.

The answering machine was already full when we walked into the house. The phone started ringing immediately and never stopped. Media calls from all around the world were going into the church office as well, and by Wednesday the church phone system blew up. "The church has a sizable staff," Steve Riggle says, "but we just couldn't keep up with all the calls. It was impossible."

It quickly became apparent that each family was going to need a backup CACO to help in the aftermath, and Steve called Scott Parazynski. (Scott was on the John Glenn flight with Steve and had also been the family escort for Rick's first mission in 1999. Rick and I had selected him to back up Steve in the role of CACO.) They were gentle and professional and asked what I needed them to do. They jumped in and helped by picking up family and friends at the airport, and they turned off the phone that wouldn't stop ringing and rerouted all calls to Steve's cell. (I teased Steve later that it would be a good test to see if cell phones cause brain tumors because his phone was attached to his head for weeks.) They filtered news from NASA to us, talked to the media, and in general protected our family.

Steve informed me that my parents would be in Houston in ninety minutes, but I didn't think I'd make it. I needed them desperately to help me through the nightmare that wasn't ending.

I heard Matthew in his bedroom and knew something was wrong. I went up to see him. "Do you see why I'll never be an astronaut?" he said, frustrated. He was so angry, but it was the first emotion he'd shown since he learned that Rick was dead. I held him in my arms.

"Matthew," I said, "Daddy never would have put us through this on purpose. He loved being an astronaut, but he never would have wanted to die this way. He never would have wanted to do this to you or me or Laura." He was quiet. "Matthew, why don't you see if Danny can play?" I knew he needed something to be normal on such an unreal day. I asked David Jones to walk Matthew across the street to Danny's house.

Laura was in her room sitting on her bed. I stood in her doorway. "Sweetie, are you okay?" She wasn't crying. She was just very quiet and solemn. She looked up at me with lost eyes.

"I think I'd like to be alone," she said quietly.

I sat down and hugged her. "Let me know when you need me," I said, holding her. "Grammy and GaGa will be here soon, and Nanny, Keith, and Kathy are coming tomorrow." She nodded and I left the room.

Laura sat for the longest time, but then she took the calendar off her wall. She started writing on February 1 and wrote to the bottom of the calendar. She wrote,

My dad dies as the best dad in the whole world! I love him so much and I will see him in heaven. He died as a hero and he loved my family sooo much. He loved Jesus and he led me to Christ. He loves Jesus with all his heart and said and did everything he could to get us to love Jesus as much as he did and still does. I love you, Daddy! Love, from your biggest fan and daughter, Laura.

Bd, dd, pd, tt [This was code that Laura and Rick had between each other.]

P.S. My goal will try to be like you and do everything you taught me and witness. I love you!!!!!!!!!!!!!!!

I don't know how she had the frame of mind to write anything down, but Laura has always been so good with words that it seemed only natural that she would express what was in her heart that day. Laura has a way of stating things that seem obvious, things that I can't articulate, but she can make sense of them. I didn't fully process it at the time, but weeks later, it hit me that Laura and Matthew never questioned where Rick was. They knew he was in heaven. It was already part of the legacy that Rick had left with us. Someone once said that the memory of a faithful life speaks more eloquently than words, and on February 1, Laura remembered her father's faithful life.

We muddled through the next few hours as best we could. I confiscated Laura's big Winnie the Pooh bear and sobbed into it. I was in such tremendous pain that I didn't know what to do. It was excruciating to walk through our home and know Rick was gone. Everywhere I looked, there were his things: his clothes, his books, his Bible, his notes. I couldn't take it all in and just wept, holding on to that bear.

My parents arrived at 5:30 and were still in shock. Mother and Daddy walked into our entryway, and I let my guard down when I saw them. I felt like a small child again. I remember times when I would hurt really bad as a girl but wouldn't cry until I saw either Mother or Daddy. Then when I'd see them, I'd start wailing. It was like that on February 1. I saw them and started to cry all over again.

"I'm so happy to finally be able to hold you," Mother said.

Daddy pulled me closer. "Evelyn," he said. "I'm so sorry, Darlin'. I'm so sorry." They had always adored Rick; they loved him like a son.

Texans excel at funeral foods, and in hours, our house had more than enough food to feed every Texan in the state. The police and NASA were protective of the people they let into our home, but before long the house was filled with dear friends who were organizing my refrigerator and getting things in order for us. My two roommates from college, Cherie January Stowe and Pam Keffer, organized the stacks of casseroles that came to the house, labeling them and making room in the refrigerator and freezer. They kept track of all the flowers, unpacked our suitcases, did our laundry, cleaned the house, and did all of it effortlessly. I don't know what I would have done without them.

I had called Richard and Janetta Curtis around 4:30 and said I wanted them to come over. I put their names on the police list so they would be allowed into the house. Years earlier they had advised Rick and me on our finances, helping us to get on a workable budget, and had continually helped us with all aspects of our finances and investments.

"When we got there," Janetta says, "David and Risa Jones were there along with Steve Lindsey and Scott Parazynski, Beth Cotten and Dan and Jean [Dan and Jean are my parents]. Everyone was quiet. There was an enormous amount of grief, but there was also an incredible sense of the presence of the Lord. It was almost tangible. It was a peace, a grace that kept everyone from losing it all together."

Rick had flown a cross into space that belonged to Richard. It hung on a chain, and when Richard arrived at the house, I gave him the chain back. Rick had asked Richard to be the executor of our will before his first flight in 1999. "I never expected in my wildest dreams that I'd have to do it," Richard says. "When I got to the house, I saw my name on a sheet of who does what in case something happens, and it really impacted me when I saw my name in Rick's handwriting. It was almost surreal. I expected Rick to walk through the door any minute, but when I saw my name on that sheet, I knew he wasn't going to, but it was too much to wrap my mind around. Dan [my father, Dan Neely] took me to the side and said, 'I don't want her to have to work, Richard.' I told him that Rick was a good steward of what God had given them and had taken care of all those things. Rick was always thinking of his family."

"Laura came down the stairs," Janetta says, "and asked me, 'Are we going to have to sell the house? Are we going to have to move?' I was able to say no, and that gave her great peace. She had to know there was going to be some stability."

Glenn and Becky Gault came over that night as well. "There wasn't a sense of gloom," Becky says. "There was grief, but there was always an underlying peace because everyone knew that Rick was in heaven."

"Rick was always a great encourager," Glenn says. "He saw the best in everyone, and he really would have seen everyone's best in those days following the tragedy. Nobody ran around holding their heads like, *What are we going to do?* There was never that sense. There was always a great calm."

Almost immediately, gifts of all kinds started to flow into our home: stuffed animals, CDs, afghans, quilts, books, and mail by the bin full. "It was so overwhelming for everybody," Janetta says. "We knew right away that it was going to require constant organization. The mail came in so fast that we could barely keep up with it. There were five hundred e-mails alone by Monday morning."

In the days following Rick's death, Richard and Steve Lindsey did all the paperwork and refinanced the house for me. Rick had been intending to do it for two years but could never complete it because of his training duties.

It was too much to grasp. Everything that was taking place was supposed to happen to a widow who had lost her husband, but I was too young to have lost my husband. I couldn't be a widow at forty-four. It was unimaginable. It was like a bad dream that wouldn't end. But it wasn't a dream; it was real. And it was happening to me.

14

A World Without Rick

What really set Rick apart was his faith. I wish I had half of it.

—Bob Cabana, chief of Flight Crew Operations

THE NEXT MORNING, LAURA, MATTHEW, AND I STAYED HOME from church. I knew that a video tribute of Rick and Mike was going to be played during the service, but I just couldn't go. My grief was too heavy, and I wasn't ready to face the media. The sermon that morning was titled "Triumph and Tragedy," and several people from the media interviewed church members afterward. They were perplexed about the hope that was evident in the midst of such tragedy. How could they feel that way when two of their dear friends were dead? Everyone responded the same: "Because we know where they are!" They were clinging to God's promise in 1 Thessalonians 4:13: "Brothers, we do not want you to be ignorant about those who fall asleep, or to grieve like the rest of men, who have no hope." They didn't wonder where Rick was; they knew. Their hope was secure in God's Word.

Immediately following the service, two special families came to our home; both have daughters Laura's age who go to school with her and are dear friends. Yvana Rivera, the oldest of four children, had traveled with us the summer before to sing in the Honors Choir in San Antonio; she came over and loved Laura that day along with Emily Harvey, Laura's very first friend in Houston. The three of them disappeared in Laura's room to laugh and giggle as only teenage girls can. Both girls sent Laura the unspoken message that said although her world had been turned upside down, it was possible to still laugh and be a teenager.

While the girls enjoyed each other, their parents, Maria and Julio Rivera and Jim and Lori Harvey, loved and restored me and communicated in spoken and unspoken ways that they valued me as a person . . . they enjoyed being with me . . . the absence of Rick would not harm our deep friendship. It is a true turning point for a new widow when she realizes that friendships are still intact, even though she is no longer part of a "couple."

Julio and Jim played with Matthew at church and loved him through some tough weeks. They could never replace Matthew's father, but they could be strong male role models for him, and I was grateful for their kindness and attention.

Lori was another friend who stealthily moved about my home taking care of things after Rick's death. She made sure that laundry was done, floors were swept, and food was put away. She never asked if I needed anything; she saw what was needed and did it. For seven straight weeks, she tirelessly organized all the meals that were brought into our home.

I said good-bye to our friends and prepared for the arrival of the crew families that afternoon. When they arrived, we went up to Matthew's room, the only place in the house that wasn't occupied. "Hey, why's everybody in my room?" Matthew asked.

"We needed someplace quiet to talk," I said. "Should we pay you rent?"

He smiled and I gave him a dollar, which made him very happy. The crew children also came over that day, and they were thrilled to be with each other again. There was already such a connection with the children—all had lost a parent in the same horrible tragedy—and I knew they would be able to draw strength from one another. The spouses felt the same way toward one another. We felt like a family; we had always been as close as the crew. We cried and laughed and shared many stories. We were all in the same boat, so there was a great sense of understanding and comfort. Our spouses had died together; we would be forever bonded.

The media had been requesting a statement from the families, and I thought, *They just died yesterday!* It was hard for me to understand why a statement had to be released so soon. We sat in Matthew's room and worked on a statement. I had been asked to appear on the *Today Show* the next day, and I would read it on behalf of all the families.

On the morning of Monday, February 3, I was exhausted from lack of sleep and grief and nervous to be speaking on national television, but I really wanted to step up to the plate and do a good job for the families and be a clear reflection of God. An NBC camera crew set up their equipment in Building 9 of Johnson Space Center. A week earlier I had driven on-site for the last video conference with Rick, and now I was driving back on-site to talk about his death.

Before I went in, I prayed with Steve Lindsey—I knew that walking into that building was going to be emotional. It was one of the buildings where the crew did much of their training. Rick had even taken Laura's class on a tour in that building. Somehow, although I know that I was tired and nervous, I never felt any of that when I was on the air. I know that God stepped in and took over, giving me the strength I needed.

Katie Couric welcomed me and asked how all the families were doing, and I told her that everyone was doing remarkably well. "One of the blessings that came out of all of this was the launch was delayed so many times that it gave us an incredible amount of time to get to know each other and become very close," I said. Katie mentioned the statement, and I read it on the air:

On January 16, we saw our loved ones launch into a brilliant cloud-free sky. Their hearts were full of enthusiasm, pride in country, faith in their God, and a willingness to accept risk in the pursuit of knowledge, knowledge that might improve the quality of life for all mankind. *Columbia*'s sixteen-day mission of scientific discovery was a great success cut short by mere minutes, yet it will live on forever in our memories. We want to thank the NASA family and people from around the world for their incredible outpouring of love and support. Although we grieve deeply, as do the families of *Apollo One* and *Challenger* before us, the bold exploration of space must go on. Once the root cause of this tragedy is found and corrected, the legacy of *Columbia* must carry on for the benefit of our children—and yours.

The most difficult part of the interview came when Katie said, "Let's listen to what Commander Rick Husband had to say about this mission." For the first time since Rick's death, I could hear his voice in my earpiece. I held my breath to keep from crying.

At the end of the interview, Katie asked how I would like Rick to be remembered. I said, "When Rick autographed pictures for people, he always put a Scripture on it that was Proverbs 3:5–6, which says,

'Trust in the LORD with all your heart and lean not on your own under-standing; in all your ways acknowledge him, and he will make your paths straight.' And that has been a blessing to me and Rick. And now it's a tremendous blessing to me because I don't understand any of this, but I do trust the Lord. And so that's been a tremendous comfort."

The cameraman turned his camera off, and I sighed. It was over. God had gotten me through it. I had never imagined myself in this position; Rick was the public figure in our family, not I. I didn't know that the appearance would be the first of many public appearances I would make in the next few months.

While the families mourned, NASA engineers and investigators paid special attention to a piece of foam that broke off from the exter-nal tank and hit the left wing eighty-two seconds after liftoff. They determined that the foam had hit the leading edge of the orbiter's left wing and punched a hole in the reinforced carbon-carbon surface, which protects the wing from the tremendous heating encountered during entry. When the 3,000 degree Fahrenheit heat of entry hit the damaged surface, it penetrated the underside of the left wing, melting it from the inside out, eventually causing the left wing to fail struc-turally. (As of May 2003, it was my understanding that approxi-mately 30 percent of the scientific experiments aboard the *Columbia* were saved—primarily downlinked information. Additional science was discovered in the wreckage, but I don't know at this time if any of it will add to the results.)

Because of the constant activity and planning at our home, I didn't get the one-on-one time that I would have liked with Laura and Matthew. Matthew occupied himself with friends, and I'd see him in passing, giving a hug and holding him. I'd say, "Matthew, have you brushed your teeth today?" "Matthew, have you eaten?" "Matthew, can I have a kiss?" The children's pastor at our church, Susie Dennard, made Matthew and Laura her focus that first week. Kathy Baden, a friend from church who had once lived in Clear Lake and worked with Rick and me in children's ministry, flew in from her home in North Carolina to be with Laura and Matthew as well. They took the kids to movies and out to pizza and just let them talk for as long as they needed. They were a tremendous blessing to me, but there were still times that Laura needed to pull me aside because she wanted a hug and I wanted one too. She and I needed time alone to mourn together.

Laura was filled with questions: "Mama, have they been able to find Daddy yet?"

My heart broke. "No," I said. "But I know they will."

"Why are there so many meetings in our house?"

"We're trying to plan a memorial service at the church for Daddy and Mike. Plus, NASA is trying to keep us updated with any news. They want to deliver that news personally. Especially because Daddy was the commander."

"When do you think everybody will leave?"

"After the memorial service on Wednesday, Sweetie," I said. "Grammy and GaGa will leave Saturday."

"So nobody will be in our house after that?"

"There will be people here for quite a while who have to help with all the different things that have come up since Daddy died."

"What are they helping with? I can help you."

I held her hand. "We can't handle everything on our own, Laura. There's just too much involved. But I'll never be too busy for you and Matthew, and I absolutely love your hugs."

She hugged me tight, and I silently prayed that both she and Matthew would make it through the next few days as we went to the memorials and that they'd lean into God for a comfort that not even I could offer.

A national memorial service was going to be held the next day at Johnson Space Center in Houston. We were also planning a memorial service at our own church for Rick and Mike on Wednesday. I just prayed that we would all have the strength we needed to get through them and handle them with grace. I even dared to ask God that I would be steeled up enough so I wouldn't cry through them, and He answered that prayer. I wanted to have the presence of mind to know what was being said during those services.

On Tuesday, February 4, three days after the disaster, Laura, Matthew, and I got ready to attend the national memorial service for the crew at Johnson Space Center. I woke up and said, "Okay, I need to get through this today." In the weeks previous to the launch I had grown accustomed to a regimented schedule: "You have to be here at this time; you have to do this at this time." I was able to switch on and off emotionally for the events I needed to get through. After Rick died, it seemed as if I was still following that pattern of being told where to be and at what time. I would face each day looking at things from the perspective of, "Okay, I need to do these two things, and then I'm done." On February 4, the national memorial was one of those things.

I looked out the window and saw that all the cars in the caravan and our police escort were waiting on the street. Laura wasn't ready, and I wasn't up for pushing her out the door. Rick had always called leaving our house "attempting to achieve escape velocity," a space term that meant things just kept going round and round but never could break free. Three of us could be ready, but then Matthew would run back upstairs for something. Then he'd come down, and I would run into the bathroom for something. It was always impossible to leave. I turned to Becky Gault, who was helping me get Laura and Matthew ready for the service, and said, "Becky, would you go tell Laura she needs to get down here right now?"

Becky went upstairs and found Laura in the bathroom meticulously combing her hair, making sure it was just right. She tried to help, but Laura wanted to do it herself. Moments later, Laura appeared with perfect hair.

"Mom, Mrs. Gault used a stern voice," Laura said.

I knew that Rick had to be smiling. For once in our lives we were actually leaving on time.

On the drive to Johnson Space Center I looked out my window at very familiar places: the church where I used to take Matthew to Mother's Day Out, the Kroger I always shopped at, the apartments where Rick and I lived when we first moved here, and for the first time in years, I felt that Houston was my home. I had always assumed that we would grow roots here until Rick's time at NASA was complete and then we would move on: it's what military families do. We move on. But on that day, I knew that it was home. Laura and Matthew and I had grown roots here.

Moments before walking out to take our seats at the service, Matthew had to go to the bathroom. Steve Lindsey ran with Matthew down a very shiny hallway, and their suits flailed and flapped at the speed. A Secret Service agent looked down at his watch. I felt terrible but wanted to say, *When you gotta go, you gotta go.*

President and Mrs. Bush walked to their seats, and a few minutes later the crew's families walked out. Steve escorted Laura, Matthew, and me to our seats and then took his seat among the astronaut corps. When I took my seat, I met the president, and he took my hand and squeezed it. I looked at him and said, "We're going to be okay," and he looked at me with great compassion. Mrs. Bush was on his other side, next to Lani McCool. Keith noted later that Rick's childhood heroes, Neil Armstrong, the first astronaut to walk on the moon, and former senator and astronaut John Glenn, were attending the crew's memorial. It was touching to know that they had taken time to honor the crew that day.

It was a beautiful, clear afternoon. We sat in the middle of Johnson Space Center, the same spot where President Reagan eulogized the crew of the *Challenger* seventeen years earlier. Onlookers gathered in a plaza called "the mall," and NASA estimated the crowd was between ten thouand and fifteen thousand.

The service opened with the singing of the hymn "O God, Our Help in Ages Past." A rabbi from the navy spoke and prayed in both Hebrew and English before NASA Administrator Sean O'Keefe spoke. He said, "The bond between those who go into space and those on the ground is incredibly strong. Today, our grief is overwhelming." He went on to say, "Our duty now is to provide comfort to the brave families of the *Columbia* crew. We also have the tremendous duty to honor the legacy of those fallen heroes by finding out what caused the loss of the *Columbia* and its crew. We will keep this solemn pledge."

I held tightly to Laura's hand, praying I would get through the service. The astronaut corps sat nearby, and their grief was visible. It was still so hard to understand what happened.

Kent Rominger, Rick's friend and commander of his first shuttle mission in 1999 and now chief of the Astronaut Office, delivered the eulogy, which was a wonderful tribute to the crew. He said, "This diverse crew functioned flawlessly together." Rick had such deep respect for Kent; he would have been honored to hear him speak of the crew that way. How the crew functioned as a team was one of the things in which Rick took great pride. Kent finished his eulogy by saying, "Please know you are in our hearts and we will always smile when we think of you."

At one point in the service, Matthew sneezed, and I could see out of the corner of my eye that he needed a Kleenex. I looked at him, and he shrugged his shoulders as if to say, "What are we gonna do?" There was a bank of cameras in front of us so I didn't want to move because I knew they'd take pictures of me wiping Matthew's nose, but it had to be done; Matthew was running his hand over his nose, trying to clean himself up. I slowly reached across Laura and ran my finger under his nose.

"Do you need a handkerchief?" President Bush asked me.

"That would be great," I whispered.

The president took his handkerchief out of his pocket and handed it to me, and I slid it across Laura to Matthew. He wiped his nose and face and handed the handkerchief back to me. I gave it to the president, and he slid it back into his pocket. I never once in my life thought that the president of the United States would help me wipe my son's nose on national television, but he was very gracious.

President Bush got up to speak:

Their mission was almost complete, and we lost them so close to home. The men and women of the *Columbia* had journeyed more than six million miles and were minutes away from arrival and reunion.

The loss was sudden and terrible, and for their families, the grief is heavy. Our nation shares in your sorrow and in your pride. And today we remember not only one moment of tragedy, but seven lives of great purpose and achievement.

To leave behind Earth and air and gravity is an ancient dream of humanity. For these seven, it was a dream fulfilled. Each of these astronauts had the daring and discipline required of their calling. Each of them knew that great endeavors are inseparable from great risks. And each of them accepted those risks willingly, even joyfully, in the cause of discovery.

Rick Husband was a boy of four when he first thought of being an astronaut. As a man, and having become an astronaut, he found it was even more important to love his family and serve his Lord. One of Rick's favorite hymns was "How Great Thou Art," which offers these words of praise: "I see the stars. I hear the mighty thunder. Thy power throughout the universe displayed."

David Brown was first drawn to the stars as a little boy with a telescope in his backyard. He admired astronauts, but, as he said, "I thought they were movie stars. I thought I was kind of a normal kid." David grew up to be a physician, an aviator who could land on the deck of a carrier in the middle of the night, and a shuttle astronaut. His brother asked him several weeks ago what would happen if something went wrong on their mission. David replied, "This program will go on."

Michael Anderson always wanted to fly planes, and rose to the rank of lieutenant colonel in the air force. Along the way, he became a role model—especially for his two daughters and for the many children he spoke to in schools. He said to them, "Whatever you want to be in life, you're training for it now." He also told his minister, "If this thing doesn't come out right, don't worry about me. I'm just going on higher."

Laurel Salton Clark was a physician and a flight surgeon who loved adventure, loved her work, loved her husband and her son. A friend who heard Laurel speaking to Mission Control said, "There was a smile in her voice." Laurel conducted some of the experiments as *Columbia* orbited the Earth, and described seeing new life emerge from a tiny cocoon. "Life," she said, "continues in a lot of places, and life is a magical thing."

None of our astronauts traveled a longer path to space than Kalpana Chawla. She left India as a student, but she would see the nation of her birth, all of it, from hundreds of miles above. When the sad news reached her hometown, an administrator at her high school recalled, "She always said she wanted to reach the stars. She went there, and beyond." Kalpana's native country mourns her today, and so does her adopted land.

Ilan Ramon also flew above his home, the land of Israel. He said, "The quiet that envelops space makes the beauty even more powerful. And I only hope that the quiet can one day spread to my country." Ilan was a patriot, the devoted son of a Holocaust survivor, and served his country in two wars. "Ilan," said his wife, Rona, "left us at his peak moment, in his favorite place, with people he loved."

The *Columbia*'s pilot was Comdr. Willie McCool, whom friends knew as the most steady and dependable of men. In Lubbock today, they are thinking back to the Eagle Scout who became a distinguished naval officer and a fearless test pilot. One friend remembers Willie this way: "He was blessed. And we were blessed to know him."

Our whole nation was blessed to have such men and women serving in our space program. Their loss is deeply felt, especially in this place, where so many of you called them friends. The people of NASA are being tested once again. In your grief, you are responding as your friends would have wished—with focus, professionalism, and unbroken faith in the mission of this agency. Captain Brown was correct: America's space program will go on.

This cause of exploration and discovery is not an option we choose; it is a desire written in the human heart. We are that part of creation which seeks to understand all of creation. We find the best among us, send them forth into unmapped darkness, and pray they will return. They go in peace for all mankind, and all mankind is in their debt.

Yet some explorers do not return. And the loss settles unfairly on a few. The families here today shared in the courage of those they loved, but now they must face life and grief without them. The sorrow is lonely, but you are not alone. In time, you will find comfort and the grace to see you through. And in God's own time, we can pray that the day of your reunion will come.

And to the children who miss your mom or dad so much today, you need to know they love you, and that love will always be with you. They were proud of you, and you can be proud of them for the rest of your life.

The final days of their own lives were spent looking down upon this Earth. And now, on every continent, in every land they could see, the names of these astronauts are known and remembered. They will always have an honored place in the memory of this country. And today I offer the respect and gratitude of the people of the United States.

May God bless you all.

The navy bell tolled seven times for the crew, and then there was a flyby of four NASA T-38s in missing man formation. All four flew over, and then one of them pulled off and soared up and away.

"Throughout the service," Janetta Curtis says, "some part of my brain kept thinking, *Nah, they'll be back. They missed an orbit turn.* It's a trick your mind plays. But then when that missing man formation flew overhead, I don't know, it's extremely emotional and you know it's final."

"I was strong throughout the memorial," David Jones says. "But I broke down when the missing man formation flew overhead. I never expected it to affect me the way it did, but I just lost it."

After the memorial, the crew families met with President and Mrs. Bush. They sat down and talked with each family individually and spent time with them. We had no sense that the president had anything else to do because he was so focused on us. I mentioned to President Bush how much I admired both him and his parents. He smiled and said, "Maybe you can meet them sometime."

After President and Mrs. Bush left, we met with the families of the *Challenger,* and I asked Kathie Scobee Fulgham, Dick Scobee's daughter, if she would say something to Laura, Matthew, and the rest of the crew children. I didn't know it, but she had taken the time to write a beautiful letter from her and the children of the *Challenger* disaster. Kathie knew firsthand what our children were going through and that they had been thrust into a club they never wanted to join. She, too, struggled with the scary, unanswered questions again and again when her father died on the space shuttle *Challenger.*

Feb. 1, 2003

To the children of the *Columbia* crew,

We, the *Challenger* children and all the children of public disasters, are hearing your hearts break, holding your hands and hugging you from afar. You are not alone. Our nation mourns with you. But yours is also a personal loss that is separate from this national tragedy.

We hope this letter will bring you some comfort now or in the future, when you are strong enough and old enough to read it. We want to prepare you for what's to come and help you on grief's journey. We want you to know that it will be bad—very bad—for a little while, but it will get better.

Why does the TV show the space shuttle streaking across the sky over and over again? What happened? Where is my mom or dad? Yours is a small voice in a crashing storm of questions. And no answers will bring you comfort.

Seventeen years ago, before some of you were even born, I watched my father and his crew die in a horrible accident. Our loved ones were astronauts on board the Space Shuttle *Challenger,* which blew up a few minutes after takeoff. It all happened on live television. It should have been a moment of private grief, but instead it turned into a very public torture. We couldn't turn on the television for weeks afterward, because we were afraid we would see the gruesome spectacle of the *Challenger* coming apart a mile up in the sky.

My father died a hundred times a day on televisions all across the country. And since it happened so publicly, everyone in the country felt like it happened to them, too. And it did. The *Challenger* explosion was a national tragedy. Everyone saw it, everyone hurt, everyone grieved, everyone wanted to help. But that did not make it any easier for me. They wanted to say good-bye to American heroes. I just wanted to say good-bye to my daddy.

You've discovered by now that you won't be able to escape the barrage of news and the countless angles of investigation, speculation and exasperation. The news coverage will ebb and flow, but will blindside you in the weeks, months and years to follow when you least expect it. You will be watching television and then, suddenly, there will be that image of the shuttle—YOUR shuttle—making its tragic path across the sky. For other people watching, this will all be something called "history." To you, it's your life.

Just know that the public's perception of this catastrophe isn't the same as yours. They can't know how painful it is to watch your mom or dad die several times each day. They can't know the horror you feel when they talk about finding your loved one's remains. If they knew how much pain it caused, they would stop.

You may feel sick when you think about his or her broken body. You will be afraid to ask what happened because the answers might be worse than what you imagined. You'll torture yourself wondering if they felt pain, if they suffered, if they knew what was happening. They didn't. In the same way your brain doesn't register pain immediately when you break your arm, your mom or dad didn't know pain in their last moments of life on this earth.

You will think about the last things you said to each other. You might worry that you didn't say enough or say the right things. Rest easy. Their last thoughts were of you—the all of who you are—not the Feb. 1, 2003, you. And they were happy thoughts, all in a jumble of emotions so deep they are everlasting.

Everyone you know will cry fresh tears when they see you. People will try to feed you even though you know it all tastes like cardboard. They want to know what you think—what you feel—what you need.

But you really don't know. You may not know for a very long time. And it will be an even longer amount of time before you can imagine your life without your mom or dad.

Some people, working through their own grief, will want to talk to you about the catastrophe, the aftermath, the debris recovery, or the actions that will be taken by NASA. Others will whisper as you walk by, "Her dad was killed in the space shuttle disaster." This new identity might be difficult for you. Sometimes you will want to say to the whisperers, "Yes! That was my dad. We are so proud of him. I miss him like crazy!" But sometimes you will want to fade into the background, wanting to anonymously grieve in your own way, in your own time, without an audience.

When those who loved your mom or dad talk with you, cry with you, or even scream with frustration and unfairness of it, you don't have to make sense of it all. Grief is a weird and winding path with no real destination and lots of switchbacks. Look on grief as a journey—full of rest stops, enlightening sites and potholes of differing depths of rage, sadness and despair. Just realize that you won't be staying forever at one stop. You will eventually move on to the next. And the path will become smoother, but it may never come to an end.

Ask the people who love you and who knew and loved your mom or dad to help you remember the way they lived—not the way they died. You need stories about your mom or dad from their friends, co-workers, teachers and your extended family. These stories will keep your mom or dad alive and real in your heart and mind for the rest of your life. Listen carefully to the stories. Tell them. Write them. Record them. Post them online. The stories will help you remember. The stories will help you make decisions about your life—help you become the person you were meant to be.

Please know that we are with you—holding you in our hearts, in our minds and in our prayers.

With love, Kathie and the children of *The Challenger* crew

We went home, and I began praying for the memorial service at church the next day. *One day at a time,* I told myself. *God will get me through this one day, one step, at a time.*

Prior to launch, each astronaut fills out papers containing information for the Astronaut Office to keep on file in the event of an accident. The packet includes financial and personal information such as loans, bank accounts, personal and spiritual advisers, extended family, and so on. It's also where the crew member designates CACOs. (On Rick's sheet Steve Lindsey is named as the primary CACO, with Mike Anderson listed as the alternate. However, since Mike was on the flight with Rick, Steve arranged with administrators for Scott Parazynski to assist him as backup CACO.) On the last page of this packet titled "Special Instructions for Funeral Services," there's a section called "Other Special Instructions." In this section, Rick wrote,

> Tell 'em about Jesus!—That He is *real* to me.
> Proverbs 3:5–6
> Colossians 3:23

That's what Rick wanted done in case something happened: he wanted people to know about Jesus and His love. Rick's request has now become my life's mission statement, and I communicate that every chance I get.

Angus Hogg had flown in from England, and I asked him to speak at the church memorial service. Steve Green also flew in, and he was to sing "God of Wonders," the wake-up song that greeted Rick and the Red Team in space. Months earlier I had contacted Jimmy Logan, a member of our church, and asked if he would put together a video of Rick for the reception in Florida, prior to the launch. I gave him family photos and video of Rick in space during his first mission, and he compiled it into a beautiful video. Steve sang "God of Wonders" at the reception with the video playing in the background and sang it again at the memorial. I cried as I looked at the screen and saw Rick. I couldn't believe he wasn't there with me. I just couldn't believe he was gone.

A videotape of Rick singing "Were It Not for Grace" during Easter weekend was also played. "When Rick sang on videotape that day," Steve Green says, "it was very powerful. I'd never heard him sing before. There's something about hearing someone sing that gives a view into his heart that you can't have any other way. When I heard him sing, my affection for him instantly grew. He was very transparent; you could see his love for God, and I thought, *What a testimony.*

It wasn't just the church family that was there: it was people from NASA and the community. The other astronauts were witnessing a very intimate part of Rick's world—discovering another side they'd never known—and it was very moving."

A videotape played of Rick speaking with Pastor Riggle before the flight of the *Columbia,* and David Jones later commented that only Rick could sing *and* speak at his own memorial service. It was so painful to watch Rick on the screen, but in the middle of my immeasurable grief, something amazing happened: I worshiped. I got lost in God's holiness and provision. I was swept away by His faithfulness and presence. In the depths of my agonizing heartache, God was there, comforting and holding me. Although it felt as if half of me had been ripped away and the pain in my heart would never end, I knew that God would take care of me. I knew that He would take care of Laura and Matthew. I thought, *When Laura and Matthew are grown, I want them to look back at this time and say that God never left us; He was always there. Yes, Mom cried all the time, but through it all, God was there.*

That evening we broke away from the stacks of casseroles that were in the refrigerator. Friends and family were sitting around our kitchen table, and I stood in the center of the kitchen and said, "We are going out for Mexican food tonight. We are *not* eating funeral food!" We went to a Mexican restaurant to celebrate my father's seventieth birthday. The wait staff sang "Happy Birthday" to him and put a sombrero on his head.

It was a great getaway. There were moments that I actually felt normal. I thought, *I'm still here. I can still have fun.* It was the first time I had done something that wasn't official; it had nothing to do with STS-107. We talked about other things, and it was very freeing. We had a great time, and at one point, my neighbor Beth's son called and said his head was bleeding. "Is there a lot of blood?" she asked. No one wanted the fun to end. It was the first time since Rick died that I actually felt hungry and the first meal that I enjoyed. It was a turning point for me because it was my first new fun memory without Rick.

Angus had to fly back to England the next day. In two weeks, he would return for Rick's funeral in Amarillo. A longtime friend of ours and of Angus's took him to the airport. This friend had been at our home for a few days after Rick's death and had witnessed everything that was taking place. He was with us the previous evening for the great time at the Mexican restaurant. He and Angus had had spiritual talks in the past, so Angus asked him where he was spiritually, and he looked at Angus and said, "I want what Evelyn has. I want that peace."

"Then you want Jesus," Angus said. "Because He's where that peace comes from." Our friend pulled off to the side of the road, and Angus prayed with him as he asked Jesus into his heart. Angus called me from the airport and told me, he was so excited. Already, Rick's life was bringing people to Christ.

Another memorial was held that day at the National Cathedral in Washington, D.C., but I couldn't attend. It was physically impossible. Dave Brown's parents attended, along with Jon and Iain Clark. Some of the family members sent representatives, and they included Mike Anderson's brother-in-law and Rick's cousin, Janet McCormick. NASA dignitaries from the national headquarters in D.C. were also there along with members of Congress. I received a videotape of the service, and it was lovely. Patti LaBelle sang a beautiful song called "Way Up There," written specifically for the space program. Bob Cabana, chief of Flight Crew Operations, walked to the podium to speak of the STS-107 crew. He said, in part:

> There was nothing flashy about them. They performed flawlessly with understated excellence and were an example for us all of what we can accomplish when we work together as one. I'd like to share with you the faith that they had and the strength I've gained from them. It all began before leaving the suit room on launch day to head for the Astro van on the way to the pad. The commander, Rick Husband, stopped before exiting, turned to his crew, and the seven embraced as one: Jew, Hindu, Christian together, and Rick led them in prayer. As they rode to the pad, they were filled with joy, anticipation, excitement, and an inner peace that they were ready for whatever may lie ahead.

Bob spoke of each crew member and finished with thoughts about Rick. He said,

> Colonel Rick Husband, United States Air Force. Why break the mold with this crew? Another mild-mannered antithesis of what one thinks of as a fighter pilot, a leader of the highest caliber. But what really set Rick apart was his faith. I wish I had half of it.

Bob concluded his beautifully written thoughts of Rick and the crew and took his seat. Vice President Dick Cheney stood to speak.

They were soldiers and scientists, doctors and pilots—but, above all, they were explorers. Each of them followed his or her own path to the space program. Each led a life of high purpose and high achievement.

The crew of the *Columbia* was united not by faith or heritage, but by the calling they answered and shared. They were bound together in the great cause of discovery. They were envoys to the unknown. They advanced human understanding by showing human courage.

The men and women aboard the *Columbia* were driven by a fierce determination to make life better here on earth by unlocking the mysteries of space . . . The *Columbia* is lost, but the dreams that inspired its crew remain with us . . . While many memorials will be built to honor *Columbia*'s crew, their greatest memorial will be a vibrant space program with new missions carried out by a new generation of brave explorers.

America and all the world will always remember the first flight of the *Columbia* in 1981. And we will never forget the men and women of her final voyage: Willie McCool, Kalpana Chawla, Ilan Ramon, Michael Anderson, David Brown, Laurel Clark, and Rick Husband.

May a merciful God receive these seven souls. May He comfort their families. May He help our nation to bear this heavy loss. And may He guide us forward in exploring His creation.

On Friday, Laura and Matthew and I had an important mission: I felt both of them needed to walk through the doors of their school for the first time after their daddy's death. They attend a small Christian school, and the entire student population had signed a banner that they were going to take to Ellington Field to welcome the crew back to Houston. It saddens me to think they were never a part of the homecoming they had envisioned. Laura and Matthew were not the only astronaut children in the school. Laura's science and English teacher was Martha Tanner. Her husband, Joe, is part of the astronaut corps and had prayed with me prior to Rick's first launch of STS-96. Martha had the seventh-grade class write letters to Laura, and she was able to read those the week of Rick's death. Matthew's class had colored pictures for him.

To be at the school in time for lunch with Matthew's class, we needed to be on the road. I went through the usual drill with them: "Come on! Get ready. Get your shoes on. We need to leave."

"I don't want to go," Matthew yelled down the stairs.

I knew he was nervous about his first day back. "Come on, Matthew. I'm going with you," I said.

Laura was dragging as well. She was usually the more social of the two, but she was dreading the spotlight and the sympathy.

"Do I have to tell every single story of what we've gone through this week?" Laura asked. "I don't want everybody to cry on me."

"They just want to be with you and give you a hug because we're not the only ones going through this," I said. "They're mourning Daddy too."

She and Matthew reluctantly got into the van.

I escorted them to the lunchroom where Matthew's teacher, Mrs. Johnston, and the entire class greeted us. They burst into applause when they saw Matthew, making him feel very welcome. I wanted all of the children to see that we were okay. "I'm sorry your husband died," one little girl said, hugging me.

"I'm sorry he did too," I said. Sometimes it's not as complicated to talk with a seven-year-old—not as many words are needed.

Laura's classmates, many of whom had already been at our home, were thrilled to see her. As I watched from afar, I could see Laura smiling and laughing with Yvana and Emily, and I thanked God that some things were the same. We had just gotten over another hurdle.

My parents stayed with us for a week and left on Saturday, February 8. A couple of days after the memorial at Johnson Space Center I got a call from Steve Lindsey saying President George Bush and his wife, Barbara, wanted to have lunch with us in Houston on the eighth. After my parents left, Matthew, Laura, and I, along with Steve, toured the president's office, took pictures, and had lunch at a nearby club. President and Mrs. Bush were gracious and kind as they spoke with us, and it was a great honor to meet them. I was amazed at how loving they were toward us. A lot of people think that Southerners automatically have great hospitality, but that's not true. Not every Southerner can make someone feel at ease, but George and Barbara Bush have that gift. They were interactive with Laura and Matthew and very comfortable talking with them. It was obvious they had grandchildren!

At one point, I heard Matthew talking with Mrs. Bush about boogers, and she looked over at me and said, "Too much information." I couldn't have agreed more. I couldn't believe Matthew was talking about boogers to a former First Lady, but I thought, *She has grandchildren. Hopefully, she's heard about them before.* She had the traits of a very loving mother and grandmother and never acted shocked or put off but took the conversation with great humor.

That Saturday I knew that Matthew, Laura, and I had to somehow get back to normal, or rather, we had to find a new normal. I sat the kids down at the kitchen table and said, "The four of us didn't die. Daddy did. We've got to find a way to live in this new life we have now." Of course, none of us knew how to do that. I was a widow at forty-four—that was my new normal. Rick and I were no longer a couple—it was just me as a single parent to the kids. Laura and Matthew no longer had a daddy; they had just me. That was their new normal.

I felt like a ninety-five-year-old woman who was finished with her life but still had the rest of her life to live without her husband. I couldn't imagine living without Rick. There was a great emptiness inside me without him. I loved being in his company. I loved hearing him tell stories. It was a great sadness to realize that I wouldn't be able to hear all his stories from space with the rest of the STS-107 crew. It was always so wonderful to hear him talk and share stories about his job. I knew that we would have to continue to create stories for our family; even since Rick's death we already had some new ones under our belts—not the least of which, we met two presidents in one week.

That evening we ate the first meal in our house alone. It was incredibly painful. I had to figure out where we would sit now.

"Am I the new spiritual leader of the home?" Matthew asked.

"No, Matthew," I said. "I guess I am, with God's help. But I'll need for you and Laura to help me as we walk through each day." I realized that Matthew was thinking about Rick, even though he wasn't talking about him. I wanted to answer his questions in a loving, gentle way.

"Am I the man of the family now?" he asked.

My heart sank. I grieved that Matthew was only seven and would no longer have Rick's leadership in his life. My prayer is that Matthew will always have memories of the influence that Rick provided.

"No, Sweetie. God is the head of our family. I need you to help Mama all you can and be a good boy for me, but more than that I just want you to be a little boy. You don't need to worry about being the leader of our home. God will help me do that. Plus, I had a great example with Daddy." I sat down in Rick's chair, and we made it through our first meal alone.

I cleaned the kitchen and ran the water for Matthew's bath. Evenings could be so painful. Rick and I had always worked as a team to get the kids ready for bed, and he always prayed with each of them before good-night kisses. I struggled through those evenings without him and fell into my bed alone, praying for the strength to get up and do it all again the next day.

I was so thankful the children were young because they had a schedule that I had to maintain with them. A routine was already in place, and I was forced to get up and going each day. We discovered that there is a lot of comfort in sameness: our church was the same; the neighborhood was the same; the school was the same; we still had the same sense of humor. We kept to our routine, but the dinner hour and weekends were our most vulnerable times because that was when Rick was always with us and there was this big, gaping hole without him. But we kept moving; we kept breathing. Laura and Matthew had soccer so we kept up with their game schedules. I was amazed at their strength and ability to carry on with life. I guess they realized that life was going to keep moving anyway.

We knew there was nothing that any of us could do to change what had taken place, but we did have control over how we handled it. I determined that I didn't want to be bitter. I didn't have any bitterness toward NASA because I knew that if they thought for a second that the *Columbia* wasn't safe on January 16, that liftoff would never have happened. Rick had confidence in all the men and women of NASA and was confident the mission would go well. I didn't want to have an ounce of anger toward anyone. I never wanted to look back at that

time and say, *I wish I hadn't done that. I wish I hadn't acted that way.*
I knew that I could trust God. He had proved Himself faithful to me
again and again throughout my life, and I knew that He would continue to be faithful. He has never left me. He didn't leave Rick on
February 1. He opened His arms and welcomed him home.

15

Steps of Faith

I stood at the door of the New Year and I said, "Give me a light that I might see my way safely into the unknown." But a voice came to me and said, "Instead, step into the darkness and take the hand of God—for it will be to you better than light and safer than a known way."

SOMETIME AFTER OUR RETURN FROM FLORIDA, I DEVELOPED THE film from our camera and saw the picture of the three of us standing in front of the landing clock that showed 11:21:00. We were all smiles because we thought the shuttle was eleven minutes from landing. I put that picture on my refrigerator, and above it I put a political cartoon drawn by Jeff Parker of the *Columbia* flying through the gates of heaven. There are seven stars in the sky—one is the Star of David of Israel, honoring Ilan. They're shining brilliantly as the *Columbia* flies through beautiful, golden gates. We didn't know it then, but as Laura, Matthew, and I posed for the picture, Rick was already at the gates of heaven. I looked at the photograph and felt my heart sink. It was still so unbelievable. I felt my emotions rising and grabbed my purse. I didn't want to break down in sobs again. I needed to get to the grocery store.

I slid into the driver's seat in the van and noticed I had messages on my cell phone. I put the phone to my ear to retrieve them and heard Rick's voice from the calls I had stored in previous messages. He left it on the day we were going to visit him in crew quarters, and he was trying to track us down. It was the first time I'd heard it since the day I saved it. I listened to his message and began to sob. Tears blurred my vision, and I couldn't see the road. I pulled over into a parking lot and wept. The sound of his voice made me ache; I missed it so much. *Lord, when will this get easier? Will it* ever *get easier at all?*

During the week of the tenth, Steve Lindsey came to the house and said he needed to talk with me. Poor Steve, he looked so tired; the nightmare was never-ending. Steve is a kindhearted man, and I felt awful that doing things like that was now part of his life. We sat down at the kitchen table, and he was quiet. I knew he had something important to say.

"We found the remains of all seven of the crew, and Rick's are among them," he said. "I have all the details if you want to know them. It's completely up to you."

I nodded for him to go ahead. Steve told me specifically what had been identified. An astronaut at the site knew it was Rick when the remains were discovered. I could feel my chest tighten. I was looking forward to the day when there would be no more bad news. It was information I needed to hear, but it was extremely difficult.

"There was a chaplain at the site of Rick's remains," Steve said. "The process was very dignified and respectful. Before the remains were removed, the chaplain prayed and read Joshua 1:6–9." It was what Rick had quoted the night before launch.

"Did they find Rick's wedding ring?"

He looked at me somberly. "No."

"Excuse me," I said. I could feel the tears coming and didn't want to cry on Steve's shoulder.

He let himself out.

I went upstairs and fell onto the bed, weeping, and cried for two hours, holding on to Laura's huge Winnie the Pooh. It seemed that every single day I had to say good-bye to Rick all over again, and the pain was almost unbearable. I missed him every second of the day, and something would inevitably happen that would break my heart again. I had given Rick my wedding band to take into space, just as I had done on his first mission, and now it was gone, along with his wedding band. In the middle of my grief I kept thinking about those rings. It was devastating to think that both were lost. Years ago, Rick had bought two bands of small diamonds that we soldered to my engagement ring, but I still always wore my wedding band with them. I never felt complete unless I had it on, but now it was gone. I couldn't get it out of my mind and sobbed, thinking that the symbols of our love were destroyed along with our marriage. There are days that I twist my ring on my finger and feel that the band is gone, and the pain grieves me again. I think of Rick's band on his finger and mourn the memory of putting the ring on his hand at our wedding. *Oh, Rick, how I miss your touch.*

The next day, I was in the playroom working on the computer when Laura came up the stairs looking for me. She plopped down on the couch and watched me read through some e-mails. "Mama," she said, "can we talk for a minute?"

"Sure," I said. I got up and sat next to her.

She asked, "Mom, why did Daddy die?" That was a question I had repeatedly asked myself.

"Laura, Daddy had a very dangerous job," I said.

She gave me the strangest look. "He did?"

I realized then that Rick and I had protected Laura and Matthew from the stark reality of his job. We never talked with them about the possibility of something happening because we wanted to shelter them from unnecessary fear.

"I've been doing a lot of thinking, and I think I would rather have Daddy die than you and Daddy get a divorce." Her words caught me off guard.

"Why, Laura? What do you mean?"

"I couldn't stand not seeing you and Daddy loving each other anymore. You and Daddy loved each other so much. Daddy leaving would be worse than Daddy dying."

I had to think about what she said. I was amazed that she thought death was a better option than divorce, but then I realized that Rick and I set an example of a godly marriage for her and I was very thankful. She had known other families that had gone through divorce and the pain it caused. She knew that would be a pain that would never heal. On that day, I knew I was blessed that Laura and Matthew had so many great memories of their dad.

We were quiet in the van as we drove to church that Sunday, then I heard Matthew's little voice from the backseat. "Mom, what does Dad *do* all day in heaven?" He sounded exasperated, as if he'd already given it much thought but wasn't coming up with any answers.

I turned to look at him. "He gets to hang out with Jesus, and I bet he sings all day. He doesn't hurt, though, and he never cries."

He thought for a moment. "If Daddy could come back, would he?"

My heart sank. I knew Matthew was trying so hard to figure out what was happening. "That's a good question, Matthew, but time in heaven is different from time on earth." Whenever Rick went on a trip, Laura would always sleep with me and say she was saving Daddy's place. I looked back at Matthew and said, "Daddy is saving our place in heaven, and I think that instead of his coming back here, he'd rather us be there with him."

I wondered when the questions would get any easier.

After the service, a sweet couple asked Matthew if there was anything they could do for me. Matthew thought for a moment and said, "You could pick her up."

I was so touched that that was what Matthew thought of—that he had remembered his daddy picking me up whenever I was sad. I had noticed that Laura's and Matthew's ways of mourning were different. Laura was like me and could easily cry. Matthew was quiet, observing things in his own way, but his thoughts would come out in profound ways. I smiled and assured the couple that they did not have to pick me up!

That afternoon, I finally got around to emptying Rick's bags he had packed and left in crew quarters before the mission. I pulled out his flight suits, boots, and helmet and held on to them. His flight suit still smelled like his cologne, and it brought floods of fresh tears. It amazed me how each of our senses is used to mourn and how each sense comes with its own memories. That day, it was the memory of smell: I smelled his shaving cream, cologne, even his body odor that was on his workout clothes, and all of them brought a flood of memories and fresh aches for his presence. I clutched his shorts and T-shirt to my chest and thought, *Rick, even your dirty clothes bring me comfort.*

I found his wallet and looked through all of his perfectly folded receipts, coupons he had been saving, and photos of us. I pulled out all the money that was inside: one lone dollar bill. *Where did he get this?* I thought, laughing. *He never had any money!* I am grateful for a God who brings laughter in the middle of great sorrow. I knew that there would be many tears in the long days ahead, but that in the middle of our anguish, God would continue to bring laughter to our hearts.

Rick's funeral was in Amarillo on February 21. People came from around the country and the world, including Rick's former Boscombe Down squadron commander, Nigel Wood, who flew in from England. All of the crew spouses flew on a NASA plane. Dr. Jim Bankhead of the First Presbyterian Church officiated along with Dr. James R. Carroll, who had led us through our marriage vows twenty years earlier in that same church. He had become my pastor when I was five and served my first Communion.

We took a small private jet to Amarillo. Glenn and Becky Gault watched over Laura and Matthew as I sat in the back and finished Rick's eulogy. Matthew wanted to sit on my lap, but I was balancing my Bible and notes and there just wasn't any room. "I can't hold you right now," I said, kissing him. "But I love you. Can you go up front and look at the clouds?"

Matthew took his seat next to Glenn and was quiet as he looked out the window. "That cloud looks like a clown," Matthew said to Glenn and Becky. "That one looks like a dog." Then he looked out and said, "I think I see my daddy's face."

I was so grateful I couldn't hear him. Writing the eulogy was so emotional for me. If I had heard Matthew say he saw his daddy in the clouds, I wouldn't have been able to handle it.

We landed in Amarillo at TAC Air, a private and military airport adjacent to the public airport. Rick had always flown to TAC Air in his T-38. Walking through the small building, I was reminded of all the warm welcomes and send-offs we had experienced there with Rick. Today was no exception: T-38s dotted the landscape belonging to astronauts who were there to help us. We caravanned to my parents' home and waited for Rick's casket to arrive, but the weather was bad and detained the plane. It was nine o'clock that evening when the funeral home finally called.

Paul Lockhart, a close friend and astronaut who is also from Amarillo, accompanied Rick's casket from Dover Air Force Base in Delaware and stood guard beside it. Jane and Keith went to the funeral home first, and I arrived after they had paid their final respects. I left Laura and Matthew at my parents' home with friends during that time. I asked Steve Lindsey to go into the room first; I needed to know if anything was going to be upsetting or shocking before I went in to say good-bye to Rick. The military had put a full-dress air force uniform with all of Rick's medals and ribbons pinned to it inside the top portion of the casket. His remains had been carefully placed inside a bag and rested below a blanket. Steve exited the room and nodded, assuring me that everything was all right, and I went in alone.

I was trembling as I approached the casket and began to sob. I felt as if my heart was breaking. I began to wail and hoped no one could hear me. *Lord, how am I ever going to get through this? How am I going to live without him?* This was a moment I had anticipated for days and had discussed at length with my grief counselor. He explained to me that women, especially, have a strong need for touch and that it could help me with closure. I had waited on February 1 to touch Rick, and here I stood three weeks later under extraordinarily difficult circumstances with him in reach. I stretched out my hand and felt his remains beneath the uniform, and as I gently touched him, I wailed, feeling the man I had loved for twenty-six years. "I love you, Rick," I sobbed. "I love you so much." I tucked letters that Laura, Matthew, and I had written to Rick inside the pocket of the uniform and told him we would always love him.

The next morning, I wanted the graveside service to be intimate so we held a small private burial service at the cemetery with a handful of family and friends before Rick's funeral in the afternoon at First Presbyterian Church. Rick had listed six pallbearers on his contingency sheets: David Jones, Steve Schavrien, Angus Hogg, Larry Moore, Carl Lorey (a singing buddy from high-school choir), and Kent Rominger; they stood in front of us, with their wives (Carole Hogg was still in England at that time) standing directly behind them.

The flag-draped coffin was only two feet away, and Laura sobbed when she saw it. Matthew sat quietly, his eyes as big as saucers, looking at it. It was the first and only time they saw their dad's casket. I gave myself permission to cry throughout the ceremony. A military flyby and a twenty-one-gun salute took place, and Jane and I were each presented with the American flag. As we were leaving, Laura,

Matthew, and I paused and put our hands on Rick's coffin and prayed that God would get us through this new life without Rick. He was buried right across the street from Tradewinds Airport where he had learned to fly twenty-eight years earlier.

That afternoon, we rode to the church for the funeral in yet another police-escorted motorcade. I prayed that I wouldn't cry throughout the service, especially during my tribute to Rick. *Please help me, Father,* I prayed. *Please get me through this.*

After the choir sang a few hymns, Dr. Carroll took hold of his cane and walked to the podium. He was gray and frail and years had slowed his steps, but when he spoke, my heart filled.

> Rick lived by these words in the Proverbs: "Trust in the Lord with all your heart and do not rely on your own insight. In all your ways acknowledge Him and He will make straight your paths."
>
> His name and those of his crew are written forever in the annals of the human effort to explore the universe. God loved him. Rick loved his Lord.
>
> He lived his faith. He did not hesitate to put in a good word for Jesus. His life was his sermon. By his life and his love and his faith, in life and in his death, he has witnessed to the whole world . . . Countless thousands, because of Rick, look up beyond the stars and see the face of God.
>
> For him, death is swallowed up in victory. Heaven is his eternal home. I would be surprised if God has not asked the commander of the *Columbia* to help Him in the management of His stars and solar system and all of outer space. And, surely, Rick is singing in the heavenly choirs.
>
> The apostle Paul asked, "Who shall separate us from the love of Christ? Can trouble, pain or persecution? Can famine or lack of clothes, or peril or sword? Nay, in all these things we are more than conquerors through Him who loved us. For I am persuaded that neither death, nor life, nor angels, nor principalities, nor powers, nor anything else in all Creation shall be able to separate us from the love of God in Christ Jesus our Lord."
>
> And Jesus said, "I am the Resurrection and the Life. He who believes in me, though he died, yet shall he live and whoever lives and believes in me shall never die."
>
> All is well. Hallelujah!

I stood to deliver my eulogy and prayed again that I could get through it. I took a breath and walked up the steps to the podium.

My spiritual journey began here over forty-four years ago. My parents stood at this altar and held me as a newborn. They made a covenant to God to raise me in a home that believed in Jesus. I thank God for my parents' dedication to me. Rick's parents made a similar pledge before God to raise him in the grace and knowledge of Jesus Christ at Polk Street Methodist. I thank God that my future husband's life began with such a covenant. Legacies are important.

This church has much significance to me. Seventy-three years ago, my grandparents pledged their love to each other in this sanctuary. My parents stood before God and witnesses and pledged their love to each other forty-five years ago. And almost exactly twenty-one years ago, Rick and I began our marriage in this sanctuary before God and many who are here today. Legacies are important.

I spoke to Jane and Keith and to my parents, then addressed Laura and Matthew. I felt a lump in my throat. When I looked at their little faces, my voice started shaking:

The legacy your father has left you is this . . . He prayed for you every single day that he lived. He loved you with all of his heart. His pride and joy for you were immeasurable. He will always be in your heart as we treasure all of our memories of him. Daddy's prayers and desires for you will be honored by God throughout your lives. His legacy is with you.

I looked out and saw the faces of the crew spouses and spoke to them:

Our destiny together has been laid before us. Many kind words have been spoken recently of the closeness of the crew. That bond, that closeness, now lives in our hearts forever—we have shared a horrible tragedy—may we also share many triumphs.

I spoke to the NASA family and to our extended family and friends and then closed:

I still cannot completely comprehend that Rick is in heaven and not here . . . that I will never see his beautiful face come in the door from work, I will never feel his warm embrace or hear his voice saying my name. We will not experience growing old together or raising our children together or being grandparents together.

So where does my anguished soul turn? Where can I find strength to love and nurture our two precious children that we prayed for, for so long? As I cried out in pain to Jesus last Saturday that the cost of losing Rick was too much . . . too painful to withstand, an answer flooded over me: *Evelyn, I know what pain is . . . I died on the cross for you.* He died on the cross for all of our sins. It doesn't matter whether you believe or not, whether you accept it or not . . . it does not alter the fact that it is true. This is God's legacy to us. He took our punishment for sin so that we could be eternally in God's holy presence. Rick believed in Jesus. He was real to Rick. Rick is in God's holy presence right now. What a legacy!!!!

My precious Rick is now safely home.

I sat down, and Angus came forward. At one point he made the packed church laugh during his eulogy. "I used to joke that he wasn't an astronaut but in Houston selling burgers," Angus said that morning. It was a light moment, and I was so grateful for Angus and his wonderful sense of humor. He went on:

He was a great patriot. He loved his country and would never speak ill of someone else's country. He was thrilled to be part of the space program but loved his family more. He was aware of his faults but was the last person to tell you of your faults. He never wanted to embarrass or make people feel awkward about what he did for a living. He was totally committed to the things of God. He made people feel as if they mattered. When you were with Rick, he made you feel as though you were the most important person at that moment. He saw himself as someone who had put his faith in God, and God had done wonderful things through him and fulfilled his every dream with his family and what he was doing. He had no inclination as to what would happen; yet he believed utterly that he would stand before his Maker without fear. I saw him in November. He spoke of nothing but praise for every crew member. He said, "They're the best of the best." Whatever the unknowns are, I know with certainty that Rick stands in heaven with his Savior, Jesus Christ.

In 1999, Rick was asked to give his testimony at First Presbyterian, and the church recorded his words. A portion of the thirty-minute talk was replayed during the service. Laura and Matthew leaned their heads on my shoulders, and we sat and listened to the tape. I felt tears in my eyes when I heard Rick's voice.

I asked Jesus to be my Savior when I was a freshman in college. I didn't really do much about it for quite a long time after that. I attended church, but I didn't experience any spiritual growth. I didn't really get to know God . . .While we were in England I really had a tremendous opportunity to sit and listen to God. I started figuring out what it meant to give my life to Jesus . . .

When I think of the times I got to tuck my daughter in at night and sing to her and have her ask me questions about things she's thinking about or when our little three-year-old runs in completely naked to give me a kiss after his bath, I think I wouldn't trade any of those things for a ride in space because it wouldn't be worth it. There's nothing more important than our relationship with Jesus because God loved us enough to send Him to die for our sins so that we might not perish but have eternal life. Every day we trust in things that are made by human hands. How much more should we trust in God who created us, and in Jesus, His Son, to be Lord of our lives?

Dr. Bankhead stood at the front and talked candidly with everyone:

When I got the news, it drove me to my knees and I said, "Lord, can I trust You in this? You promised to be with me. You promised to never leave me or forsake me. Can I trust You to do this in the death of all of these astronauts and the pain on all of their families?" And very quickly He began to prove Himself to me again.

In that moment, I was reminded that God can be trusted. He has always proved faithful and true with His promises.

Steve Green stood and sang a song I had requested called "Safely Home." Hearing Steve sing the song was always emotional for me, but I knew it had to be sung at Rick's funeral.

Children, precious children
I know you're shaken
A loved one taken

Oh but hear Me
Come, draw near Me
Their pain is past now
They rest at last now
Safely home

They are strong and free
They are safe with Me

This life is merely shadow
Today there's sorrow
But joy tomorrow
Safely home
They are strong and free
They are safe with Me

One day you will join them
All together
This time forever
Safely home
Safely home

The day after the funeral, Matthew, Laura, and I went to Palo Duro Canyon in Amarillo with about twenty family and friends, and we hiked all day to a rock formation called the Light House. Steve Lindsey was thrilled as we drove into the canyon because his cell phone showed no service. We were cut off from the world, and it was incredible! It was therapeutic for all of us because it was the first time we had really been outdoors in weeks. Our bodies needed to move. Matthew refused to walk a single step. He was exuberant to be set free from a suit and grown-ups and ran the whole way. We laughed throughout our hike, and it was an early lesson for Matthew and Laura that we could have fun without Daddy. God was providing opportunities for us to laugh again, and I was grateful.

Early the next morning I flew to Las Vegas so that I could meet the other crew spouses at Zion National Park in the southwest corner of Utah. Steve and Scott Parazynski picked me up at the airport for the two-hour drive. We were dressed casually because we had to hike up a hillside to where K. C.'s funeral service was going to be held. It was a favorite place of hers, and if something happened, it was her final wish that the service would be held there. It was hard to say good-bye, to know that we would never hear K. C.'s sweet voice again.

On the bus ride back to the air force base where we would all board a NASA plane, I looked out the window and looked up at the sky. Every time I saw the condensation trail left by aircraft, it was a painful reminder of not seeing Rick come home from the sky and what the sky must have looked like that last day for him. We flew back to Houston and arrived at midnight. Laura had left a sweet note on my pillow and laid my nightclothes out for me. Even in the middle of heartache, she is able to give me so much love. I went into her room and kissed her and prayed and went into Matthew's room and did the same. I fell into bed and thought, *Did I do all that in one day?* I realized the pace that Rick had held for years was now my pace. I used to envy all the traveling he did, but as I fell to sleep that night, I believed him when he said it wasn't all that it was cracked up to be. I was exhausted.

February 27 marked what would have been our twenty-first wedding anniversary. It was my first anticipated milestone date that I knew was coming and expected to be difficult. I woke up and looked at our wedding pictures hanging on the bedroom wall. "We should be together today, Rick," I said, looking at his face. "We were always together on our anniversary!" I couldn't believe it had been a year since our trip to San Francisco. "I miss you so much," I sobbed. I always thought our marriage would last longer than twenty years. When you lose a spouse, all your future memories together die as well. Rick and I would never create another memory together. I buried my head into the pillow and wept. I didn't want to spend that day without him. Before Laura left for school, she came into the bathroom as I was getting ready for the day.

"Laura, this would have been my and Daddy's twenty-first wedding anniversary," I said.

"I know, Mom," she said. "I remember." She paused for a moment. "Please promise me that you'll never marry again."

I couldn't believe it. The pain of that day was so unbearable I just couldn't believe, of all the days to pick, she had said that on our anniversary, but I knew Laura was protecting Rick and his memory. She didn't want anyone swooping in, trying to take his place, and it broke my heart. No one could ever take Rick's place.

"Laura," I said, "I can't promise you that, but I will promise you that I will be a moral woman and I will be obedient to God."

I managed to get through the day and looked forward to Mexican food that night with Angus and Carole and my neighbor Beth. Angus and Carole had invited Matthew, Laura, and me to visit them in England, and Beth and her son, Justin, were going to go with us, so we talked about what we would do while we were there. It was an enjoyable evening, but I missed my husband. I was looking forward to going home and having a good pity party for myself, but first I needed to pick up a few things at the drugstore. A woman who worked there pulled me off to the side and told me how much Rick's death had affected her. She attended his memorial service and, as a result, wanted to renew her relationship with Jesus. I prayed with her that she would seek Jesus and that her relationship with Him would come alive. It was a privilege to talk about God so comfortably with someone. I drove home and realized that God wasn't going to let me have a pity party after all—He had blessed me instead.

The next day, February 28, the crew spouses flew to Annapolis on a NASA plane for Willie's funeral. I left Matthew and Laura behind in Houston, promising to call them when I arrived. We stayed at Andrews Air Force Base, and the base kindly gave us rooms in the Officer Temporary Quarters. I walked in and thought, *I'm staying in one of the most beautiful rooms I've ever been in and I'm by myself.* It would have been such a wonderful place to celebrate our anniversary. I called Rick's mom that night and talked to her about adjusting to widowhood and the loneliness of it. I dreaded going to sleep in that big four-poster bed all by myself. I unpacked a little teddy bear a friend had given me and slept with it. The next morning I showered and dressed for Willie's funeral at nine o'clock in the chapel at Annapolis. I flew back to Houston that evening.

On Friday, March 7, Laura, Matthew, and I, along with the rest of the crew families, flew to Washington, D.C. Sandy Anderson and her daughters had flown in earlier to prepare for Mike's funeral at Arlington National Cemetery, which would take place that afternoon. I felt so sad, especially for Sandy and the girls. Before the service began, we were all brought into a special room, and I was given a medal that Rick had received—the Defense Distinguished Service Medal given for extraordinary meritorious service for the armed forces of the United States. The citation reads:

> Colonel Rick D. Husband, United States Air Force, distinguished himself by exceptionally distinguished service as Commander aboard The Space Shuttle Columbia, STS-107, National Aeronautics and Space Administration, from 16 January 2003 to 1 February 2003. In a duty of great responsibility, during the mission of STS-107, Colonel Husband's outstanding leadership directly led to the flawless preparation and on-orbit execution of this ambitious scientific research mission totaling more than 80 experiments. In addition, Colonel Husband's diligence and attention to detail ensured the seamless integration of the first Israeli Astronaut, Colonel Ilan Ramon, into the crew of STS-107, despite the concerns over terrorism in Israel and the United States. The distinctive accomplishments of Colonel Husband and the dedication of his service to his country, reflect great credit upon himself, the United States Air Force, and the Department of Defense.

I was incredibly proud, and it meant the world to me to have the other spouses in the room. I had been there when awards were given to other crew families, and it was a great honor to be a part of those ceremonies.

The crew families walked behind the caisson carrying Mike's casket. As we approached the site where Mike would be buried, we passed the Challenger Memorial. Two years earlier I had stood with Laura beside that memorial on a class field trip, and I prayed that we would never experience such a tragedy. Almost exactly two years later, here I was living out my deepest fears. It felt as if we were moving in slow motion as we passed it. It was unbelievable and surreal.

Following Mike's funeral, we visited the White House and met with President and Mrs. Bush for two hours. They greeted each family individually and were both so warm and genuine, taking their time with each of us, making us feel welcome. Matthew played with Barney, their Scottish terrier, in the Oval Office and outside in the Rose Garden. In addition to Barney, we met Spot, a daughter of Millie (President George and Barbara Bush's dog during their time in the White House), and Wilson, a black cat. The younger children loved chasing the pets around. Laura sat on the couch with Mrs. Bush, and Mrs. Bush was attentive and gentle as Laura spoke.

President Bush was incredibly caring and easygoing. We sat in the Oval Office and listened as he explained the significance of the room and what an honor it was to work there and to be our president. He said the sunrise is particularly beautiful as he sits at his desk (the same one Presidents Roosevelt and Kennedy used) and works. The children wanted autographs for their teachers, and President Bush signed as many as they needed. Before we went into the White House, Lani McCool suggested that we give the president a signed picture of the crew that each of the spouses and children had also signed. I presented him with the photo, and he was very appreciative, telling us he would save it in his archives.

The Bushes gave us a tour around the first floor of the White House. We saw the room where they have state dinners, and Matthew and Barney crawled under the table. I apologized to Mrs. Bush, and she raised her hand and said, "Don't worry about it. This is the people's house. Let him enjoy it."

One of the Bushes' most endearing qualities is their ability to make you feel comfortable; they have such an incredible gift of hospitality. They were very gracious, just like his parents. As I toured each room, I had to keep reminding myself, *The president is taking me through the White House.* For so long I had hoped Rick and I would be able to tour the White House together with the rest of the crew and spouses. This wasn't the way I had imagined the to visit.

On Sunday we went to the Challenger Center Headquarters for lunch. June Scobee Rodgers was there, wife of the *Challenger* Commander Dick Scobee, along with former astronaut Joe Allen and other staff members. They told us about the purpose of the center: to educate students about science and space through educational equipment and classes. I walked in to see a huge picture of the *Challenger* crew on one wall and an eight-by-ten-inch picture of the *Columbia* crew on another wall. As I felt tears come to my eyes, I thought, *This is not a club that I ever wanted to belong to*. The staff of the center was compassionate and encouraging, but it was painful to be there. I had watched the *Challenger* disaster on TV when it happened, and I didn't like to fast-forward seventeen years later and realize that I was now part of their world.

The next day, Monday, March 10, Laurel's service was at Fort Myer, adjacent to Arlington National Cemetery. The kids and I and Steve Lindsey toured Mount Vernon for the rest of the day, and Steve had a huge snowball fight with Laura and Matthew in the parking lot. Matthew drew a picture of the snowball fight that evening, and he had Rick in heaven, watching it. When I saw it, it made my heart ache for Matthew, Laura, and me.

Two days later, we went to Dave's funeral at Fort Myer. All the funerals were now over (Ilan's took place in Israel on February 11, so it was the only one we were unable to attend), and in many ways it was a tremendous relief. We were able to grieve for each member of the crew during a special service.

We flew back to Houston and I unpacked our bags. I was so tired. Saying good-bye to the crew over the past few weeks was emotionally exhausting and painful. My heart still breaks for all of them. I miss them so much.

A few weeks after Dave's funeral, I received a CD in the mail from Steve Green. He had written a song for me called "Evelyn's Song" and had recorded it in the little work studio inside his home. It wasn't intended to be a song for the public, just a gift for me, but it was meaningful and moving in ways I can't describe. When I listened to it the first time, I started to weep. It was touching areas of pain that I hadn't even explored yet.

> A mother wakes her sleeping child, says
> We have to leave in just a little while,
> Today's the day that Daddy's coming home
> We'll see him soaring through the sky,
> You know how much your daddy loves to fly
> Hurry now it's almost time to go

Daddy's comin' home; I can almost see him smile
He'll wrap us in his arms and hold us for a while
Then he'll tell us all about his time up there
But now let's say a prayer, honey, don't be scared
Daddy's comin' home

We watched and we wondered what went wrong
Then felt death's shadow send a chill across the dawn
They're gone

A mother holds her weeping child, says
We have to leave in just a little while
Today's the day that Daddy's gone home
He was soaring through the sky
You know how much your daddy loved to fly
When all at once Jesus called him home

Daddy's gone home; I can almost see him smile
He's safe in Jesus' arms and He'll hold him for a while
You know he'll tell the Lord all about his time up there
But now let's say a prayer; we'll need God's loving care
Daddy's gone home

I know right now it seems so far away
But we'll be together for all time some day
Some day

We will all be home; I can almost see him smile
He'll wrap us in his arms and hold us for a while
Then he'll tell us all about his time up there
We'll tell him how the Lord answered every prayer
We'll never have to cry, 'cause there'll be no more good-byes
And we will all be home

The song makes my heart ache because I know that for Rick, there
is no time in heaven; but on earth, time drags on without him. There
is a sense of hope in the song—my children know that Rick has gone
home to be with Jesus and that we will someday be with him again.

I love the end of the song that talks about the promises found in the book of Revelation that states we will have no more sorrow: "He will wipe every tear from their eyes. There will be no more death or mourning or crying or pain, for the old order of things has passed away" (21:4). It took me more than a dozen times to listen without crying, but now when I hear the song, I feel the promise of hope and look forward to our family's reunion in heaven when there will never be another good-bye.

It was late when we got home one hot spring night. The kids and I should have been in bed, but dinner with friends went longer than expected, making bath time later than usual. I ran the bathwater for Matthew and walked downstairs to the living room where our friends waited to say good night. Before they left, I pulled out a videotape, slid it into the VCR, and pressed play.

"This is one of the tapes Rick did for Matthew," I said. Everyone was quiet as Rick faded onto the screen, wearing a white polo shirt with the shuttle emblem embroidered on the front. I stood at the side of the television and watched with the others as Rick looked into the camera. I smiled watching him, remembering the day he filmed it. He pushed the button on the remote, and when the light flashed on the camera, he looked into the lens and smiled.

"Hi, Matthew," he said. "I wanted to tell you how much I love you and I wanted to make this tape for you so that you and I could have a devotional time for every day that I'm in space. So, what I am doing is I'm looking at your devotional book and I'm starting on the sixteenth of January, which is our launch day, and what I will do is read through this book and read the Bible verse also and go through the whole thing just like you and I are sitting here on the couch together. I just wanted to do this because I love you so much and I'm going to do one for your sister as well. So here we go. This will be our first day," he said, looking down at the book. "It says to read Isaiah 61, verses 1 through 3."

I realized I hadn't seen the first day of Matthew's videos. I never took my eyes off the screen as Rick read the Bible verses:

The Spirit of the Sovereign LORD is on me,
because the LORD has anointed me to preach good news to the poor.
He has sent me to bind up the brokenhearted,
to proclaim freedom for the captives
and release from darkness for the prisoners,
to proclaim the year of the LORD's favor
and the day of vengeance of our God,
to comfort all who mourn,
and provide for those who grieve in Zion—
to bestow on them a crown of beauty instead of ashes,
the oil of gladness instead of mourning,
and a garment of praise instead of a spirit of despair.
They will be called oaks of righteousness,
a planting of the LORD for the display of his splendor.

I couldn't believe what I was hearing and shook my head. When Rick read, "He has sent me to bind up the brokenhearted . . . to comfort all who mourn, and provide for those who grieve . . . to bestow on them a crown of beauty instead of ashes, the oil of gladness instead of mourning, and a garment of praise instead of a spirit of despair," I felt tears in my eyes and sat down. Rick was reading Scripture that was bringing me comfort on that night!

He picked up Matthew's devotional book and read the story of a little boy who wanted to oil his mother's kitchen cupboards so they'd stop squeaking. Playing in his neighborhood, he noticed that several neighbors had complaining, bitter spirits. He decided that they could use some oil too. His father suggested that the little boy start spreading some oil of gladness whenever he ran into any of the neighbors. I watched Rick read through the story and smiled through my tears. Oh, how I missed his voice, his love, his presence in this home!

Once he finished the story, Rick looked back into the camera at Matthew. "I'm going to say a prayer for you today, the first day we're doing these devotionals." Rick closed his eyes and said, "Lord, I pray that You'll help Matthew to spread gladness today. Help him to be helpful and lend a helping hand and help him to just spread his happy spirit with everybody he sees. Thank You, Lord, for Matthew. We pray that You'll watch over him and Laura and Mama and our family. And we ask this in Jesus' name, amen." He finished the prayer and looked back in the camera. "Okay, that was our first day. I love you very, very much, Matthew, and I hope that this goes very well for all the different devotionals we're going to do. You can save the next one until tomorrow. I love you, bye."

Rick pressed the stop button on the remote, and the screen went black. Everyone was quiet in the living room; no one knew what to say. We said our good-byes, and I turned off the TV and climbed the stairs to my bedroom. I sat on the bed and rubbed my face. What will I do for the rest of my life without you, Rick? I prayed for our family, climbed into bed, and turned off the light, but I was so lonely for Rick. Seeing the video and hearing his voice made the ache in my heart throb. *How do I do this, Lord? How do I go on without him?*

I remembered something that had been written months earlier on a card for me and turned on the light. I had placed the card inside my Bible. I took it out and read the words:

I stood at the door of the New Year and I said, "Give me a light that I might see my way safely into the unknown." But a voice came to me and said, "Instead, step into the darkness and take the hand of God— for it will be to you better than light and safer than a known way."

I turned off the light, took hold of the hand of God, and fell asleep.

Epilogue

ON APRIL 1, MATTHEW THREW OUT THE OPENING PITCH (ALONG with other crew children) at the season opener for the Houston Astros. He wore a jersey that swallowed him (it hung down to his calves) with the crew patch on a sleeve, just like the players wore all season. The back of the jersey had "Husband" written in huge letters and the number "107." Matthew wore a ball cap pulled down to where you could barely see his eyes. I smiled looking at him because it was just how Rick wore his ball caps when he was little. Matthew pitched to Craig Biggio, who later signed his baseball. Former President George Bush signed the ball as well. The highlight of the evening for Matthew was that the cotton candy was free!

As planned before Rick's death, Keith married Kathy in April in a beautiful outdoor ceremony in the hill country of Fredericksburg, Texas. Matthew was best man, taking his father's place. He did a great job, and in true Husband tradition, he even escorted me after the ceremony. (Rick escorted his mother out of the church after we were married.)

In May (Mother's Day) I was asked to speak at the Crystal Cathedral along with June Scobee Rodgers, widow of Space Shuttle Challenger Commander Dick Scobee. That evening, I spoke at the Billy Graham Crusade in San Diego at Qualcom Stadium. I had never imagined myself speaking before such large crowds and had done it twice in one day.

Shortly after Keith and Kathy were married, they asked us to go on a one-week Alaskan cruise with them in May. Matthew thought it sounded fun as long as we wouldn't have to witness them kissing that week! Keith and Kathy were happy to oblige, so they honored Matthew's request. It was difficult to see couples having so much fun, but God provided another woman who was also taking the cruise to be a prayer partner that week. It reminded me again that God is faithful in all circumstances.

A few weeks after the cruise, we were blessed to spend a month in England with Angus and Carole Hogg. My next-door neighbor, Beth Cotten, and her son, Justin, went with us, and I felt that I was given some needed rest away from my schedule. My life had been so busy since Rick's death that it was really the first time that I could just sit and do nothing at all. Matthew had never been to England before and was very intrigued with all the castles, cathedrals, and weapons! I found it very comforting to be surrounded with friends I hadn't seen in so long, but everywhere I looked, memories flooded my mind of things Rick and I had done together when we had lived there.

On many days I would exercise or jog and become overwhelmed with grief, but I felt that I had the freedom to cry and think about Rick any time I wanted to. Those runs were very cathartic.

The most difficult day included a drive we took past our former home at Boscombe Down. I was overcome with memories, and the tears flowed freely. Laura and I both had a good, long cry when we took a short walk to the playground that she and Rick had frequented on a regular basis. The gaping, empty spot in each of our hearts reminded us again of what a wonderful husband and father he was.

Our trip was a time of tremendous healing. There were no distractions and very few responsibilities! Angus and Carole were loving hosts, providing comfort, prayers, and much laughter.

In July, Laura began work on a very special project. She wanted to write down her thoughts of Rick. To the world, Rick will forever be remembered as the commander of the ill-fated space shuttle *Columbia*, but to Laura, he will always be remembered as Daddy.

My Daddy

When I think of my dad, I think of how he helped me take my first steps and then years later talked with me about boys. My dad was a loving father who told me very often that I was beautiful. He had such great enthusiasm and was very interested in our lives. He enjoyed spending time with us. One of my memories of Daddy is the way he would put sunscreen on me. He would try to put it on gently, but sometimes it was still too rough and he would call himself a rough, old bear.

He was a very strong Christian man. He helped me accept Jesus when I was four years old. I am glad that his priorities were straight by putting God first, his family second, and work third. He was humble in everything he did, and I enjoyed his sense of humor. He made me feel special. I would love it when he would come home from work, open the door, and say, "Hello, family!" He used to be in choir in church and sometimes would sing solos or sing in quartets. One of my favorite songs he sang was "Man of Sorrows." I was blessed to have such a great dad even though it was a shorter time than I would have liked it to be. I love him very much and miss him a whole lot. But, I am so glad to know that he is safe in heaven and that I will see him again and this time we'll never have to say good-bye.

Four months after the crew's deaths, a mountain peak in Colorado was named in their honor. The 13,980-foot Columbia Point is close to Challenger Point, on the east side of Kit Carson Mountain. Naming the peak after the *Columbia* crew was Scott Parazynski's suggestion. He's an avid mountain climber and climbed Challenger Point four years ago. Scott had remembered how much the STS-107 crew loved their time in the Wyoming mountains on their NOLS expedition and thought naming a peak after the crew was a fitting tribute. I think he's right.

On August 6, 2003, Laura, Matthew, and I, along with most of the crew families, flew into Pueblo, Colorado. We were going to climb Columbia Point! I was thrilled to do something outside my comfort zone, and with the amazing help of Steve Lindsey, Scott Parazynski, Terry Virts, Smith Johnston, and John Kanengieter and Andy Cline (the NOLS instructors from the crew's climb), we were able to create memories and share a unique time together. I had never met Andy and John, but because they had gotten to know the crew so well and from the stories Rick brought back from his time in the mountains with them, I felt as if we had known each other for a long time. Andy's wife, Molly, also a seasoned NOLS instructor, was with us as well.

The next morning we went off-road and four-wheeled by Jeep into the mountains to the trailhead of our base camp. The road was very rough, and for two solid hours our heads bobbed and banged back and forth. At the trailhead, we sorted our gear and began our 1.4-mile hike to the base camp, which was at 11,500 feet. (Andy and John, along with several astronauts and other NASA folks, set up our base camp in advance.) There were eleven tents scattered around a beautiful area with a breathtaking backdrop of the Sangre de Cristo range.

Shortly after arriving at the base camp, we began to settle into our tents and sort our belongings. About the time I felt that we were up and running in our new home, the heavens began to unload buckets of rain for three hours. Our little sanctuary was hanging on for dear life and was on its way to becoming a study in mud! I had *never* camped in my entire life and felt somewhat scared but determined to have fun. At one point during the storm, we heard a woman's voice outside our tent. I peeked out and saw a hiker who had been caught in the storm. Laura, Matthew, and I maneuvered around the center pole, which was holding up the tent to make room for our soggy new friend. She stayed with us till the rain started to taper off and told us her story, and we told her why we were there. I'm sure she hadn't expected to see tents filled with astronauts when she began her hike that day.

Early the next day, we were scheduled to make the climb beginning around 4:30 A.M., but because it was still raining, it was decided that we would begin at daylight. When we began our climb, Laura and Matthew remained behind at base camp and went fishing with other astronauts who stayed with them.

I had been exercising for months and had begun training for the climb but was concerned about the altitude. I just knew we were all going to be short of breath. Fortunately, it didn't bother me and the climb was incredible. We made it to Humboldt Saddle, which is at about 13,100 feet, but the weather was not favorable to summit Columbia Point. We had climbed as far as we were going to get. We stayed at the saddle for a couple of hours and built seven rock piles in honor of the crew. Lots of tears were shed during our time there as everyone shared stories and memories.

Before we began our descent, a prearranged four-ship of F-16s blasted through the valley. Tears filled my eyes as the flight lead pulled up in the missing man formation over the top of Columbia Point and almost immediately disappeared in the clouds. It was breathtaking.

The next day I was able to see a sunrise all alone on the mountain range. It was bathed in red, and I knew why Rick loved his time with the crew in the Wyoming mountains. God's beauty in nature is spectacular! We packed our things and headed out of the base camp and back to the trailhead. I was so tired I actually dozed while my head bobbed and banged for the two-hour trip! After we arrived at our home in Clear Lake, I began to unpack the smelliest clothes I have ever attempted to clean. I should have done a laundry detergent commercial right there in my kitchen because load after load I was shocked and amazed that the clothes could actually be clean again.

I fell into bed that night and thought of our time on Columbia Point as one of the best experiences in my life. It was a time of many tears and laughs but also a time of great healing for me as I hiked the peak named after Rick and the crew. It was yet another mountain I have climbed since February 1.

After our return from Colorado, we prepared for another school year, the first full year since Rick's death. Laura turned thirteen in October and is in the eighth grade this year. One of her first questions to me on February 1 was, "Who will help me with math?" Now one of my fears is upon me in full force . . . she has algebra this year! I have never really understood algebra (though I am assured by people like Steve Lindsey that it can be useful), but day by day we plod through her homework. Laura's favorite subject is science. Her teacher is Martha Tanner, the wife of an astronaut. Laura is taking band and learning how to play the clarinet. She is also in choir and is getting to use the beautiful voice she inherited from her dad. She is continuing piano lessons and has started baby-sitting. Laura also volunteers in the children's ministry at our church. She and Matthew are signed up for fall soccer again; this will be their sixth season. Laura is like me in that she freely cries and shares her feelings of loss and pain. Although her grief has been great since she lost her father, Laura has always fallen into God's arms for help. I'm so proud of the young lady she is becoming.

Matthew is eight and in the second grade. He has started piano lessons, and at the beginning of them he negotiated with his piano teacher that the recital next spring will be optional for him! Matthew is like his father in that he loves math, and unlike his mother in that he's really good at it! I hope this means I get to coast through the second round of algebra. Matthew loves to fish and play outside with our neighbor, Danny. He has really enjoyed collecting souvenirs from all the places we have been this year.

One Sunday, we went to Scott Parazynski's home for lunch with his family. After lunch, Scott took us over to Rice University, which is close to his home, where he and his son Luke showed Matthew how to ride a bicycle in a huge parking lot at the stadium. Within a few minutes, Matthew was riding on his own and thrilled out of his mind. Rick had tried to teach him before his flight, but Matthew couldn't quite do it, and he was absolutely thrilled to finally master this new skill. Now I can't keep him off his bicycle! Matthew is a good little boy, and I know Rick would be so proud of how he has conducted himself in the many difficult circumstances in which we have found ourselves since February 1. It is my prayer that Matthew will grow up to be a godly man like his father.

Six weeks before the launch, I began to work out at the YMCA every weekday and continue to this day. I have lost more than fifty pounds and feel stronger physically than I have in years. I now see that it was God's provision to build me up physically so I could handle the new demands in my life. My trainer, Lanette DeLoach, suffered through the loss of her first husband. She was left with three little children and eventually married again. Lanette is a godly woman, and my time with her allowed me to talk about hurts few could relate to firsthand. I still work with her two days a week, and one of her newest clients is Laura!

Before the launch, I was leading a Moms in Touch prayer group at Laura and Matthew's school and still do that. My greatest responsibility in this life is to pray for Laura and Matthew.

In addition to Rick's death, this year has seen other challenges in our family. My father is battling cancer that was discovered this spring, and my last living grandparent, my mom's mother, died in September on her ninety-fourth birthday. She was a wonderful, Christian woman whom I adored. She had suffered from dementia the last few years and had no knowledge of our family tragedy this year. I joked with my mom that when she stepped into heaven and saw Rick she probably thought, *Did I miss something?* Her last words were "Would someone please turn off that bright light."

My aunt Doris (my dad's sister) died the day after my grandmother's funeral. She had been ill for years. With only a week to live she asked Jesus into her heart with my mom and dad present. My mom baptized her in the hospital and said, "I probably did it wrong." I said, "I don't think there's a wrong way to do it!" I was with Aunt Doris when she died. It was very peaceful. My family rejoiced in her salvation. Rick and I had prayed for her for years to know Jesus personally. On that day, God taught me to never give up praying for someone. After losing five family members in eighteen months, (three grandparents, my precious Rick, and Aunt Doris) I am ready for a break. Heaven is being populated with the people I love.

The day I returned home to Houston after Aunt Doris died, Matthew wanted me to watch him ride his bicycle up and down the street. It was a picture of stark reality—two completely different worlds—the end of life and the beginning of life with my children. I prayed, "Lord let me *live* until the day I die." In other words, I don't want to waste any days that are given me.

I have been honored since February 1 to speak at different women's conferences, and it is thrilling to share God's faithfulness. I am trying to limit my personal appearances because first and foremost I want to be the best mom I possibly can be to Laura and Matthew. They need my undivided attention, and I need them. There are days when I'm so sad and lonely for Rick that I don't want to do anything else but be with him. Laura and Matthew keep me grounded. They gently remind me in their smiles, laughter, and tears that there's still a life to be lived here. I am learning that life does go on and that new experiences, good and bad, will be on my journey.

Throughout this year I have been blessed with friends who have lifted me in prayer on a daily basis. They have walked me through these days in practical, helpful ways and have helped keep my head above water. They are people of integrity, character, strength, and comfort, and I am blessed to call them friends. I have told many people that I have experienced the worst of the worst and the best of the best this year.

People have asked me if I blame God for what happened, and I always tell them no. God has a plan for each person's life; I may not understand that plan, and it may grieve me, but I am not bitter toward God. He has been too good to me, to Rick, and to our families. I have a long history with God, and I cannot turn my back on that history of God's faithfulness, provision, and grace. He has always loved me when I was unlovable and continues to love me today through the greatest sadness of my life. He has carried me through dark times and continues to carry me through the darkest of days without Rick.

I have lost all sense of politeness with God. I have cried and wept and yelled at Him, but I know He's big enough to handle it. He has drawn me closer than I ever thought possible. He has held me close to His heart and let me cry for as long as I've needed. My sweet sister-in-law, Kathy, told me on February 1 that God would walk me step-by-step through this sorrow, and He has. Time and again, what the Lord said in the Bible has proved faithful and true.

Isaiah 53:3 tells us that Jesus was a man of sorrows and acquainted with our grief. He really does know how I feel. Psalm 147:3 declares that God "heals the brokenhearted and binds up their wounds." Revelation 21:4 says, "He will wipe every tear from their eyes. There will be no more death or mourning or crying or pain" in heaven. Matthew 11:28 states, "Come to me, all you who are weary and burdened, and I will give you rest." Psalm 56:8 reminds us that God keeps track of our sorrows. He has collected all my tears in a bottle and has recorded each one in a book. Verse after verse reflects God's love for me and helps carry me through painfully dark days.

Although I am lonely for Rick and will be for the rest of my life, I am never alone; I will never be alone. God is always with me. I know that I will see Rick again in heaven, but I still mourn for him and miss him terribly. There are days that my heart feels it's literally going to break because the pain is so deep, but because I have put my hope in Christ, I am assured of the eternal hope of heaven.

Rick and his crew never would have chosen this ending to their very successful mission. They were headed home—yet their destination was forever changed only sixteen minutes from the landing. Looking back on the days previous to the STS-107 flight, I know that God held all four of us and was preparing us for what was ahead. Rick had no idea that he would die on February 1, but his belief in God would sustain him through his last breaths. Laura and Matthew and I would be sustained through those first horrifying moments when we knew that we lost Rick because we knew he went straight into the presence of the Lord. Even though there was great shock and our grieving process had not yet begun, we knew that God would somehow take care of us.

In one of my e-mails to Rick in space I told him that Laura was praying for the most perfect landing ever. People have said that our prayers weren't answered, that God didn't listen, and although God didn't answer our prayers the way I wanted because I would rather Rick still be here with us, God answered our prayers another way. In the days after Rick's death I talked with Laura about her prayer. "Daddy did have a perfect landing," I said. "He landed right in the presence of Jesus. His landing in Florida could not have been perfect. It could have been outstanding or excellent but not perfect. When he stepped foot into heaven, that was his perfect landing. He landed in God's holy presence, and I know that for now he's saving our place in heaven." Those aren't trite, shallow words—something a grieving widow grabs onto for comfort; they are words of truth, God's truth, and I'll cling to them for the rest of my life.

On the last day of Rick's journal entries, he wrote,

Lord—I want to do Your will and I want to be a godly man. Please help me to seek and know Your will and obey You in what You want me to do. I want to be happy and joyful and see that reflected in my family, my work, and especially in my relationship with You.

As Rick's wife and best friend, I can affirm that his heart's cry to God was answered in his lifetime. He was a godly man. He was not a perfect man, but he sought God every day of his life and he obeyed God's Word, teaching it to our children. In everything, Rick was a happy and joyful man. That joy and contentment was reflected in our home and on our faces; it was reflected in the care and discipline with which Rick did his work; it was especially evident in his relationship with Christ.

As Dr. Carroll said at Rick's funeral . . .

All is well. Hallelujah!

About the Author

Evelyn Husband lives with her two children, thirteen-year-old Laura and eight-year-old Matthew, in Houston, Texas. Prior to February 1, 2003, Evelyn was a self-described "ordinary stay-at-home mom" who never imagined the extraordinary circumstances in which she would find herself.

"Never in my wildest dreams did I think what Rick and I did—how we lived our lives and raised our family—would become a national story," says Evelyn. "And honestly, I would give it all up to just have my husband and my old life back. But I want to be faithful to how God wants to use this tragedy to bring hope to people."

In the weeks and months following the Columbia tragedy, Evelyn learned that it is possible to have peace and hope in the midst of the deepest despair. She now shares that message through this book, as well as with tens of thousands of women across the U.S. as a guest speaker for Women of Faith, America's largest women's conference.

Evelyn and Rick Husband met as students at Amarillo High School in Amarillo, Texas, where they both grew up. They were married for twenty years.